UNIVERSITY OF YORK
BORTHWICK INSTITUTE OF HISTORICAL RESEAR

Yorkshire Returns of the 1851 Census of Religious Worship

Volume 1:

Introduction, City of York and East Riding

**Edited by
John Wolffe**

BORTHWICK TEXTS AND CALENDARS 25

FIRST PUBLISHED 2000
© University of York 2000
ISBN 0-903857-95-2

CONTENTS

ABBREVIATIONS

ExW   Used exclusively as a Place of Worship (except for Sunday School)

F   Female

GC   General Congregation

M   Male

OPE   Other Permanent Endowment

P   Parish synonymous with Township

SEB   Separate and entire Building

SS   Sunday Scholars

INTRODUCTION

This edition of the 1851 Census of Religious Worship for Yorkshire renders accessible in a new way a major portion of a detailed and unique survey, covering a substantial region of northern England. As an offshoot of the regular decennial census of population, schedules were distributed to all identified places of worship in England, Scotland and Wales, requesting a return of seating, attendance on Sunday 30 March, and answers to various other questions (see the reproduced specimen forms). The main objectives appear to have been to obtain indications of the extent and denominational distribution of religious practice, and to assess the adequacy or otherwise of the amount of accommodation available in places of worship.

The task of collecting the returns was assigned to the 30,610 enumerators responsible for the population census. These officials first compiled lists of places of worship within their respective districts and delivered forms to 'the minister or other official party competent to give intelligence'. The enumerators then collected the forms on Monday 31 March, and forwarded them to local registrars, who were responsible for taking further steps to obtain missing returns for places of worship whose existence had been noted by the enumerators. Registrars then returned all the forms for their district to the Census Office, from where further enquiries were made to fill up remaining gaps. Subsequently a report with extensive statistical tables was compiled by Horace Mann, a young barrister, and published as a parliamentary paper in December 1853.[1]

The results of the census generated great interest and controversy, in fuelling rivalries between the Church of England and Nonconformity, in documenting serious deficiencies in overall pastoral provision, and in indicating widespread non-participation in organized worship. The contemporary debate has been revived in recent decades among historians who recognize in the religious census, for all its acknowledged deficiencies, a vitally important source for the study of early Victorian religious life.[2] Much of this discussion, however, has been based primarily on the statistics in the printed report, and has not been properly informed by study of the individual returns themselves. Nevertheless the latter have largely survived (although in Yorkshire the entire registration district of Halifax is unfortunately missing[3]), being stored in the Public Record Office under class HO129. It is hoped that this edition of the remaining Yorkshire returns, especially when used alongside the recent

[1]   *Census of Great Britain, 1851: Religious Worship, England and Wales – Report and Tables* (London, 1853; House of Commons Sessional Papers, 1852-3, Vol. 89, pp. clxix-xx and *passim*; reprinted (1970), Irish University Press Series of British Parliamentary Papers, Population, Vol. 10) [hereafter *Census Report*].

[2]   For an excellent recent survey of the literature, containing detailed references, see Clive Field, 'The 1851 Religious Census of Great Britain: a Bibliographical Guide for Local and Regional Historians', The *Local Historian*, 27 (1997), 194-217.

[3]   The Public Record Office logged the Halifax file (HO129/498) as missing in 1955, so there appears no realistic prospect that it will be found.

editions available for other counties[4], will serve to stimulate constructive new directions in the use of the census by historians and hence new insight into early Victorian religious life as a whole.

Yorkshire was not only England's largest county, but also its most populous and diverse. The historic county stretched from the Tees in the north to beyond the Don in the south and from Spurn Head in the east to within ten miles of the Irish Sea in the west. Within its 3.75 million acres and among its 1.8 million people, there was enormous geographical, social, and economic variety, fertile lowlands, bleak fells, burgeoning industrial centres, historic market towns, and isolated rural and upland settlements. In 1851 there was industrial decline as well as industrial growth, particularly as waterpower gave way to steam; rural depopulation as well as urban overcrowding. More than any other single county, Yorkshire was a cross-section of England.[5]

The Yorkshire returns for the Religious Census serve as a mirror held up to a diverse society. In particular they illuminate the rich variety of organized religious life, the continuities of village Anglicanism alongside the rise of rural Dissent; the belated efforts of the Church of England to reclaim the towns in the face both of Nonconformist growth and widespread popular indifference. The tiny attendances at Quaker Meeting Houses in the Dales were redolent of a decline both in spiritual and community life, even as the over-crowded Roman Catholic chapels of the towns serve as evidence of the importance of their church in the lives of recent Irish immigrants. Yorkshire too provides ample illustration of the schismatic dimensions of English religion, notably in the secession of the Wesleyan Reformers following the flysheets controversy of 1849, and also of its capacity for continual innovation, as evidenced by the arrival of the Mormons. Meanwhile the institutional legacy of

---

4   The following editions have now been published: D.W. Bushby, 'The Ecclesiastical Census, Bedfordshire, March 1851' in Bedford Historical Record Society, Vol. 54 (1975); Ieuan Gwynedd Jones and David Williams, The Religious Census of 1851 A Calendar of the Returns Relating to Wales, 2 vols. (Cardiff, 1976, 1981); R.W. Ambler, Lincolnshire Returns of the Census of Religious Worship 1851, The Lincoln Record Society, Vol. 72 (1979); Kate Tiller, Church and Chapel in Oxfordshire 1851 The returns of the census of religious worship, The Oxfordshire Record Society, Vol. 55 (1987); Michael Watts, Religion in Victorian Nottinghamshire: The Religious Census of 1851, 2 vols. (University of Nottingham Centre for Local History Record Series, 1988); John A. Vickers, The Religious Census of Sussex 1851, Sussex Record Society, Vol. 75 (Lewes, 1989); Michael J.L. Wickes, Devon in the Religious Census of 1851 (privately published, 1990); Edward Legg, Buckinghamshire Returns of the Census of Religious Worship 1851, Buckinghamshire Record Society, No. 27 (1991); John A. Vickers, The Religious Census of Hampshire 1851 (Winchester, 1993); Judith Burg, Religion in Hertfordshire 1847 to 1851, Hertfordshire Record Publications, Vol. 11 (1995); Margery Tranter, The Derbyshire Returns to the 1851 Religious Census, Derbyshire Record Society Vol. 23 (1995); Cliff Webb and David Robinson, The 1851 Religious Census: Surrey, Surrey Record Society, Vol. 35 (Guildford, 1997); T.C.B. Timmins, Suffolk Returns from the Census of Religious Worship of 1851, Suffolk Records Society, Vol. 39 (Woodbridge, 1997); Janet Ede and Norma Virgoe, Religious Worship in Norfolk: The 1851 Census of Accommodation and Attendance at Worship, Norfolk Record Society, Vol. 62 (1998); J.C.C. Probert, ed., 1851 Religious Census: West Cornwall and the Isles of Scilly (n.p., n.d.).

5   Cf. David Hey, Yorkshire From AD 1000 (1986).

previous revival movements lived on in the many branches of Protestant Nonconformity.

Ever since the first publication of the report in 1853, both contemporary observers and subsequent scholars have been preoccupied with attempts to calculate from the census overall rates of attendance and non-attendance. Such endeavours are valid and useful up to a point: they lead to the broad but indisputable conclusions that between a third and a half of the population of England attended church on census Sunday, but that within that figure there was enormous regional and local variation. More precise statistical calculations, however, have been apt to seem like attempts to build a house of cards on board a small boat riding in a heavy swell.

Study of the individual returns indicates that while the majority of respondents attempted to complete the forms conscientiously, some were not in a position to provide crucial information, and many failed properly to understand the somewhat confusing instructions they were given. Many of the figures recorded were suspiciously round numbers, and were evidently estimates rather than exact headcounts. Many respondents failed to distinguish between the general congregation and Sunday scholars. It is also likely that on many occasions Sunday scholars were incorrectly counted when they were only present in a separate meeting place for the school and not in the main worship service in church or chapel at all. Even when the forms were correctly completed there was usually no way of telling how many people attended two or three services on census Sunday and hence were counted two or even three times. Not only did some attend the same place of worship more than once, but there were quite numerous reports, especially in rural areas, of individuals attending both Church of England and Wesleyan worship on the same day. At Bishop Burton (near Beverley) the vicar remarked on a three-way interchangeability of congregations between his own church, the Baptists and the Wesleyans.[6] Occasional such respondents gave valuable additional information of this kind, but in general statistical solutions had to be arbitrary ones.

A further set of difficulties arises when the individual returns are aggregated to provide overall figures for attendance on a district, regional or national basis. There was no legal requirement to return the forms and, in particular, a substantial minority of Anglican clergy declined to do so on principle, although churchwardens sometimes stepped into the breach. For example, initially returns were missing or inadequate for six out of twenty-eight churches in the Skipton district, while at Whiston near Rotherham, the piously blunt rector responded that as he was 'occupied when at Church with saying my prayers' he could not provide attendance figures.[7] In the York district only three or four[8] out of sixty-four Anglican returns were left to the registrars, but four of the others had been completed by churchwardens, one of whom, at St Denis, Walmgate, regretted that he was 'very imperfectly informed: the

---

6   Vol. 1, 317. For another example of Anglican-Wesleyan interchange see Warter (Vol. 1, 190-1).
7   Vol. 3, 2326.
8   The status of the respondent at St Michael, Spurriergate (Vol. 1, 17) is uncertain.

Rector ... declining to cooperate'.[9] Subsequent enquiries dropped the request for information on endowments and thereby won the participation of those clergy who had taken particular exception to that enquiry, but others still refused to co-operate. In such cases figures for attendance were liable to be dependent on hearsay or even guesswork. Moreover it is probable that some, perhaps many, places of worship, especially smaller and more remote Nonconformist meeting houses, were inadvertently missed by the enumerators. It has been estimated that in Suffolk 15% of all places of worship and over a quarter of Nonconformist ones were not recorded.[10] There are good grounds for suspecting that in Yorkshire with its burgeoning new industrial settlements, many in comparatively remote areas, the rate of omissions was at least as high as in East Anglia.[11]

The printed summary tables included in the census report were also subject to distortion through simple clerical and computational errors.[12] The problems were compounded when Mann attempted to translate attendances into an overall national figure for individual worshippers. In order to allow for dual or triple attendance he adopted an arbitrary formula of the morning attendance plus half the afternoon, plus one third of the evening.[13] This crude approach obviously failed to account for the fact that at many places of worship, especially Nonconformist chapels, the sole or main service was in the afternoon or evening. Moreover many Anglican churches in rural Yorkshire, as in country districts in the south, reported higher attendances in the afternoon than in the morning.

---

[9]   Vol. 1, 35. In W.F. Hook's immediate sphere of influence in the Leeds and Hunslet registra-
       tion districts, there was an impressive 100% initial response rate for Anglican churches, but
       this was exceptional.

[10]   Timmins, *Suffolk Returns*, pp. xii-xiii. Numerous omissions have also been noted in Norfolk
       (Ede and Virgoe, *Religious Worship in Norfolk*, pp. 12-13).

[11]   Mark Smith has noted that in the districts of Oldham and Saddleworth, partly within Yorkshire,
       and partly immediately adjoining it, the enumerators missed one out of four Independent
       Methodist preaching places and five out of thirteen Primitive Methodist ones (*Religion in
       Industrial Society: Oldham and Saddleworth 1740-1865* (Oxford, 1994), p. 206). The surviving
       educational census Sunday School returns for the Keighley and Todmorden districts suggest
       that even a few quite sizeable places of worship were missed in the religious census, for example
       Lees Chapel (Wesleyan Methodist), near Haworth with a Sunday School attendance of 168
       and Millwood Chapel (Particular Baptist) at Stansfield, with a Sunday School attendance of
       72. There were also free-standing Sunday Schools, significant in relation to any general
       assessment of religious influence, but not covered by the religious census at all unless they also
       normally provided public worship services. In the rural East Riding a comparison of the returns
       with David and Susan Neave's *East Riding Chapels and Meeting Houses*, East Riding Local History
       Society, 44 (1990) suggests that in that part of the county few, if any, purpose-built chapels
       were missed, but one cannot be so confident that the record of Methodist and other services
       in cottages and school rooms, numerous as they were, was a comprehensive one.

[12]   For example the figure for seating accommodation for the Society of Friends in Hull was
       magnified by a factor of ten thus significantly distorting the overall figures. Michael Watts (*op.
       cit.*, p. xi) has noted similarly crude errors in Nottinghamshire. The unreliability of the printed
       tables, as well as constraints of space, has led to a decision not to reproduce them systematically
       in this edition.

[13]   *Census Report*, p. cliii.

It is also open to serious question how meaningful attendance figures for one day taken in isolation can be as an index of religiosity. As many respondents pointed out, congregations were significantly affected by factors such as the weather, illness, local events, the presence or absence of a popular preacher, and building or repair works on the churches themselves. The overall impression emerges that, even when allowance is made for some special pleading by respondents, the state of the roads following the winter, poor weather on 30 March itself, and widespread colds and influenza, generally depressed attendances, especially in rural areas. Even if the attendance on 30 March were to be regarded as representative, taken in isolation it still leaves open the question of how regularly individuals attended church. A headcount of 100 on 30 March might represent a highly committed body of regular weekly attenders amounting to little more than 100, or might make up less than half of a much larger number of people who attended worship fortnightly, monthly or even more infrequently, but still maintained a significant sense of identification with organized religion. Several Yorkshire returns to the census indicate that such a pattern of attendance was noticeable, especially in the Church of England. [14]

A rare specificity was provided by the curate who reported attendances at the Church of England School Room at Farnley Iron Works, near Leeds, on 30 March of 25 in the morning and 60 in the afternoon, with 60 and 95 Sunday scholars respectively. Applying Mann's formula of morning + half afternoon, this would give a figure of $25 + 60 + 0.5(60+95) = 167.5$ individuals. The respondent however remarked that 'many who attend this Place of Worship attend frequently but not regularly. The entire number of persons attached to this place of worship may be set down at 250.'[15] Thus in this case the number of 'attached' might be held to exceed the number of attenders by a factor of 49%. Were such a ratio to be applied across the country it would significantly shift our assumptions about levels of participation in religious worship.

Such generalization from a single case would naturally be exposed to the same justified charge of arbitrariness as that levelled against Mann's original report. The single case does however generate a hypothesis worthy of further exploration, with reference in the first instance to the other returns where information of this kind is given. Although relatively rare, there may well be sufficient examples across the country to provide a statistically valid sample. Other data from the forms, notably those for average attendances and for appropriated pews, might then be used as a basis for further valid inferences about the numbers of people 'attached' to particular places of worship. Such an investigation would also be served by data from the Sunday School returns which additionally survive for the registration districts of Keighley and Todmorden, and which provide useful corroboration both of the numbers of attenders at Sunday School, and of the numbers of pupils on the books of churches and chapels.

The above example is advanced in order to illustrate the way in which study of

---

[14] See, for example, below Vol. 1, 187, 283, 395, 399, 432, 592; Vol. 2, 933, 1427. For a converse case, where it was remarked that the congregation was 'particularly uniform and invariable', see Vol. 2, 1335.

[15] Vol. 2, 1458.

the individual returns can lead to potential reassessments of much more than local significance. It is thus possible to envisage that, in this and other ways, future computer-based analysis of the raw data would permit the generation of much more sophisticated statistical conclusions than have been available in the past.

At the same time more traditional modes of historical scholarship will have a crucial part to play in using the returns to generate insights into the role of religion in communities large and small, which can then be tested and developed by reference to other evidence. In serving such an endeavour the returns can provide valuable qualitative as well as quantitative information, in indicating, for example, the pastoral efficiency of clergy and ministers, not only through their explicit remarks, but also through the numbers of services held, and whether or not they were resident in the immediate vicinity of the place of worship in question. Information on Anglican endowments is also significant insofar as it shows the extent of the resources clergy had available to support their ministries. Many Nonconformist signatories gave their occupations and addresses, thus providing a significant clue to the social composition of the congregations that they represented. Further evidence of this kind is provided by the returns made by women, or by illiterate, or barely literate, respondents. The very descriptions of places of worship – in particular whether they were known by the name of the place or district where they were located – gives an indication of their standing and prominence, or otherwise, in their local communities. Moreover although the census was a snapshot taken on one particular early spring day, it still provides clues to longer-term patterns of development, notably in documenting quite systematically the dates at which churches and chapels had been erected and opened during the preceding half century. At some points too the timing of the census meant that it captured the impact of more dramatic short term changes, notably the nature and extent of the contemporary ferment in Wesleyan Methodism, and the renewal of Anglicanism in the Leeds area under the leadership of the town's remarkable vicar, Walter Farquhar Hook. [16]

The very weaknesses of the original printed report on the census render it doubly important to make the surviving manuscript returns accessible in a form where they can be widely utilised in future research, by local, religious and social historians alike. Such further investigation might be based primarily on the census itself, or it might very constructively employ its evidence in connection with other sources, such as the printed reports and manuscript enumerators' returns of the population census, Anglican parochial records and visitation returns, or Nonconformist chapel minutes and membership records. There is much scope both for intensive local studies and for broader regional and national comparisons. The editor will be well content if over the coming years the current publication makes a worthwhile contribution to such endeavours. [17]

---

[16]   Cf. Nigel Yates, 'The religious life of Victorian Leeds', in Derek Fraser, ed., A History of Modern Leeds (Manchester, 1980), pp.250-69.

[17]   My own further analysis of the Yorkshire material will be provided in a Borthwick Paper, which will be published to accompany this edition.

Coverage, Organization and Structure of this Edition

For the purposes of the census Yorkshire was divided into the fifty-three districts used for the registration of births, deaths and marriages. These districts were normally centred on the county's major towns, but varied greatly both in size and population according to locality. In general the coverage of the districts was rational enough, but it is important to note that the registration districts of Hull, Leeds and Sheffield only covered the central sections of their conurbations: suburban areas are to be found in Sculcoates, Hunslet and both Eccleshall and Penistone districts respectively. Conversely, the York registration district comprised not only the whole of the administratively distinct City of York, but also extensive adjoining rural areas from all three Ridings. The districts were in turn divided into subdistricts concentrated on smaller centres, within which the original returns were filed according to civil parish and township divisions, and by wards in larger towns. This sequence of the manuscript returns is generally preserved in this edition, in faithfulness to the integrity of the archive, in order to facilitate comparisons with the printed report, and with a view to placing contiguous parishes and townships within parishes close to each other in the text.

The organization of the material into the four volumes of this edition also follows the original in reflecting the division into Ridings there employed. The division of the West Riding between its two volumes is perforce an arbitrary one in order to balance the size of the volumes, but the reader may be assisted by noting that in the western part of the Riding it corresponds approximately to the modern line of the M62 motorway. Any attempt to reorganize the material to reflect the changed administrative subdivisions of Yorkshire at the end of the twentieth century would have been not only extremely complicated and prone to error, but also of very questionable utility given the potentiality in the long term for further reorganization of local government. An alphabetical organization of the returns was considered, but rejected as liable to generate more problems for both editor and user than it would solve.[18]

The organization of the returns by registration district is complemented by full indexes, by denomination in each volume, and overall indexes by place and personal names in the final volume. The index by denomination should also allow the reader who has only one volume to hand quickly to locate the returns for particular places; but reference will have to be made to the overall placename index when the reader is unsure in which volume to look, or in order to trace all the returns for large parishes, and to identify placenames which occur in returns for locations other than the place in question.

It is important to note that 'Yorkshire' as defined by the fifty-three registration districts did not conform exactly to the administrative county and Ridings. On the borders, a number of parishes from neighbouring counties were included in Yorkshire

---

[18] Such an arrangement works reasonably well in the volumes for Buckinghamshire (Legg, *op. cit.*) and Oxfordshire (Tiller, *op. cit.*) but even in these relatively small counties it is open to objection as rendering more difficult comparison of contiguous parishes, a problem that would be greatly magnified if applied to a county the size of Yorkshire.

registration districts, and conversely, some Yorkshire parishes were returned in the registration districts of Clitheroe (Lancashire), Worksop (Nottinghamshire), and Darlington, Stockton, and Teesdale (Durham). This edition adopts a comprehensive approach by normally including in full all registration districts centred on towns which were then in Yorkshire (thus including significant areas now (2000) in other counties), together with the parishes then in Yorkshire in the five above non-Yorkshire based registration districts. One exception to this policy has been made in relation to the registration district of Thorne, where two entire subdistricts were both then and now in Lincolnshire. Accordingly, only the Yorkshire subdistrict of Thorne itself has been included.[19] A similar complication occurs on the boundaries between the three Ridings, but here editorial policy has been simply to follow the registration Ridings, while noting the administrative status of such border parishes as necessary. Thus the reader familiar with the administrative Ridings should be aware that a number of parishes will therefore be found in the 'wrong' volume, and will accordingly need to be located by reference to the placename index.[20]

Headings and subheadings in the text indicate the civil status of settlements. Municipal boroughs have been noted where applicable. For townships, the civil parish is indicated in parenthesis (a 'P' signifying that parish and township are synonymous). In cases where a whole district or subdistrict was in the same parish or township this information is given in connection with the applicable level of heading. This information will be useful to the reader in that it serves to indicate the probable actual or historic ecclesiastical affiliation, significant information especially in cases where there was no Anglican church, or a chapelry or daughter church of recent date. It should be noted, however, that formally constituted chapelries and district parishes were normally independent of their mother churches for all practical day to day ecclesiastical purposes. Headings also provide population figures, as recorded in the printed main census report for 1851, and footnotes indicate settlements for which there is no extant return. It should not be automatically assumed, however, that these settlements had no place of worship, omissions by enumerators and registrars being a real possibility.

In the great majority of cases, the sequence of the forms together with the information recorded on them provides satisfactory and consistent evidence of location. In a few instances however the forms themselves suggest that filing errors were made by the original Census Office clerks, which were then perpetuated by later Public Record Office numbering. In such cases the sequence as printed has been adjusted in order to conform to the internal evidence of particular forms.

---

[19]   The Lincolnshire parts of the Thorne district have already been published in Ambler, *op. cit.*, pp. 272-8.

[20]   There are indications that the system confused officials in 1851. Returns for several Anglican churches in the North Riding section of the Ripon district (otherwise West Riding) were erroneously filed under the adjoining North Riding registration district of Thirsk: see below Vol. 2, 974, 978, 982, 985. Two returns for the church at the deserted village of Wharram Percy survive, one made by the curate and filed under the East Riding district of Driffield (Vol. 1, 608); the other by the churchwarden and filed under Malton district in the North Riding (Vol. 4).

Where the numbering of a district is inconsistent with the sequence of subdivisions followed in the printed census tables, the sequence has similarly been adjusted. The reader will be alerted to cases where such alterations have been made by changes in the sequence of PRO classification numbers, as recorded at the end of each return, and by explicit notes where it has been found necessary to move a return to an entirely different registration district. Other gaps in the sequence of PRO classification are normally accounted for by summary listings by contemporary clerks, preserved in the PRO, but not transcribed here. For the purposes of indexing and cross-referencing, in this edition each return has been assigned a unique number, printed at the beginning of the entry.

Editorial Method

The returns were initially transcribed from the microfilm copies held at the Borthwick Institute in York, the Durham County Record Office in Durham and the Public Record Office at Kew. Transcriptions were then checked against the microfilm, with the originals only being consulted in order to resolve particular details that were unclear on the microfilm. It should be noted that this approach arises from current Public Record Office policy on access to originals which have been microfilmed, rather than from the editor's own choice: it is possible that enforced over-reliance on microfilm copies has given rise to transcription errors that would not have occurred had more extended work with the originals been possible.

The sheer size of Yorkshire (with more than twice as many returns as for any other county yet published) has rendered necessary a less ambitious editorial strategy than that which has been applied to the returns for some other smaller counties, in the cause of producing within a reasonable timescale a consistent and coherent text under the control of a single editor. Accordingly crosschecking of the returns against other sources has been limited. Information from the main census regarding population and the status of localities has, however, been added. Placenames have been verified when necessary and modern spellings normally used in headings, though not in the returns themselves. Dedications of Church of England churches thought to have been in use in 1851 have been added when recorded in a card index available in the Borthwick Institute. (It is interesting to note that many incumbents were ignorant or unsure of the dedications of their churches, probably an indication of ingrained Protestant attitudes to the veneration of saints.) Anglican clergy have been checked against the <u>Clergy List</u>. On the other hand, the names of lay and non-Anglican signatories have not been verified against other sources, although where the reading is uncertain, indication has been made to that effect. Where returns have been manifestly misfiled or the location of a particular place of worship remains uncertain, every effort has been made to rectify errors and deficiencies from internal evidence, but no attempt has been made to pursue investigation on the ground or in other sources.

The editorial objective has been to produce a text which conveys not only the information contained in the original returns, but also something of their character as documents. Accordingly the spelling of originals has been retained, with only the minimal adjustments to punctuation and capitalization necessary to ensure readability for the modern user. Italics are used to designate the main headings on the printed forms. Redundant repetition and words and phrases such as 'in the year' (in dates) and 'persons' (in attendance figures) have been cut. Throughout the text round brackets '( )' have been used for three purposes: to reproduce brackets in the original; to indicate that words present in the original have been moved; and in order to enhance clarity. Square brackets '[ ]' have been used for editorial interpolations. Where there is serious doubt about the reading of a word, figure, or name a query has been added thus '[?]'; where a single word is wholly illegible or missing due to torn edges the gap is indicated thus '[...]'; an explicit editorial note is made in relation to longer gaps in the text. Where a word or figure is clear but seems inconsistent with other information on the form, a 'sic' has been interpolated in square brackets. Words or figures which have apparently been deleted by the respondents themselves, and other ambiguous marks on the forms have been ignored, except when explicitly noted.

Four examples of the standard forms used for the census are here reproduced,[21] one used for Anglican churches, another for Quakers and a third for all other denominations. The latter form was thus used by Roman Catholics and Jews – who returned figures for the Sabbath, Saturday 29 March – as well as by all varieties of Protestant Nonconformity. The Quaker form differed from the standard non-Anglican one in requesting a figure for floor area, and not asking for any differentiation of Sunday School attendances. Two further, simplified, forms – one for Anglican churches, the other for all non-Anglicans – were used to follow up places of worship which had initially failed to make a return. The Anglican version, here reproduced, omitted the questions on building costs and endowments and redefined the categories of sittings as 'Free' and 'Appropriated' (rather than 'Other' on the main form). This was a significant difference in that it clarified the point, more open to misunderstanding on the main form, that 'Free' did not mean absence of payment, but freedom of general access. The simplified forms merely asked for a single set of figures for the 'Usual Number of Attendants'. They also differed from the initial forms in not requiring the date nor the address of informants, who were often local registrars rather than church officials. In this edition, where returns have been made on the simplified forms this has been noted at the end of the entry following the PRO classification numbers, as is any other abnormality in the form of the return (such as the use of the wrong form for the denomination in question). The note 'Registrar's Enquiry' signifies that the information is not on a census form at all, but was supplied in response to a specific manuscript enquiry from the Census Office and/or the local registrar, usually many months after the census date.[22]

Where duplicate forms exist for a single place of worship, a note to that effect has been included in the text, and any significant differences between them have

---

21   See p. xv et seq.
22   For a full account of the process by which the data was collected see Timmins, *Suffolk Returns*, pp. ix-xii.

been noted. In instances where differences are substantial, both forms have been transcribed in full, either following each other, or with cross-references.[23]

The following policies have been adopted in relation to particular divisions of the forms:

Names, Denominations and Locations The name of a place of worship is recorded as stated on the form, although sometimes abridging cumbersome phraseology. Names that are solely generically descriptive, such as 'dwelling house' or 'school' have been repositioned to follow the heading rather than forming part of it. In cases where the denomination is not clear – or not fully clear – from the name of its church or chapel, additional denominational information as recorded on the form is added in round brackets.[24] Thus ' *Name* Zion Independent Chapel' would be recorded exactly as written on the form but ' *Name* Zion Chapel ... *Denomination* Independent' would appear as 'Zion Chapel (Independent)'. '*Name* Wesleyan Methodist Chapel' would appear as written, but '*Name* Wesleyan Chapel ...*Denomination* Wesleyan Methodist' as 'Wesleyan (Methodist) Chapel'. Anglican returns are not explicitly identified as such, unless confusion might arise from the absence of a dedication. The location is then stated in the heading, following the name and denomination, retaining the spelling and nomenclature of the original, but avoiding redundant repetition of the names of large towns. The levels of detail provided by respondents varied greatly, some giving a precise address, others merely identifying a sizeable town or parish in which the place of worship was located. In such cases, more exact indications of location are suggested by the position of the return in the sequence and by the address of the respondent. Neither test, however, is wholly conclusive, in the light of the vagaries of the contemporary Census Office clerks, and the possibility that the respondent lived at some distance from the place of worship in question. Anglican dioceses are omitted unless other than Ripon or York.

Anglican Building Costs and Endowments are recorded as stated. Explicit zeros or words such as 'none' or 'nil' are recorded, as are total figures when these provide implicit evidence of nil returns for other categories. The category 'Private Benefaction or Subscription or from other sources' is abbreviated to 'Private Benefaction etc.' and that of 'Other Permanent Endowment' to 'OPE'.

Nonconformist Buildings Affirmative responses to the questions as to whether a separate and entire building and whether used exclusively for worship (except for a Sunday School) are recorded with the following abbreviations: 'SEB ExW'. Answers have been construed as straightforwardly affirmative if they are a 'yes' or if they

---

23   Such instances provide telling incidental evidence of the haphazard nature of some returns. For example, in relation to the Wesleyan chapel at Langtoft near Bridlington (Vol. 1, 622, 657), the minister, who was not present, gave an exaggerated estimate of the evening congregation, evidently not realizing that his own absence, as reported in the other return by the steward, had had an adverse effect on numbers.

24   It is important to recognize that denominational designations and structures were in some cases still fluid in 1851, and it is therefore important to assess the evidence of the census returns on their own terms without imposing descriptions which might not have been owned by the respondents themselves. Cf. Vickers, *Religious Census of Sussex*, pp xix-xxi.

repeat the form of the question without significant alteration. Other explicit answers such as 'Dwelling house', 'Separate building' and 'Also a day school' are transcribed verbatim. Simple 'no' answers to these questions, very often implicit in responses to other questions on the form (such as the description of the building as a day school or dwelling house) are indicated by the absence of any statement in the text. On the rare occasions where the question was not answered and the nature of the building is not otherwise clear from the rest of the form an, editorial note has been added to that effect.

Sittings On Anglican forms, where a 'Total' figure confirms a nil count for the 'Free' or 'Other' categories it is included, but is otherwise omitted.

Attendances Respondents were asked to record an 'X' at periods of the day when no service had taken place, and such Xs are duly recorded here, as are other explicit negatives such as a zero, or the words 'none' or 'no service'. Other marks such as dashes, lines or dots have, however, been ignored as open to various interpretation. On numerous forms where only one attendance figure was given for each service, its position makes it impossible to determine whether or not it was for a general congregation, without any Sunday scholars; for a Sunday School; or a composite figure for both general congregation and Sunday School. In such cases the figure is recorded in the following format 'Morning 75', but where clear separate figures for general congregation and Sunday School are present, they are recorded in the following manner 'Morning GC 40 SS 35'. Similarly, in the less frequent cases where the positioning of the figures renders it uncertain to what period of the day an attendance should be attributed, this has been left unspecified in the transcript. Total attendance figures have only been given where they suggest inaccuracies or confusions in the individual figures.

In a number of returns inconsistencies and implausibilities suggest that it is very possible that figures were wrongly positioned or instructions misunderstood. Policy has, however, always been to reproduce the apparent import of the form, leaving possible reinterpretation to the reader, although a '[sic]' has been interpolated in cases where it seems to the editor that the form may well have been incorrectly completed. Figures for averages are particularly open to various interpretation, especially in cases where only average figures for one service are given (even if there had been two or three services on 30 March), usually in the left hand 'Morning' column. In such instances it is possible, especially on the non-Anglican forms where the layout was confusing, that respondents were offering an overall average of attenders or attendances for the day as a whole. On the other hand it is also possible that they were carefully following instructions that implied that averages need only be given when they differed from attendances on 30 March.[25] A further confusion arose on the simplified Anglican forms that were apparently interpreted by some respondents as requiring an overall figure for attendants, as well as a breakdown by service. This

---

25   Cf. Webb and Robinson, *1851 Religious Census: Surrey*, pp. li-lii. For examples of cases where such confusion is apparent see the returns for the Wesleyan Methodist Chapels at Elvington (Vol. 1, 100) and Huggate (Vol. 1, 188).

obviously useful additional information is included where given before the individual service figures.[26]

Date and Signature The date is omitted for the great majority of forms where it was March 30, the day of the census, or the following day, Monday March 31. Other dates are recorded, but with the year omitted unless other than 1851. The simplified forms used in the second trawl for information were not dated. The style 'Revd.' is omitted when it is otherwise clear that the respondent was an Anglican clergyman, but is included where it appears on non-Anglican forms. On non-Anglican schedules respondents frequently gave their 'Official Character' as 'manager' of the place of worship in question: accordingly the description of a respondent as a 'manager' should be assumed, unless otherwise stated, to relate to their ecclesiastical responsibilities rather than a secular profession.

Address Addresses are recorded as given, except that the county is omitted, unless other than Yorkshire or an immediately neighbouring county. 'Near' is consistently abbreviated to 'nr' even if written in full in the original.

Accompanying Correspondence A number of respondents sent covering or supplementary letters with their forms. The content of these letters is sometimes very illuminating, as in the case of the vicar of South Cave (Vol. 1, 283), but on other occasions is of limited interest. Accordingly these documents have been treated on their individual merits, being sometimes transcribed in full and sometimes merely summarized, but their existence has always been noted.

The user is reminded that the compilation of this edition, like any other printed transcript of a manuscript document, is to a significant extent an interpretative as well as a mechanical process. The translation of information from the original forms to a printed text involves the interposition of editorial judgements, which although fully defensible, might still be open to legitimate difference of opinion from other scholars. Accordingly researchers interested in the fine detail of the return for a particular place of worship, are still advised to consult the original.

Acknowledgements

More than a decade ago, when I was a member of staff at the Department of History at the University of York, Bill Sheils was kind enough to suggest that I might undertake this edition. Edward Royle has also encouraged me to pursue the project and has, over the years, provided much invaluable stimulus and advice drawing on his own deep knowledge of religion in nineteenth-century Yorkshire. We have all, however, had to be patient until a suitable opportunity arose. The means have now be provided by the Faculty of Arts Research Committee at the Open University, which has generously funded research assistance, primarily for the initial transcription of the returns; the British Academy which has made a grant for indexing and publication

---

[26] See for example All Saints, Kirby Underdale (Vol. 1, 129) where the initial figure of 90 corresponds to the sum of the morning, afternoon and Sunday School attendances.

costs; and the Borthwick Institute of Historical Research, which by appointing me to a Visiting Research Fellowship for the Summer Term of 1998 has provided essential research facilities and a congenial working environment. I am most grateful to them all.

I am indebted above all to Nicholas Bird, my research assistant for this project, for his meticulous attention to detail, and unfailing commitment and cheerfulness. I have benefited much from his advice, ideas and encouragement. He undertook the initial transcription of the great majority of the returns, and compiled much of the index. The text has, however, subsequently been fully checked and revised by me, and responsibility for the final format and for any remaining errors is therefore mine alone. I am also very grateful to David Smith, Chris Webb and to all the staff of the Borthwick Institute for their insights and assistance, and to my colleagues in the Religious Studies Department at the Open University, especially Gerald Parsons and Susan Mumm, who have willingly shouldered some of my usual responsibilities during my study leave.

Census of Great Britain, 1851.

(13 and 14 Victoriæ, Cap. 53.)

510-1-2-3 4

A RETURN

the several Particulars to be inquired into respecting the undermentioned CHURCH or CHAPEL in England, belonging to the United Church of England and Ireland.

[A similar Return (*mutatis mutandis*,) will be obtained with respect to Churches belonging to the Established Church in Scotland, and the Episcopal Church there, and also from Roman Catholic Priests, and from the Ministers of every other Religious Denomination throughout Great Britain, with respect to their Places of Worship.]

NAME and DESCRIPTION of CHURCH or CHAPEL.

I. *Parish Church of the Parish of Tickhill*

II. WHERE SITUATED.	Parish, Ecclesiastical Division or District, Township or Place	Superintendent Registrar's District	County and Diocese
	in the Town of Tickhill	*Doncaster*	*York*

III. WHEN CONSECRATED OR LICENSED	Under what Circumstances CONSECRATED or LICENSED
at its building Some Centuries back	

In the case of a CHURCH or CHAPEL CONSECRATED or LICENSED since the 1st January, 1800; state

IV. HOW OR BY WHOM ERECTED	COST, how Defrayed
	By Parliamentary Grant .... Parochial Rate .... „ Private Benefaction, or Subscription, or from other Sources......} Total Cost......£

The Vicarage is endowed as follows

V. HOW ENDOWED		VI. SPACE AVAILABLE FOR PUBLIC WORSHIP
The Church has no endowment	£	
Land .... *yes*	Pew Rents .... *none*	Free Sittings *366*
Tithe .... *yes*	Fees .... *small*	Other Sittings *545*
Glebe .... *yes*	Dues .... *none*	
Other Permanent Endowment ....} *yes*	Easter Offerings ...... *none* Other Sources .... *none*	Total Sittings... *911*

VII. Estimated Number of Persons attending Divine Service on Sunday, March 30, 1851.				AVERAGE NUMBER OF ATTENDANTS during — Months next preceding March 30, 1851. (See Instruction VII.)			
	Morning	Afternoon	Evening		Morning	Afternoon	Evening
General Congregation } Sunday Scholars	*141*		*98*	General Congregation } Sunday Scholars	*No minute*		*kept.*
Total..				Total...			

VIII. REMARKS	*Congregations vary so much according to Season & general Health as makes this no sure statistical return. Church is quite sufficient – average Congregations fair.*

I certify the foregoing to be a true and correct Return to the best of my belief.

Witness my hand this —— *31* —— day of *March* 1851.

IX. (Signature) *Edwd H Brooksbank*

(Official Character) *Vicar of Tickhill* of the above named,

(Address by Post) *Rotherham Yorkshire.*

Facsimile 2: Simplified form for returns from Anglican churches

570 - 3 - 1 - 2 57

Superintendent Registrar's District _Doncaster_

Registrar's District _Doncaster_

Parish or Township _Doncaster_

1. Name of Church — _Christ Church in Doncaster_

2. When erected (as near as may be known) _first Stone laid 9 Octr 1827_

3. No. of persons who might be accommodated........ { Free Sittings................. _210_
{ Appropriated Sittings .... _790_

Total...... _1000_

4. Usual Number of Attendants upon the Sabbath :—

	General Congregation	Sunday Scholars
Morning	800	220
Afternoon	100	
Evening	700	

Signature of Informant. _Charles P. Alford_

2000. 11-51.

Facsimile 3: Form for returns from Quaker Meeting Houses

510-3-1-

CENSUS OF GREAT BRITAIN, 1851.

(13 and 14 Victoriæ, cap. 53.)

A RETURN

OF THE SEVERAL PARTICULARS TO BE INQUIRED INTO RESPECTING THE UNDERMENTIONED

MEETING-HOUSE OF THE SOCIETY OF FRIENDS.

I. Where Situate; Specifying the			II. When Erected	III. Whether a Separate and Entire Building	IV. Whether used exclusively as a Place of Worship	V. Space available for Public Worship in Meeting Houses used on Sunday, March 30, 1851.		VI. Estimated Number of Attendants on Sunday, March 30, 1851			VII. REMARKS
Parish or Place	County	District				Admeasurement in Superficial Feet (4)	Estimated Number of Persons capable of being Seated (5)	Morning	Afternoon	Evening	
(1)	(2)	(3)									
West Faithorpe Doncaster	Yorks.	Doncaster Union	Before 1806	Yes	Yes	On the Floor or Area...... 1155	222	34	24	—	
						In the Galleries 483	114				
						Total ... 1638	336				

I certify the foregoing to be a true and correct Return to the best of my belief. Witness my hand this 31st day of 3 mo 1851.

Name   *[signature]*

Address   *Friends [signature] Doncaster*

Signed by special appointment.

(For instructions, see adjoining Page.)

N.B.—The Particulars to be inserted may be written longitudinally or across the columns, as may be more convenient.

Facsimile 4: Form for returns from all other places of worship

Census of Great Britain, 1851.

(13 and 14 Victoriæ, cap. 53).

A RETURN

OF THE SEVERAL PARTICULARS TO BE INQUIRED INTO RESPECTING THE UNDERMENTIONED

PLACE OF PUBLIC RELIGIOUS WORSHIP.

[N.B.—A similar Return will be obtained from the Clergy of the Church of England, and also from the Minister of every other Religious Denomination throughout Great Britain.]

I.	II. Where Situate; specifying the			III.	IV.	V.	VI.	VII.	VIII.			IX.
Name or Title of Place of Worship	Parish, or Place (1)	District (2)	County (3)	Religious Denomination	When Erected	Whether a Separate and Entire Building	Whether used exclusively as a Place of Worship (Except for a Sunday School)	Space available for Public Worship — Number of Sittings already Provided	Estimated Number of Persons attending Divine Service on Sunday, March 30, 1851			REMARKS

Columns for VII: Free Sittings (4), Other Sittings (5); VIII: Morning, Afternoon, Evening.

								Free Sittings	Other Sittings	Morning	Afternoon	Evening	
General Congregation								70	110	50	72	36	
Sunday Scholars										54			
Total										54			

Average Number of Attendants during months (See Instruction VIII.)

	Morning	Afternoon	Evening
General Congregation	—	80	50
Sunday Scholars	50	—	—
Total	50	80	50

Free Space or Standing Room for —

I certify the foregoing to be a true and correct Return to the best of my belief. Witness my hand this 30 day of _March_ 1851.

X. (Signature) ...... _John Spears_

(Official Character) _Baptist Minister_

(Address by Post) _Rev. John Spears_

of the above-named Place of Worship.

The particulars to be inserted in Divisions I. to VI. inclusive, and in IX., may be written either along or across the columns, as may be more convenient.

YORK DISTRICT: CITY OF YORK (HO 129/515)

Bootham Subdistrict[1]

ST GILES IN THE SUBURBS (Part Parish, Population 2059)

1   St Giles' Licensed Room, Clarence Street. *Licensed* September 1850 to afford accommodation as a place of worship for a large and poor district – the population of the entire parish exceeding 4000 souls. *Erected* The Revd William Henry Strong. *Cost* Private Benefaction. *Sittings* Free 150. *On 30 March* Morning GC 65 Afternoon X Evening GC 150. *Signed* William Henry Strong, Incumbent of St Olave's & St Giles, Lord Mayor's Walk, York. [515/76]

ST WILFRED (Parish, Population 319)

2   Festival Concert Room (Wesleyan Methodist (Reformers)), Museum Street. *Erected* Hired as a temporary place for religious worship on Sundays. SEB. *Sittings* Free 1050 Other 550. *On 30 March* Morning GC 885 SS 173 Evening GC 1317. *Average during 9 months* Morning GC 870 SS 180 Evening GC 1450. *Remarks* The office-bearers connected with this place of worship wish it to be distinctly understood that they are Wesleyan Methodists, only separated as a branch for a time, in order to bring about a change in matters of discipline in the Wesleyan body. *Signed* George Hope, Circuit Steward, 3 Castlegate, York. [515/77]

3   St Wilfrid's [Roman] Catholic Chapel. *Erected* 1802. SEB ExW. *Sittings* Free 80 Other 410 Free Space 50. *On 30 March* Morning GC 861 [more than one service] SS 130 Afternoon GC 70 SS 181 Evening GC 362. *Signed* Joseph Render, Roman Catholic Priest, Little Blake Street, York. [515/78]

ST MICHAEL LE BELFREY (Part Parish, Population 1115)

4   St Michael le Belfrey. Probably consecrated as Saint Michael at the Belframes – Now called Saint Michael le Belfrey – or commonly "Belfrey's". An ancient parish church for the Parish of St Michael le Belfrey & the Parishes united, viz St Wilfrid, Minster Yard & Clifton. *Consecrated* before 1800. *Endowment* Land £35 OPE £65 Fees about £20 Easter Offerings about £25 Other Sources £2.2.0. *Sittings* Total 1000. *On 30 March* Morning GC 420 SS 160 Afternoon GC 475 SS 160 Total 630 [sic]. *Signed* W. H. Oldfield, Incumbent, 33 Bootham, York. [515/79]

5   Grape Lane Chapel (Primitive Methodist). *Erected* before 1800. SEB ExW. *Sittings* Free 120 Other 380 Free Space 200. *On 30 March* Morning GC 125 SS 16 Afternoon GC 76 SS 16 Evening GC 500. *Signed* Jeremiah Dodsworth, Minister, 34 Union Terrace, York. [515/80]

---

[1]   No returns for the extra parochial area of New Street and Davy Gate (population 24) or the parishes of St John Delpike (population 386), St Andrews (population 365) and St Peter the Little (population 294).

ST MARTIN LE GRAND (Parish, Population 523)

6 St Martin le Grand, Coney Street. An ancient Parish church. *Consecrated* before 1800. *Sittings* Free 105 Other 515. On 30 March Morning 150. *Average during 6 months* Afternoon 350. *Signed* A. W. Dorset Fellowes, Incumbent or Vicar, York. [515/81]

7 New Street Chapel (Wesleyan). *Erected* 1815. SEB ExW. *Sittings* Free 350 Other 650. On 30 March Morning GC 375 SS 99 Afternoon GC 120 Evening GC 500. *Average during 12 months* Morning GC 350 Afternoon GC 100 Evening GC 500. *Signed* Saml. Tindall, Minister, 7 New Street, York. [515/82]

ST HELEN, STONEGATE (Parish, Population 551)

8 Lendal Chapel (Independents). *Erected* 1816. SEB ExW. *Sittings* Free 400 Other 760. On 30 March Morning GC 220 SS 135 Evening GC 216. *Remarks* The Minister of the Chapel Mr Evan has been absent some month in consequence of Ill Health. *Signed* William Robinson, Deacon, Solicitor, York. [515/83]

9 St Helen, Stonegate. An ancient Parish Church, the Oldest in the City of York. *Consecrated* some 1400 years – Before 1800. *Endowment* Land £88.12.6 OPE Parliamentary Grant £21.8.0 Fees £4 Easter Offerings £7. *Sittings* Free 60 Other 340. On 30 March Morning GC 45 Afternoon X Evening GC 110. *Average* Morning GC 70 Afternoon X Evening GC 153. *Remarks* As there are very few poor children in the Parish, these go or may go to one or other of the National Schools, placed in different parts of the City, and as all these schools are also Sunday schools, they take all the children of each school to the nearest church when there is room. I have therefore no Sunday School. In 1815 when I received the appointment to the vicarage of St Helens, the first time I did the duty, the congregation consisted only of 7 persons. Having got the Church repewed, in a short time every sitting was occupied. I then commenced an Evening Lecture – this also became the same till about 1846. My voice then having failed me, and two, adjoining Churches, which before then had only afternoon service, being required to have morning service also, about half of my congregation consisting of persons belonging to these two parishes gradually left, and took their place in their own Churches. These, my advanced years, the failure of my voice, and several other evening Lectures having since been commenced in different parts of the City, and one very near, where there is a popular preacher, were the chief causes why my congregation are now so much reduced. The numbers taken yesterday do not I consider amount to the general avarage of the last 12 months. 8 of this months I take it would be about 70 in the morning and 153 in the evening. This, here, I consider the most unfavourable part of the year – so very many people being poisoned by colds & [prevented from] attending their place of worship. *Signed* John Acaster, Queen's Villa, Heworth Grange, nr York. [515/84]

10 Little Stonegate Room, Little Stonegate, Christians meeting together for worship as such without any denominational name or title. ExW. *Sittings* Free 150 Other None. On 30 March Morning GC 80 Afternoon SS 20. *Average during 12* *months* Evening GC 150. *Remarks* "Little Stonegate Room" being part of a Building hired for the purpose of a Meeting-Room, the date of its <u>erection</u> is not known. It was opened for the above purpose in March 1849. On Sunday March 30th the evening meeting was held in a larger Room instead – viz, Merchant's Hall, Fossgate: hence the return is made below. *Signed* William Trotter, one of the Ministers of the Gospel preaching in the above-named Place of Worship, 32 Palmer Lane, York. [515/85]

MINSTER YARD WITH BEDDERN (Extra Parochial, Population 1108)

   11   <u>Cathedral & Metropolitical Church of St Peter of York [York Minster]</u>. *Sittings* Free 879 Total 879. *On 30 March* Morning GC 275 Afternoon GC 411. *Average during 12 months* Morning GC 600 Afternoon GC 1000. *Remarks* The inclemancy of the weather and the prevailing epidemic will account for the comparative smallness of the Congregation on the 30 March 1851. *Signed* Charles Alfred Thiselton, Chapter Clerk, Minster Yard, York. [515/86]

HOLY TRINITY, GOODRAMGATE (Parish, Population 526)

   12   <u>Holy Trinity, Goodramgate</u>. An Ancient Parish Church. *Consecrated* before 1800. *Sittings* Free 100 Other 300. *On 30 March* Afternoon GC 193 SS 52. *Signed* Edw. J. Raines, Rector, York. [515/87]

   13   <u>New Church or Swedenborgians</u>. *Sittings* Free 60 Other none Free Space 20. *On 30 March* Evening GC 13. *Average during 12 months* 20. *Signed* William Heppell, Leader, 3 Vicars' Terrace, Layerthorpe, York. [515/88]

HOLY TRINITY, KING'S COURT (Parish, Population 720)

   14   <u>Holy Trinity, King's Court, King's Square</u>. *Sittings* Free 15 Other 310. *On 30 March* (alternate during Summer) Morning X Afternoon GC 46 SS 26 Evening X. *Average* (alternate during Summer) Morning GC 50 SS 24 Afternoon GC 50 SS 24 Evening X. *Remarks* Presuming that the 5th Heading "How Endowed" has reference to Churches consecrated since 1800, & not being able to give a correct Return, I have left the Column blank. *Signed* Isaac Grayson, Curate, 44 St Andrewgate, York. [515/89]

ST SAMPSON (Parish, Population 758)

   15   <u>St Sampson's</u>. An ancient Church, nearly rebuilt in 1847 & 1848, chiefly by subscription & the Tower not finished through want of funds there being a Debt of £300 still remaining. Till the reign of King Edward III the Patronage was in the Archdeacon's of Richmond. Then it came to the Crown & in 1393 King Richard 2d granted the Advowson to the Vicar's Choral of York Minster to be united & appropriated to their College, & they are still the Patrons. *Sittings* Free 200 Other 300. *On 30 March* Morning 150 Afternoon X Evening 210. *Average* Morning GC 170 Afternoon X Evening GC 22. *Remarks* The Dissenters having particularly urged a full attendance at their Chapels, I believe, occasioned my congregations to be rather smaller than usual. *Signed* Wm. Bulmer, Incumbent Curate, York. [515/90]

ALL SAINTS, PAVEMENT (Parish, Population 423)

16   All Saints Church on the Pavement, York. *Consecrated* Before 1800. It is the Parish Church of All Saints – and also (since the Reformation) of St Peter's the Little. *Endowment* Land £11 OPE £62 Fees £3 Easter Offerings £3 Other Sources £13. *Sittings* Free 100 Other 400. *On 30 March* Morning GC 275 SS 30 Afternoon X Evening GC 363. *Average during 12 months* Morning GC 300 SS 30 Afternoon X Evening GC 500. *Signed* George Trevor, MA, Rector, Sheffield. [515/91]

ST MICHAEL, SPURRIERGATE (Parish, Population 585)

17   St Michael's, Spurriergate. *Erected* An ancient Rectory existing at the time of the Norman Conquest. Present Church of the 15th Century. *Sittings* Free 150 Appropriated 250. *Usual Number of Attendants* Morning (Service only 5 times in the year) GC 30 SS none; Afternoon (Sunday) GC 30 SS none. *Signed* Thomas Peters. [515/92 Simplified]

ST MARY, CASTLEGATE (Parish, Population 1043)

18   St Mary, Castlegate. *Endowment* Total Income £120. *Sittings* Total 600 or 800. *On 30 March* Unknown. *Remarks* The Sunday Scholars go to the Nanl School. The Day Scholars do the same. *Signed* Joseph Salvin, Minister, York. [515/93]

19   Meeting House of the Society of Friends, York. *Erected* 1816. SEB occasionally used for the annual meetings of the Religious Tract Soc: and for anti-Slavery meetings. *Space* Floor 3045 ft Galleries 1917 ft. *Estimated Seating* 1000. *On 30 March* Morning 273 Afternoon 170. *Dated* 7 April. *Signed* John Ford, 20 Bootham, York. [515/94]

Micklegate Subdistrict

ALL SAINTS, NORTH STREET (Parish, Population 1308)

20   All Saints, North Street. *Consecrated* Before 1800. *Endowment* Glebe £31.12.0 OPE £79.2.0 Fees £4. *Sittings* Free 15 Other 500. *On 30 March* Morning GC 76 SS 30 Evening GC 110. *Average during 6 months* Morning GC 100 Evening GC 250. *Remarks* Mar. 30 1851 The Rector confined by illness & the Curate unavoidably absent. *Signed* Will. Leo. Pickard, Rector, York. [515/95]

HOLY TRINITY, MICKLEGATE (Part Parish), Population 1505)

21   Holy Trinity, Micklegate. *Consecrated* Before 1800. *Sittings* Free 63 Other 362. *On 30 March* Morning 350 Afternoon 250. *Average* See letter [not extant]. *Dated* 1 April. *Signed* F. S. Pope, Curate. [515/96]

ST JOHN, MICKLEGATE (Parish, Population 915)

22   St John the Evangelist, Micklegate. *Consecrated* before 1800. *Endowment* Have only been Incumbent 2 months – Income from land only has been £170, but will not now exceed £150. *Sittings* Free 245 Other 165. *On 30 March* Church only reopened a month since after being closed 8 months, consequently Congregation not settled. Morning GC 300 Afternoon X Evening GC 350. *Average* Morning GC 300 Afternoon X Evening GC 350. *Signed* Edwin Fox, Incumbent, 4 Holdgate Terrace, York. [515/97]

ST MARTIN, MICKLEGATE WITH ST GREGORY (Parish, Population 619)

23   St Martin cum Gregory, Micklegate. *Consecrated* previous to 1230. *Sittings* Total about 1000. *Usual Number of Attendants* Morning/Evening GC very well attended; Morning SS 200 Evening SS 200. *Signed* Wm. Paver, Registrar. [515/98 Simplified]

ST MARY, BISHOPHILL JUNIOR (Part Parish, Population 3526)

24   St Mary, Bishophill Junior or New Bishophill – a Vicarage, one of the oldest Churches in York. *Sittings* No really appropriated Sittings; Total about 234. *On 30 March* Morning X Afternoon GC 150 Evening X. *Average* Morning X Afternoon GC 170 (or perhaps more than 170) Evening X. *Remarks* There is a schoolroom licensed for Divine worship in another part of the Parish which is well attended, where there is full service every Sunday Morning & Evening. The Dissenters having particularly urged, from the Pulpit, peoples' attendance at their Chapels, I believe, occasioned the attendance at my churches to be rather less than usual. *Signed* Wm. Bulmer, Vicar, York. [515/99]

ST MARY, BISHOPHILL SENIOR (Part Parish, Population 1227)

25   St Mary, Bishophill Senior. *Consecrated* prior to 1267. *Sittings* Total about 300. *Average* SS none; Morning and Afternoon GC well attended; Evening none. *Signed* Wm. Paver, Registrar. [515/105 Simplified]

26   Albion Street Chapel (Wesleyan Methodists). *Erected* 1816. SEB ExW. *Sittings* Free 300 Other 550. *On 30 March* Morning GC 196 SS 150 Evening GC 296. *Signed* Rob. R. Rocliffe, Chapel Steward, Holdgate Road, York. [515/106]

Walmgate Subdistrict[2]

ST MAURICE IN THE SUBURBS (Parish, Population 2928)

27   St Maurice, Monkgate. An Ancient Parish Church. *Consecrated* before 1800. *Sittings* Free 20 Other 318. *On 30 March* Morning GC 240 SS 41 Evening GC 200. *Signed* Edw. J. Raines, Vicar, York. [515/1]

---

[2]   No returns for the parishes of St Helen on the Walls (population 398), All Saints, Peaseholm (population 426), St Peter-le-Willows (population 588) and St Nicholas in the Suburbs (population 217)

ST CUTHBERT (Part Parish, Population 1666)

28   St Cuthbert, Peasholme Green. *Endowment* The Rector who knows & manages the Temporalities is non-resident, he living at Bishop Middleham in the County of Durham. *Sittings* Free 240 Other 30 The children sit on moveable benches in the aisle of Chancel. *On 30 March* Morning GC 245 SS 190 Afternoon GC 195 SS 188. *Average during 12 months* Morning GC 260 SS 200 Afternoon GC 220 SS 200. *Remarks* The church is uncomfortably crowded – many more would attend if it were larger. It is the only place of worship in the whole Parish & affords only 270 regular sittings for a Population now nearly 3000. *Signed* Charles Rose, Resident Curate, Park Place, York. [515/2]

ST SAVIOUR (Part Parish, Population 2538)

29   The Church of St Saviour, St Saviourgate. *Consecrated* Before 1800. *Endowment* Land £20 Tithe £10 Glebe £4 OPE £1.13.4 Fees £4 Easter Offerings £4. *Sittings* Free 450 Other 550. *On 30 March* No accurate account taken. *Average during 12 months* Morning GC 430 SS 200 Afternoon X Evening GC 650 SS X. *Remarks* The Church was restored in 1845 when additional sittings were provided for 242 persons. On many occasions the whole of the seats were occupied. *Signed* Josiah Crofts, Rector, The Rectory, St Saviourgate, York. [515/3]

30   Wesleyan (Methodist) Centenary Chapel, St Saviourgate. *Erected* About 1840. SEB ExW. *Sittings* Free 340 Other 1129 Free Space none. *On 30 March* Morning GC 703 SS 236 Evening GC 1037. *Average during 12 months* Morning GC 800 SS 250 Evening GC 1200. *Signed* James Chadwick, Steward to the Trustees, Spen Lane, York. [515/4]

31   (English Presbyterian[3]) Chapel, St Saviour[gate]. *Erected* 1692. Separate ExW. *Sittings* No distinction of this kind [i.e. between Free and other]. *On 30 March* SS none Morning GC 97 Evening GC 60. *Average during 12 months* Morning GC 120. *Signed* Charles Wellbeloved, Minister, Monkgate, York. [515/5]

32   Salem Chapel (Independent or Congregational Dissenters), St Saviour's Place. *Erected* 1839. SEB ExW. *Sittings* Free 500 Other 1100. *On 30 March* Morning GC 796 SS 182 Afternoon GC 80 Evening GC 802. *Average during 12 months* Morning GC 800 SS 180 Afternoon GC 80 Evening GC 900. *Remarks* The attendance for 30th March is given by precise enumeration. The average attendance has been diminished in consequence of the prolonged illness of the Minister. He gives his opinion that no returns can be depended on where enumeration has not been faithfully employed. *Signed* James Parsons, Minister, 28 St Saviourgate, York. [515/6]

ST CRUX (Parish, Population 920)

33   St Crux, Pavement. Ancient Parish Church. *Consecrated* Before 1800. *Endowment* Total Income £100. *Sittings* Free 168 Other 382. *On 30 March* Afternoon

---

3   This is the denominational description given by Wellbeloved. 'Unitarian' has been added in a different hand, probably the registrar's.

GC About 200. *Remarks* About 120 Sunday Scholars attend Divine Service at St Crux – but the majority are not Parishioners. *Signed* Joseph Crosby, Incumbent, St Saviourgate, York. [515/7]

34   <u>Wesleyan Methodist Association Chapel, Lady Peckitt's Yard</u>. *Erected* 1829. SEB ExW. *Sittings* Free 100 Other 450 Free Space None. *On 30 March* Morning GC 122 SS 35 Afternoon GC 25 (This is a short Service which is held always in the <u>Vestry</u>) Evening GC 194. *Remarks* The attendance on Sunday March 30th, is about the average. *Signed* William Pickwell, Trustee, Local Preacher and Class Leader, Printer, High Jubbergate, York. [515/8]

ST DENIS IN WALMGATE (Parish, Population 1479)

35   <u>Saint Dionysius [St Denis], Walmgate</u>. An Ancient Parochial Church, primarily for the use of the Parishioners of Saint Dennis only; but, since the Act of Incorporation, for those of Saint George also. *Consecrated* before 1800. *Endowment* Easter Offerings £2.10.0. *Sittings* Free 351 Other 104. *On 30 March* Morning X Afternoon GC 130 Day Scholars 208 Evening X. *Average during 3 months* Morning X Afternoon GC 80 SS 150 (scarcely more than haphazard approximation) Evening X. *Remarks* The Return'g Officer regrets that he is not in possession of the requisite material to complete this return, since of one item (that of the main part of the Endowmn't) he is altogether ignorant, & of the others but very imperfectly inform'd: the Rector (the only authority on the subject) declining to co-operate. [Certified as correct 'so far as the data given extend']. *Signed* Richard Browne, Senior Churchwarden, No 1, Foss Bridge Hosp., York. [515/9]

ST GEORGE (Parish, Population 2095)

36   <u>St George's Roman Catholic Church</u>. *Erected* 1850. SEB ExW. *Sittings* Free 100 Other 400 Free Space 100. *On 30 March* Morning GC 359 SS X Afternoon X SS X Evening GC 418 Total 481 [sic]. *Remarks* N. B. The Sunday scholars attend the Sunday schools at St Wilfrid and are returned there under from [sic] for St Wilfrids Sunday schools. *Signed* Joseph Render, Catholic Priest, Little Blake Street, York. [515/10]

ST MARGARET WALMGATE (Parish, Population 1595)

37   <u>St Margaret's Church, Walmgate</u>. An Ancient Parish Church. Date of erection not known, but the Register Books commence in 1558. St Peter le Willows' Parish was united to St Margaret's Parish in 1585. St Margaret's church serves for both Parishes, there being no church in St Peter le Willows' Parish. The united Parishes adjoin each other. *Consecrated* many centuries before 1800. *Endowment* Land £35 Glebe £17 OPE £78 Pew Rents about £4 Fees uncertain, about £5 Aggregate Annual amount £139. *Sittings* Free 450 Other 30 and Benches in the Aisles besides. *On 30 March* Morning GC 380 SS 160 Afternoon GC X SS X Evening GC 480. *Average during 12 months* Morning GC 380 SS 150 Afternoon GC X SS X Evening GC 470. *Remarks* We greatly need increased accommodation in our church. If the church were enlarged, so that the number of sittings could be doubled, there is no reason to believe they would [not] soon be occupied. Want of better accommodation now prevents many from attending church. *Signed* George Coopland, Rector and Officiating Minister, York. [515/11]

38 Wesleyan Reformers, Walmgate. SEB ExW. *Sittings* Free 100. *Remarks* But recently opened and no Service on the 30th March 1851. *Signed* John Bellerby, Steward, St George's Terrace, York. [515/12]

39 St George's School Room (Wesleyan). *Erected* 1825. SEB used chiefly as a Day and a Sunday School. *Sittings* Free 400. *Remarks* St George's School Room is used for occasional preaching; but no accurate returns as to attendance can be made. *Signed* Saml. Tindall, Minister, 7 New Street, York. [515/13]

ST LAWRENCE (Part Parish, Population 1380)

40 St Lawrence, without Walmgate Bar, Lawrence Street. *Consecrated* before 1800. *Endowment* Land £70 Tithe £45 OPE £4.12.0 Fees £10.10.0 Dues £2.12.0 Total £132.14.0. *Sittings* Free 130 Other 200. *On 30 March* Morning GC 140 SS 45. *Remarks* The above is the Gross Income, Rates amount to £5 per annum. *Signed* John Robinson, Vicar, Clifton, York. [515/14]

Skelton Subdistrict (North Riding)[1]

SHIPTON (Township (Overton), Population 416)

41   Church of the Evangelists, Shipton. *Consecrated* May 31 1849 by the Arch Bishop of York as an additional Church to the Parish Church. *Erected* By the Honble Payan Dawnay. *Cost* Private Benefaction about £3,000. *Endowment* OPE £1,000 Fees Surplice. *Sittings* Free All Total 450. *On 30 March* Morning GC 82 SS 49 Afternoon GC 61 SS 48. *Signed* James Henry Pickering, Minister, Overton with Shipton, York. [515/63]

42   Wesleyan (Methodist) Chapel, [Shipton].[2] *Erected* 1817. Separate ExW. *Sittings* Free 80 Other 70 Free Space None. *On 30 March* SS none; Morning GC 60 Afternoon X Evening GC 84. *Average during 3 months* SS none; Morning GC 55 Evening GC 70. *Remarks* This Wesleyan Chapel is open for Divine Service every Sunday evening, but only open in the morning every alternate Sabbath day; in consequence of the church being closed every other Sunday – Service being removed to the Parish church at Overton. The chapel is therefore open, when the church is closed. *Signed* John Moon, Steward, Shipton, York. [515/65]

OVERTON (Township (P), Population 45)

43   Overton Church [St Cuthbert]. *Consecrated* Before 1800. *Endowment* Land Rent charge on £58 Glebe £121 Other Sources per annum Pension from Land Revenues of the Crown £2.18.8. *Sittings* Free nearly all Other 30 Total 150. *On 30 March* Morning No service; Afternoon No service; Evening X. *Average during 12 months* Morning GC 30 Afternoon X Evening X. *Signed* James Henry Pickering, Minister, Overton with Shipton, York. [515/64]

SKELTON (Township (P), Population 347)

44   Rectoral Church of All Saints, Skelton. *Erected* unknown perhaps built about 1230 AD. *Endowment* Land £109 Glebe £5 Fees trifling & uncertain Easter Offerings uncertain. *Average* Morning GC about 60 SS about 15 Afternoon GC about 30 Evening none. *Remarks* The Parish of Skelton is one of the smallest, in extent & population in the Archdiocese of York, & the Church accommodation is sufficient for the number [of] Parishioners. *Signed* Benjamin Bass Golding, Rector, Skelton, nr York. [515/66]

---

[1]   No return for the townships of Beningbrough (population 86) in the parish of Newton-upon-Ouse or the township of Rawcliffe (population 48) in the parishes of St Olave Mary Gate and St Michael-le-Belfrey.

[2]   I am grateful to Dr Edward Royle for information on the location of this place of worship.

45   Wesleyan Methodists, Girl's School, Skelton. *Erected* 1842. SEB Sunday School & Place of worship. *Sittings* Free All. *On 30 March* Evening GC 48. *Average during 4 months* Evening GC 70. *Signed* Wm. Brown, Steward, Farmer, Skelton, nr York. [515/67]

WIGGINGTON (Parish, Population 374)

46   [St Mary and St Nicholas], Wiggington. Name not Known. Ancient Parish Church. *Consecrated* Before 1800. *Endowment* Tithe Commuted £179.16.3 Glebe 29 acres; OPE £19.5.0 Fees £1.10.0. *Sittings* Free 30 Other 90. [Certified as correct 'to the questions which I have answered'.] *Signed* James N. Corbett, Rector, Wiggington. [515/68]

HAXBY (Parish, Population 527)

47   St Mary's Chapel, Haxby. *Consecrated* Before Jany 1800. *Endowment* OPE £24.0.7 minus Inc. Tax; Fees £1.5.0. *Sittings* Free 20 Other 143. *On 30 March* Afternoon GC 77 SS 65. *Remarks* There is only one service at Haxby Chapel the Minister having to perform divine service at Strensall Church also. *Signed* Henry Harrison, Chapelwarden, Haxby, nr York. [515/69]

48   Wesleyan Chapel, Haxby. *Erected* 1800. SEB ExW. *Sittings* Free 80 Other 130. *On 30 March* Morning GC X SS 95 Afternoon GC X SS 92 Evening GC 155 SS X. *Average during 12 months* Morning GC X SS 85 Afternoon GC X SS 85 Evening GC 150. *Signed* Saml. Tindall, Minister, 7 New Street, York. [515/70]

49   Primitive Methodist Chapel, Haxby. *Erected* About 1827. SEB. *Sittings* Free 32 Other 30. *On 30 March* Morning X Afternoon GC 30 Evening X. *Average during 1 month* Morning X Afternoon GC 120 Evening X. *Signed* John Barker, Local Minister, 36 Hungate, York. [515/71]

Bootham Subdistrict (North Riding)[3]

HUNTINGTON (Township (P), Population 539)

50   All Saints, Huntington. Ancient Parish Church. *Endowment* Land £14 Tithe £123.15.6 Glebe £25.10.0 Other Sources £1. *Sittings* Free 200 Other 30. *On 30 March* Afternoon GC 116. *Average during 12 months* 80. *Remarks* Single Service, Morning and Afternoon alternately. *Signed* John Moiser, Churchwarden, Huntington, York. [515/72]

51   Wesleyan (Methodist) Chapel, Huntington. *Erected* 1825. Separate Building ExW. *Sittings* Free 40 Other 81 (23 ft by 25ft). *On 30 March* Morning none Afternoon GC 40 Evening GC 40. *Average during 12 months* 40. *Signed* John Agar, Steward, Earswick, nr York. [515/73]

---

3   No returns for the townships of Towthorpe (population 44) and Earswick (population 83) in the parish of Huntington.

CLIFTON (Township (St Olave Marygate), Population 2263)

52   The Chapel of the County Pauper Lunatic Asylum for the North & East Ridings of Yorkshire. *Consecrated* 7 April 1847 Licensed under Act 8 & 9 Victoria c 126. *Erected* By the committee of visitors. *Cost* By County rates. *Endowment* OPE By annual salary £80. *Sittings* Free 200. *On 30 March* Morning GC 172 Afternoon X Evening X. *Average during 12 months* Morning GC 110. *Remarks* The above congregation was composed of 70 female Lunatics 84 male Lunatics 6 female sane persons & 10 male sane persons. The Asylum has been this year increased from 160 to nearly 300 patients which accounts for the discrepancy between the average & the return for the 30th March. *Signed* Frederick Wm. Hayden, Chaplain, Skelton Rectory, York. [515/74]

ST OLAVE, MARYGATE (YORK) (Township, Population 677)

53   St Olave's Parish Church, Marygate. *Consecrated* In the Reign of Henry 8th On the dissolution of St Marys Abbey. *Endowment* The whole amount from every source £130. *Sittings* Free 175 Other 500. *On 30 March* Morning GC 399 SS 72 Afternoon GC 394 SS 35. *Remarks* Church accommodation much wanted for this Parish. *Signed* William Henry Strong, Incumbent, Lord Mayors Walk, York. [515/75]

Micklegate Subdistrict (West Riding)[4]

HOLGATE (Township (St Mary Bishophill Junior), Population 134)

54   [Anglican] School Room, Holgate Lane, York, licensed by the Archbishop. *Licensed* September 1848 as an additional Church for the accommodation of the inhabitants of Holgate. *Endowment* Other Sources (voluntary subscriptions) £100. *Sittings* Free All Total 250. *On 30 March* Morning GC 250 Evening GC 250. *Average during 12 months* SS none Morning GC 250 Evening GC 250. *Remarks* A new Church is building for this district, for which an endowment is required before it can be consecrated. *Signed* Wm. A. Cartledge, Officiating Minister of Holgate District, Holgate Road, York. [515/100]

UPPER POPPLETON (Chapelry (St Mary Bishophill Junior), Population 415)

55   Upper Poppleton Chapel [All Saints], being an ancient Chapel of Ease under the Parish Church of St Mary Bishophill Junior, York. *Consecrated* Before 1800. *Sittings* Free 45 Other 105. *On 30 March* Morning GC 79 The Sunday Scholars attend the School & Church at Nether Poppleton. *Average during 6 months* Morning GC 70 Afternoon GC 110. *Remarks* Copmanthorpe with Upper Poppleton are united chapels of Ease under the Ch: of St Mary Bishophill Junr. York & they are endowed with an annual Grant of £96 from the Ecclesiastical Commissioners. *Signed* Edwd. Greenhow, Minister, Nun Monkton, nr York. [515/101]

---

4   No returns for the township of Middlethorpe (population 88) in the parish of St Mary Bishophill Senior or for the townships of Angram (population 67) and Hutton-Wandesley (population 121) in the parish of Long Marston.

56   Wesleyan Methodist Chapel, Upper Poppleton. *Erected* 1817. SEB ExW. *Sittings* Free 110 Other 58. *On 30 March* Morning X Afternoon X Evening GC 92. *Signed* William Sampson, Trustee, Poppleton, Farmer, nr York. [515/102]

COPMANTHORPE (Chapelry (St Mary Bishophill Junior), Population 316)

57   Copmanthorpe Church [St Giles], an ancient chapel of Ease to the Parish church of St Mary Bishophill Junr, York. *Endowment* The church derives its Income £45 from the Ecclesiastical Commissioners. *Sittings* 109 are appropriated to the Parishioners & 45 are unappropriated for the use of Poor persons. *On 30 March* Afternoon GC 60 Evening X. *Average* Afternoon GC 50 SS 25 Evening X. *Remarks* The service is performed once on the Sunday – morning & Evg. alternately. *Signed* C. F. Buckley, Minister, Copmanthorpe, nr York. [515/103]

58   Wesleyan Chapel, Copmanthorpe. *Erected* 1821. Entire Building ExW. *Sittings* Free 64 Other 46. *Average* Morning GC 50. *Signed* Elias Hobson, Class Leader, Farmer, Copmanthorpe, York. [515/104]

DRINGHOUSES (Township (St Mary Bishophill Senior), Population 342)

59   Church of St Edward the Confessor, Dringhouses. *Consecrated* August 9th 1849 in lieu of a Donative Chapel. *Erected* The private benefaction of Mrs Trafford Leigh of Dringhouses. *Cost* Private Benefaction etc £5,000 Total about £5000. *Endowment* Land £40 All other categories 0. *Sittings* Free 200 Other 0. *On 30 March* Morning GC 63 SS 57 Afternoon GC 67 SS 58. *Remarks* No District or Parish has yet been assigned to this church. *Dated* 1 April. *Signed* Gilbert H. Philips, Perpetual Curate, Dringhouses, York. [515/107]

60   Wesleyan Chapel, Dringhouses. *Erected* 1834. Entire Building ExW. *Sittings* Free 60 Other 48. *On 30 March* Morning 14 Evening 30. *Dated* 4 April. *Signed* Robert Hick, Steward, Dringhouses, nr York. [515/108]

ACASTER MALBIS (Parish, Population 231)

61   Holy Trinity, Acaster Malbis. Ancient Parish Church. *Consecrated* Before 1800. *Sittings* Free 48 Other 132. *On 30 March* (alternate during Summer) Morning GC 47 SS 13 Afternoon X Evening X. *Average during 12 months* (alternate during Summer) Morning GC 60 SS 16 Afternoon GC 60 SS 16 Evening X. *Signed* Isaac Grayson, Curate, 44 St Andrewgate, York. [515/109]

62   Wesleyan Methodists, Acaster Malbis. *Erected* before 1770. The Service is conducted in the Parochial School. *Sittings* Free All (accommodation for about 60 persons). *On 30 March* Morning X Afternoon X Evening GC 50 (including 10 children). *Average during 12 months* Morning X Afternoon X Evening GC 40 SS 10 children. *Remarks* There is no Sunday School connected with this place of worship or belonging to the Wesleyan Methodists. *Signed* Richd. L. Dawson, Steward, Acaster Malbis, York. [515/110]

BISHOPTHORPE (Parish, Population 406)

63 <u>St Andrew's, Bishopthorpe</u>. An ancient Parish Church. *Consecrated* Before 1800. *Endowment* Land £80 Tithe £22 Glebe 16 acres £32 Fees £1 Other categories none. *Sittings* Free 260 Other (for School children) 40. *On 30 March* Morning GC 105 SS 32 Afternoon GC 73 SS 30 Evening X. *Average during 12 months* Morning GC 100 + 15 SS 30 Afternoon GC 80 + 15 SS 30 Evening X. *Remarks* The Sittings are nominally appropriated as is customary in Parish Churches, but all are really Free. The Archbishop of York is resident in the Parish during <u>eight months</u> in the year and the Vicar during <u>nine</u>. Both being absent at this time the Congregation is diminished by about 20 persons. The morning congregation was <u>above</u> and the afternoon <u>below</u> the average on Mar. 30. 15 persons are added to the average on account of the absence of the Archbishop's and Vicar's households. *Signed* Charles F. Smith, Curate, Bishopthorpe, York. [515/111]

64 <u>Wesleyan Methodist Chapel, Bishopthorpe</u>. *Erected* 1833. SEB ExW. *Sittings* Free 63 Other 61. *On 30 March* Evening 62. *Signed* Geor. Joy, Steward, Bishopthorpe, York. [515/112]

ASKHAM BRYAN (Parish, Population 350)

65 <u>[St Nicholas], Askham Bryan</u>. Name not known. An Ancient Church recently repaired. *Erected* Repaired lately. *Endowment* Land £130 Fees £1.10.0. *Sittings* Free 120 Other 30 Total about 150. *On 30 March* Morning GC 50 SS 43 Afternoon GC 40 SS 43 Evening GC X SS X. *Signed* R. A. Tuckniss [?], Curate, Askham Bryan, nr York. [515/113]

66 <u>Missionary Chapel (Wesleyan Methodists), Askham Bryan</u>. *Erected* 1836. SEB ExW. *Sittings* Free 50 Other 50. *On 30 March* Evening 42. *Signed* Wm. Stevenson, Steward. [515/114]

ASKHAM RICHARD (Parish, Population 229)

67 <u>St Mary, Askham Richard</u>. An Ancient Church. *Consecrated* Before 1800. *Erected* Good Repair by the Parish. *Endowment* Land £210 Fees £1.5.0. *Sittings* Free 100 Other 150. *On 30 March* Alternately Morning GC 80 SS 27 Afternoon GC 80 SS 27 Evening X. *Average* Morning SS 30. *Signed* Robt. Fearby, Church Warden, Askham Richard, York. [515/115]

68 <u>Wesleyan Chapel, Askham Richard</u>. *Erected* 1815. SEB ExW. *Sittings* Free 100 Other 30 Free Space 40. *On 30 March* Morning X Afternoon X Evening GC 50. *Average* Evening GC 70. *Signed* Rev W. Wilkinson; John Cundale, Steward, Askham Richard, York. [515/116]

RUFFORTH (Parish, Population 299)

69 <u>[All Saints], Rufforth</u>. *Consecrated* Before 1800. *Endowment* Land £89 OPE £10 Fees £1. *Sittings* Free 29 Other 88. *On 30 March* Afternoon GC 75 SS 11. *Signed* Will. Leo. Pickard, Incumbent Curate, York. [515/117]

70 (Wesleyan) Chapel, Rufforth. *Erected* 1843. SEB ExW. *Sittings* Free 50 Other 60. *On 30 March* Morning GC 49 Afternoon X Evening X. *Average during 12 months* Morning GC 60 Afternoon GC 60 Evening GC 65. *Remarks* Service at Rufforth Morning one Sabbath and Afternoon & Evening the other, for March 30th it was in the Morning. *Signed* Gervase Smith, Minister, 7 New Street, York. [515/118]

HESSAY (Township (Moor Monkton), Population 141)

71 Wesleyan Methodist Chapel, Hessay. *Erected* 1824. SEB ExW. *Sittings* Free 50 Other 45. *On 30 March* Morning GC 30 Afternoon GC 36. *Signed* Henry Elsworth, Trustee, Hessay, York. [515/119]

MOOR MONKTON (Township (P), Population 280)

72 St Cuthberts' Church, Moor Monkton. Ancient Parish Church. *Consecrated* before 1800. *Endowment* Glebe £544.8.0 OPE £28.5.4 Fees about £1 Other Sources £0.2.0. *Sittings* Free 143 Other 11. *On 30 March* Morning GC 80 SS 19 Afternoon GC 54 SS 16 Evening X. *Average during 6 months* Morning GC 70 SS 17 Afternoon GC 36 SS 15 Evening X. *Signed* H. W. Yeoman junior, Rector, Moor Monkton, York. [515/120]

73 Wesleyan Methodists, Moor Monkton. Granary over a stable. *Erected* before 1800. *Sittings* Free 150. *On 30 March* Evening 54. *Signed* Thomas Sampson, Society Steward, Moor Monkton, York. [515/121]

NETHER POPPLETON (Township (P), Population 255)

74 The Parish Church of Nether Poppleton, dedicated, I believe, to "All Saints". *Consecrated* The ancient parish Church. *Endowment* Tithe (money payment in lieu of small) £8 Glebe acres 53.2.4 OPE (by Q. Anne's Bounty with £1000 producing interest) £32.10.0 Pew Rents none Fees perhaps 30s or £2 Dues paid at Easter £3.16.3 1/2. *Sittings* Free 45 Other 183 (Exclusive of Sunday Scholars). *On 30 March* Morning X Afternoon GC 105 SS 80 Evening X. *Average during 6 months* when service is in morning average about 80 Scholars same; Afternoon GC 105 SS 80 Evening X. *Remarks* Divine service is Morning & Afternoon alternately with the adjoining village of Upper Poppleton, so as to give 2 Services for the inhabitants of both villages. *Signed* Chas. Jos. Camidge, Incumbent, Nether Poppleton, York. [515/122]

75 Wesleyan Methodist (Reformers), Nether Poppleton. Room. *Erected* before 1800. SEB ExW. *Sittings* Free 100 Other None. *On 30 March* Evening GC 65. *Average during 5 months* Evening GC 50. *Remarks* The office bearers connected with this place of worship wish it to be distinctly understood that they are Wesleyan Methodists only separated as a branch for a time in order to bring about a change in matters of discipline in the Wesleyan body. *Signed* John Atkinson, Manager, Farmer, Nether Poppleton, nr York. [515/123]

ACOMB (Township (P), Population 874)

76 St Stephen, Acomb. *Consecrated* Before 1800. *Erected* Rebuilt in 1831-2.

Cost By Parliamentary Grant £300 Parochial Rate £700 Private Benefaction etc £318. *Endowment* Land £24 Glebe £80 Fees £10 Other Sources £5. *Sittings* Free 212 Other 396. *On 30 March* Morning GC 230 SS 76 Afternoon GC 138 SS 54. *Remarks* There are sometimes as many as 300 or upwards on a morning; service is proportionally in the afternoon. *Signed* Isaac Spencer MA, Vicar, Incumbent Minister, Acomb, nr York. [515/124]

77   Wesleyan Methodist, Acomb. *Erected* 1821. SEB ExW. *Sittings* Free 230 Other 170. *On 30 March* Morning GC 42 Afternoon GC 47 SS 13 Evening GC 90. *Average during 12 months* SS 40 to 50 Afternoon GC 80 Evening GC 150. *Remarks* During the last twelve months there has been a considerable secession of the Society & congregation so that the returned numbers as attending this day are unusually small. *Signed* Chas. Robinson, Chapel Steward, Acomb, nr York. [515/125]

78   Providence Chapel (Primitive Methodists and Wesleyan Reformers), Acomb. *Erected* 1844 [or 1842]. SEB ExW. *Sittings* Free 150 Other 8 Free Space 20. *On 30 March* Afternoon 30 Evening 30. *Average during 12 months* Morning 50. *Remarks* The Preaching service is in the afternoon every alternatye Sunday. *Signed* Thomas Stilborn, Leader, Acomb. [515/126]

KNAPTON (Township (Acomb), Population 112)

79   Wesleyan Reformers, Knapton. Dwelling House. *Erected* Not known. *On 30 March* Evening 28. *Signed* John Wilkinson, Local Preacher. [515/127]

Walmgate Subdistrict (North Riding)

HEWORTH (Township (St Giles/St Cuthbert/St Saviour), Population 399)

80   Wesleyan (Methodist) Chapel, Heworth. *Erected* 1826. SEB ExW. *Sittings* Free 50 Other 60 Free Space none. *On 30 March* Morning no service Afternoon GC 64 Total 70. *Average during 12 months* Morning no service Afternoon GC 70 Evening no service. *Remarks* In filling up the free space or standing room, I would say there is none but a road to the seats & pulpit. *Signed* John Groves, Assistant Chapel Steward, Heworth, nr York. [515/15]

OSBALDWICK (Township (P), Population 205)

81   St Thomas, Osbaldwick. Ancient church. *Consecrated* Before 1800. *Sittings* Free 125. *On 30 March* Afternoon GC 74 SS 24. *Remarks* there are two full services every Sunday in Summer & one in Winter. *Signed* Robert Daniel, Vicar, 4 Park Place, York. [515/16]

82   Wesleyan, Osbaldwick. Dwelling House. *Usual Number of Attendants* Evening GC about 30. *Signed* Robert Robson Letley, Heslington Road, nr York. [515/17 Simplified]

Walmgate Subdistrict (East Riding)[5]

ST PAUL, HESLINGTON (Parish, Population 228)

83   St Paul's, Heslington. Church of a distinct and separate Parish. *Consecrated* Before 1800. *Sittings* Free 20 Other 180. *On 30 March* Morning/Afternoon alternately GC 100 SS 48. *Average during 12 months* Morning GC 90 SS 47 Afternoon GC 90 SS 47. *Signed* Joseph Crosby, Incumbent, No. 38 St Saviourgate, York. [515/18]

84   Wesleyan Methodist Association Chapel, Heslington. *Erected* about 1832. SEB ExW. *Sittings* Free 34 Other 34 Free Space none. *On 30 March* Evening GC 14. *Average during 12 months* Evening GC 12. *Signed* Michael Wilberfoss, Manager, Heslington, St Lawrence. [515/19]

85   Wesleyan (Methodist) Chapel, Heslington. *Erected* 1844. SEB ExW. *Sittings* Free 50 Other 52. *On 30 March* Evening GC 50. *Average during 12 months* Evening GC 45. *Signed* George Penty, Trustee, Heslington, York. [515/20]

86   Independent Chaple, Heslington. *Erected* 1847. Separate Place of Worship. *Sittings* Free 60 Other 60. *On 30 March* Evening GC 27. *Signed* James Calvert, Trustee, Heslington, nr York. [515/21]

GATE FULFORD (Township (Fulford Ambo), Population 1704)

87   St Oswald's Chapel, Fulford, being the Church of an ancient Chapelry. *Consecrated* centuries before 1800. *Sittings* Total 225. *Remarks* Presuming that the questions 4. 5. 6. 7 relate only to Churches or Chapels consecrated or licensed since 1800 – I enclose no answer to them. *Signed* Robert Sutton, Incumbent Curate, York. [515/22]

88   Wesleyan Chapel, Fulford. *Erected* 1845. SEB ExW. *Sittings* Free 120 Other 240. *On 30 March* Morning GC X SS 60 [scored through] Afternoon GC 110 SS 60 Evening GC 120 SS X. *Average during 12 months* Morning X Afternoon GC 100 Evening GC 160. *Signed* Saml. Tindall, Minister, 7 New Street, York. [515/23]

Escrick Subdistrict (East Riding)[6]

NABURN (Township (P), Population 481)

89   Naburn Church [St Matthew]. *Erected* unknown. Tradition says it was private Roman Catholic Chapel before the Reformation. *Sittings* Free 150 Appropriated 11. *Usual Number of Attendants* Morning GC 150 SS 75. *Signed* Joseph Leaf, Parish Clerk, Naburn. The above information was taken by Me at Naburn on the 4 Dec 1851. John Cooper, Registrar. [515/24 Simplified]

---

5   No returns for the township of Heslington St Lawrence (population 266) in the parish of St Lawrence or for York Barracks (population 235) and the township of Water Fulford (population 42) in the parish of Fulford.
6   No returns for the township of Deighton (population 201) in the parish of Escrick.

90   Naburn Chapel (Wesleyan). *Erected* 1818. SEB ExW. *Sittings* Free 50 Other 72. *Usual Number of Attendants* Afternoon and Evening GC from 80 to 100. *Signed* Christ. Browne, Naburn, York. The above information was taken by Me on the 4 December 1851 at Naburn. John Cooper, Registrar. [515/25 Simplified]

91   Wesleyan, Naburn Hill or White Cock Hall. A private Dwelling House. *Sittings* Free 60. *Usual Number of Attendants* Evening GC from 50 to 60. *Signed* Christ. Browne, Naburn, York. The above information was taken by Me on the 4th December 1851 at Naburn. John Cooper, Registrar. [515/25 Simplified, on same form as **90**]

STILLINGFLEET WITH MOREBY (Township (Stillingfleet), Population 419)

92   St Hellen, Stillingfleet. *Sittings* Free 127 Other 255. *On 30 March* Morning GC 96 SS 49 Afternoon GC 45 SS 29. *Signed* H. G. Pretyman, Curate, Stillingfleet, York. [515/26]

93   Wesleyan Methodist Chapel, Stillingfleet. *Erected* 1833. SEB ExW. *Sittings* Free 31 ft by 15 ft 50 Other 21ft by 12 ft 61. *On 30 March* Morning GC 12 Afternoon GC 4 Evening GC 40. *Average during 12 months* Morning GC 12 Afternoon GC 4 Evening GC 40. *Signed* Thomas Brown, Steward, Stillingfleet, Escrick, York. [515/27]

ESCRICK (Township (P), Population 700)

94   St Helen's, Escrick Parish Church, moved & rebuilt under a private Act about 1789. [1782 added in a different hand]. *Consecrated* before 1800. *Endowment* Tithe £410 Glebe £90 Fees £12. *Sittings* Free 240 Other 40 besides childrens' 140. *On 30 March* Morning GC 170 SS 118 Afternoon GC 130 SS 94. *Signed* Stephen W. Lawley, Rector, Escrick Rectory, York. [515/28]

THORGANBY WITH WEST COTTINGWITH (Parish, Population 388)

95   St Helen's, Thorganby. *Endowment* Land £35 Glebe £10.10.0 OPE £6.5.0 Fees £1.5.0. *Sittings* Free 50 Other 150. *On 30 March* Morning GC 96 SS 39 Afternoon GC 94 SS 39 Evening GC 40. *Average during 12 months* Morning GC 98 SS 42 Afternoon GC 106 SS 41 Evening no exact account kept, probably for the 12 months the average would be 50. *Remarks* There are two full services in the parish church of Thorganby and a third one in a Lecture Room set a part for that purpose. *Signed* Joseph Dunnington Jefferson, Perpetual Curate. [515/29]

96   Wesleyan (Methodist) Chapel, Thorganby. *Erected* 1815. SEB ExW. *Sittings* Free 80 Other 60. *On 30 March* 90 Evening GC 85. [undated] *Signed* John Sawyer, Steward, Thorganby, York. [515/30]

WHELDRAKE (Township (P), Population 689)

97   St Helen's, Wheldrake. The Parish Church of a very ancient foundation. *Endowment* Land/Tithe/Glebe £402. *Sittings* Free 228 Other 52 (exclusive of benches for Sunday Scholars). *On 30 March* Morning GC 104 SS 56 Afternoon GC 52 SS 58 no evening service. *Signed* Robert Bryan Cooke, Minister, Wheldrake, York. [515/31]

98   Wesleyan Methodist Chapel, Wheldrake. *Erected* 1816. Separate ExW. *Sittings* Free 60 Other 67. *On 30 March* Morning GC 5 Afternoon X Evening GC 74. *Signed* Thomas Hick, Deacon, Butcher, Wheldrake. [515/32]

Dunnington Subdistrict (East Riding)[7]

ELVINGTON (Parish, Population 372)

99   Holy Trinity, Elvington, an ancient Parish Church (Rectory). *Consecrated* 1803 In lieu of an old Church. *Erected* By the Rev Andrew Cheap, the Rector, who contributed two thirds of the expense. *Cost* Parochial Rate £300 Private Benefaction etc £700. *Endowment* Tithe (Rent Charge) £20.12.6 Glebe £209.12.0 OPE (Fixed Money Payment) £23.14.0 Fees £1.12.10. *Sittings* Free 225. *On 30 March* Morning GC 49 SS 26 Afternoon GC 57 SS 21. *Signed* Thomas Maude, Minister, Elvington Rectory, nr York. [515/33]

100   Wesleyan (Methodist) Chapel, Elvington. *Erected* About 1810. SEB ExW. *Sittings* Free 70 Other 94 Free Space 30 besides the above. *On 30 March* Morning X Afternoon X Evening GC 30. *Average during 12 months* Morning [sic] GC 60. *Signed* Thomas Lotherington, Chapel Steward, Elvington. [515/34]

KEXBY (Township (Catton), Population 150)

101   Primitive Methodist, Kexby. SEB A Schoolroom. *Usual Number of Attendants* Morning X Afternoon GC 30 Evening X. *Signed* William Dawson, Leader, Kexby, York. [515/35 Simplified]

DUNNINGTON (Township (P), Population 779)

102   [St Nicholas], Dunnington. Ancient Parish Church. *Consecrated* before 1800. *Endowment* Land £52.10.0 Tithe commuted at £348.2.0 Fees about £5. *Sittings* Free (Including sittings for Sunday School children) 70 Other 200. *On 30 March* Morning GC 86 SS 42 Afternoon GC 110 SS 43. *Signed* E. J. Randolph, Rector, Dunnington, York. [515/36]

103   Wesleyan Methodist Chapel, Dunnington. *Erected* 1805. SEB ExW. *Sittings* Free 72 Other 36. *On 30 March* Morning X Afternoon X Evening GC 40. *Average during 12 months* Morning GC X SS X Afternoon GC X SS X Evening GC 50 SS 0. *Signed* William Nelson, Steward & Trustee, Dunnington. [515/37]

104   Primitive Methodist Chapel, Dunnington. *Erected* Nov. 29 [...]. SEB. *Sittings* Free 30 Other 32. *On 30 March* Morning GC X SS 36 Afternoon GC 20 Evening GC 50. *Signed* James Bell, Steward, Dunnington, York. [515/38]

---

7   No returns for the township of Langwith (population 33) in the parish of Wheldrake, for the townships of Stamford Bridge with Scoreby (population 165) in the parish of Catton or for the township of Grimston (population 71) in the parish of Dunnington.

Dunnington Subdistrict (North Riding)

MURTON (Township (Osbaldwick), Population 167)

105 Wesleyan Methodists, Murton. Cottage. *Average* Afternoon GC 20 SS X. *Signed* Thomas Preston, occupier, Murton, nr York. [515/39 Simplified]

HOLTBY (Parish, Population 169)

106 Holy Trinity, Holtby. An ancient Parish Church. But rebuilt between 1790 & 1800 by voluntary subscription & mortgage of land left for repairs etc. *Consecrated* Before 1800. *Sittings* Free 115 Other 18. *On 30 March* Morning X Afternoon GC 75 SS 4 Evening X. *Average during 12 months* Morning GC 40 SS 13 Afternoon GC 70 SS 13 Evening X. *Remarks* As there is only one service on the Sunday alternately in the morning and afternoon I have inserted in the fourth & fifth columns what I believe to be the average alternate attendance. *Signed* Thomas Charles Price, Rector, Holtby Rectory, nr York. [515/40]

STOCKTON ON THE FOREST (Parish, Population 475)

107 St Andrew, Stockton on the Forest. Ancient Chapelry. *Consecrated* before 1800. *Endowment* Land £29 Tithe £0.6.3 Glebe £80 OPE £28.12.0 Fees £1 Other Categories 0. *Sittings* Free 86 Other 154. *On 30 March* Morning GC 69 SS 43 Afternoon GC 112 SS 43. *Average* Morning GC 90 SS 62 Afternoon GC 130 SS 62. *Remarks* Influenza is prevalent & has caused many to absent themselves from Church today. *Signed* J. G. Fawcett, Incumbent, Stockton House, York. [515/41]

108 Wesleyan (Methodist) Chapel, Stockton on the Forest. *Erected* 1815. SEB ExW. *Sittings* Free 150. *On 30 March* Evening GC 61. *Average* Morning [sic] GC 70. *Signed* John Holmes, Chapel Steward, Stockton on the Forest, nr York. [515/42]

WARTHILL (Parish, Population 169)

109 St Mary, Warthill. Ancient Parish Church. *Endowment* Land £59.10.0 Tithe £13.5.0 Glebe £58.10.0 OPE £2.3.4 Fees £9.5.0. *Sittings* Free 57 Other 72. *On 30 March* Morning GC 37 SS 21. *Average* Morning GC 60 SS 21 Afternoon GC 80 SS 21. *Remarks* The service is alternate morning & evening. Sickness accounts for the small number at Church today. *Signed* J. G. Fawcett, Vicar, Stockton House, York. [515/43]

110 Wesleyan Chapel, Warthill. *Erected* 1841. SEB ExW. *Sittings* Free 50 Other 39. *Average during 12 months* Afternoon GC 35 Evening GC 50. *Signed* John Cook, Steward, Warthill, nr York. [515/44]

UPPER HELMSLEY (Parish, Population 78)

111 St Peter, Upper Helmsley, rebuilt about 60 years ago, no chapel in the parish. *Consecrated* Before 1800. *Endowment* Land £15 Tithe £98. *Sittings* Other 140.

Average during 12 months alternate duty averaging about 50. *Signed* John Farrow, Rector, Flaxton, York. [515/45]

GATE HELMSLEY (Parish, Population 293)

112 St Mary, Gate Helmsley. An Ancient Parish Church. No chapel belonging to the Established church. *Consecrated* previous to 1800. *Endowment* Land £83 Tithe £10. *Sittings* Other 140. *Average during 12 months* Alternate duty averaging between 60 and 70. *Signed* John Farrow, Vicar, Flaxton, York. [515/46]

113 Wesleyan Methodist Chapel, Gate Helmsley. *Erected* 1814. SEB ExW. *Sittings* Free 80 Other 42. *On 30 March* Morning GC 86 SS 20 Afternoon SS 42 Evening GC 40. *Average during 6 months* 106. *Signed* Leonard Whitwall, Steward, Gate Helmsley. [515/47]

Flaxton Subdistrict (North Riding)

STRENSALL (Parish, Population 434)

114 St Mary's Parish Church, Strensall. A Vicarage. *Consecrated* In lieu of the Ancient Parish Church & on the same site. *Erected* Original endowment of the old church 1314 – Rebuilt in 1801 by the Parishioners & Rector. *Cost* Chancel By the Rector or Dr [...] The body of the Church By Parochial Rate amount not known Private Benefaction etc £64. *Endowment* Net Tithe/Glebe £160.16.0 3/4 OPE £77.2.8 Fees about £1 Easter Offerings about (£2.5.0) not collected last year. *Sittings* Free 42 Other 135. *On 30 March* Morning GC 58 SS 24. *Average during 12 months* Morning GC 85 SS 35. *Remarks* There is only one service during the day the Vicar having to perform divine service at Haxby Chapel also. *Signed* John Hodgkinson, Vicar, Strensall Vicarage, nr York. [515/48]

115 Wesleyan Methodist Chapel, Strensall. *Erected* 1823. SEB ExW. *Sittings* Free 90 Other 56. *On 30 March* Afternoon GC 100 Evening GC 60. *Signed* John Calaser senr, Steward, Strensall, York. [515/49]

116 Prim[itive] Methodist, Strensall. *On 30 March* Evening GC 16. *Signed* Robert Potter, Class Leader, Strensall, York. [515/50]

WEST LILLING (Township (Sheriff Hutton), Population 219)

117 Methodist, Lillings Ambo. Both Primitive Methodists and Wesleyan Methodists attend at separate times. *Erected* probably 6 years. SEB ExW. *Sittings* Free All. *On 30 March* Evening GC 25. *Signed* Thomas Butt, Steward, Lillings Ambo, York. [515/51]

FLAXTON ON THE MOOR (Township (Bossall), Population 381)

118 [St Lawrence], Flaxton. Chapel of Ease, belonging to the Vicarage of Bossall. *Consecrated* before 1800. *Endowment* No separate endowment. *Sittings* Free 100 Other

30. *On 30 March* Morning X Afternoon GC 89 SS 38 Evening X. *Signed* Sam. Gamlen, Vicar, Bossall, York. [515/52]

119   Primitive Methodist Chapel, Flaxton. *Erected* 1826. SEB ExW. *Sittings* Free 50 Other 40. *On 30 March* Morning X Afternoon GC 12. *Average during 12 months* Morning GC 40. *Signed* Thomas Calvert, Trustee & Chapel Steward, Flaxton, nr York. [515/53]

120   Wesleyan (Methodist) Chapel, Flaxton. *Erected* 1816. SEB ExW. *Sittings* Free 82 Other 63. *On 30 March* Morning GC 49 Evening GC 70. *Average during 12 months* Morning GC 65. *Signed* Thomas Wilson, Trustee & Chapel Steward, Flaxton, nr York. [515/54]

HARTON (Township (Bossall), Population 164)

121   Primitive Methodist, Harton. *Erected* about 4 years. *Sittings* Free All. *On 30 March* Morning GC 25. *Average during 12 months* Morning GC 50. *Signed* George Fisher, Steward, Harton, York. [515/55]

BOSSALL (Township (P), Population 72)

122   Bossall Parish Church [St Botolph]. *Consecrated* before 1800. *Endowment* No return is made to this enquiry. *Sittings* Free 130 Other 20 (Sittings appropriated to Townships). *On 30 March* Morning GC 80 SS 19 Afternoon X Evening X. *Signed* Saml. Gamlen, Vicar, Bossall, York. [515/56]

CLAXTON (Township (Bossall), Population 207)

123   Primitive Methodist, Claxton. *Erected* 1850. SEB ExW. *Sittings* Free 46 Other 46. *On 30 March* Afternoon 50 Evening 60. *Signed* Anthony Walker, Steward, Claxton, nr York. [515/57]

124   Wesleyan (Methodist) Chapel, Claxton. *Erected* 1843. SEB ExW. *Sittings* Free 60 Other 40. *On 30 March* Morning X Afternoon 43 Evening 20. *Average during 12 months* Morning [sic] GC 60. *Signed* Anthony Wright, Trustee, Claxton. [515/58]

SAND HUTTON (Township (Bossall), Population 195)

125   Sand Hutton Church [St Mary], or Chapel of Ease within the Vicarage of Bossall. *Consecrated* May 31 1847 in lieu of an old Church. No endowment. *Sittings* Free 120 Other 50. *On 30 March* Morning GC 81 SS 35 Afternoon GC 63 SS 25 Evening X. *Signed* James Griffith, Curate, Sand Hutton, York. [515/59]

BUTTERCRAMBE (Township (Bossall), Population 154)

126   [St John the Evangelist], Buttercrambe. Chapel of Ease belonging to Bossall. *Consecrated* before 1800. No endowment. *Sittings* Free 100 Other 20. *On 30 March* Morning X Afternoon GC 46 SS 22. *Signed* Saml. Gamlen, Vicar, Bossall, York. [515/60]

POCKLINGTON DISTRICT (HO129/516)

East Stamford Bridge Subdistrict[1]

SCRAYINGHAM (Township (P), Population 158)

127 St Peter's, Scrayingham. Parish Church. *Consecrated* Before 1800. *Sittings* Free 24 Other 130. *Remarks* The return respecting the Chapel of Ease at Leppington[2] in this Parish is incorrect as giving a wrong impression. *Signed* W. F. Douglas, Rector, York. [516/1]

128 Wesleyans, Scrayingham. *Erected* 7 years since. Room part of a Dweling House. No Sunday School. *Sittings* Free All; Free Space none. *On 30 March* Morning GC 10 Afternoon GC 12 Evening GC 18. *Signed* William Herbert, Local Preacher, Post Office, Scrayingham. [516/2]

KIRBY UNDERDALE (Parish, Population 335)

129 All Saints, Kirby under Dale. *Sittings* Free 77 Appropriated 129. *Usual Number of Attendants* 90 Morning GC 50 SS 20 Afternoon GC 20 SS 20. *Signed* Jos. W. Atkinson. [516/3 Simplified]

130 Wesleyan (Methodist) Chapel, Kirby Underdale. *Erected* 1796. Separate Used a Place of Worship and a Day School. *Sittings* Free 150. *Usual Number of Attendants* Afternoon GC from 40 to 50 Evening GC from 40 to 50. *Signed* John Webster, Kirkby Underdale, nr Stamford Bridge. [516/4 Simplified]

THIXENDALE (Township (Wharram Percy), Population 266)

131 Wesleyan Methodist Chapel, Thixendale. *Erected* Since 1800. SEB ExW. *Sittings* Free 30 Other 83. *On 30 March* Morning 8 Afternoon 36 Evening 42. *Average during 12 months* Morning GC 8 Afternoon GC 36 Evening GC 42. *Signed* John Richardson, C. Steward, Wesleyan Chapel. [516/5]

FRIDAYTHORPE (Parish, Population 330)

132 [St Mary], Fridaythorpe. Ancient Parish Church no name known. *Consecrated* before 1800. *Endowment* Land £150 OPE £12. *Sittings* Free 55 Other 50. *On 30 March* Morning X Afternoon GC 41 SS 42 Evening X. *Average during 12 months* Morning X Afternoon GC 50 SS 40 Evening X. *Signed* W. R. Griesbach MA, Vicar, Millington Vicarage, nr Pocklington. [516/6]

133 Wesleyan (Methodist) Centenary Chapel, Fridaythorpe. *Erected* 1840. SEB ExW. *Sittings* Free 40 Other 87 Free Space 20. *On 30 March* Morning 44 Evening 43.

---

1   No return for the hamlet of Woodhouse (population 42) in the parish of Sutton-upon-Derwent.
2   See North Riding, Malton District.

Average during 12 months Morning GC 60. *Signed* John Johnson, Chapel Steward, nr Driffield. [516/7]

134 Primitive Methodist Chapel, Fridaythorpe. Now in the couse of Erection. SEB ExW. *Sittings* Free 30 Other 80. *On 30 March* Morning X Afternoon X Evening 53. *Remarks* We are worshiping at present in a private House but think it proper to Give you [?] an Acount of the Chapel as it is So nearly finished. *Signed* Robert Pickering, Local preacher, Fridaythorpe, nr Driffield. [516/8]

BISHOP WILTON WITH BELTHORPE
(Township (Bishop Wilton), Population 652)

135 St Edith, Bishop Wilton. Ancient Parish Church. *Consecrated* before 1800. *Sittings* Free 170 Other 50. *On 30 March* Afternoon GC 70 SS 52 Evening GC 25. *Signed* Joseph Shooter[3], Vicar, Bishop Wilton, Pocklington. [516/9]

136 Bethel (Wesleyan Methodists), Bishop Wilton. *Erected* 1810. SEB ExW. *Sittings* Free 64 Other 86 Free Space 50. *On 30 March* Evening GC 80. *Average during 12 months* Afternoon GC 90. *Remarks* The services connected with this Chapel are held in the afternoon of one Sunday & in the Evening of the next alternately. The afternoon Service is generally better attended than in the Evening. *Signed* W. Walker, Steward, Bishop Wilton, Pocklington. [516/10]

137 Primitive Methodist Chapel, Bishop Wilton. *Erected* 1838. SEB ExW. *Sittings* Free 40 Other 68 Free Space None. *On 30 March* SS None Morning GC 47 Afternoon X Evening GC 60. *Signed* William Walgate Harrison, Leader of Society, Bishop Wilton, nr Pocklington. [516/11]

YOULTHORPE WITH GOWTHORPE (Township (Bishop Wilton), Population 105)

138 Wesleyan Methodists Meeting House, Youlthorpe. Dwelling House. *Sittings* Free 30. *Usual Number of Attendants* Afternoon GC from 16 to 24 Evening GC from 10 to 14. *Signed* Geo. Seller for Thomas Smith, Youlthorpe. [516/12 Simplified]

BUGTHORPE (Parish, Population 266)

139 The Parish Church of [St Andrew] Bugthorpe. An Ancient Parish Church. *Consecrated* before 1 January 1800. *Endowment* Glebe £111. *Sittings* Free 32 Other 103. *On 30 March* Afternoon GC 24 SS 14. *Average* Afternoon GC 20 SS 16 Evening GC 30 SS 20. *Signed* George Tho. Terry, Officiating Minister, Full Sutton, nr Stamford Bridge, York. [516/13]

140 Wesleyans, Bugthorpe. School. *Erected* 1840. *Sittings* Free All 19 ft by 13 ft. *On 30 March* 40. *Remarks* This School Room was Built by Sir Francis Linley Wood 11 years since for the Wesleyns to hould ther Meeting in and for a Girl's Day School.

---

3   Also Vicar of Attenbrough, Nottinghamshire.

York the Wesleyns District. Pocklington Union District. *Dated* 1 April. *Signed* Richard Smith, Class Leader, Stamford Bridge, York. [516/14]

141 Primitive Methodist, Bugthorpe. School. *Erected* 1833. *Sittings* Free All 19ft by 15ft. *On 30 March* 35. *Dated* 1 April. *Signed* William Marshall, Class Leader, Bugthorpe, Stamford Bridge, York. [516/15]

SKIRPENBECK (Parish, Population 190)

142 Skirpenbeck Church [St Mary], the Ancient Church of a distinct Parish. *Consecrated* before 1800. *Sittings* Free 28 Other 100. *On 30 March* Morning GC 52 SS 7 Afternoon X Evening GC 23. *Average during 12 months* Morning GC 60 to 70 SS 9 to 12 Evening GC 50 to 60. *Remarks* I have not filled up columns 4, 5 & 6 as I consider them to apply to Churches consecrated since 1800. *Signed* Mitford Bullock, Minister, Skirpenbeck, Stamford Bridge, York. [516/16]

FULL SUTTON (Parish, Population 165)

143 Wesleyan (Methodist) Chapel, Full Sutton. *Erected* About 1830. SEB ExW. *Sittings* Free 60 Other 40. *On 30 March* Afternoon GC 54 Evening GC 59. *Average during 12 months* Afternoon GC 50. *Signed* John Blanshard, Chapel Steward, Fangfoss. [516/17]

144 The Parish Church of Full Sutton [St Mary]. Never could learn whether dedicated or not to any particular Saint. *Consecrated* before Jan. 1 1800. *Erected* The Church was taken down rebuilt in 1845. *Cost* By Private Subscription & grant from Church Building Society £700. *Endowment* Glebe £150. *Sittings* Free 82 Other 41. *On 30 March* Morning GC 30 SS 19 Afternoon X Evening X. *Average* Morning GC 30 to 40 SS 26. *Signed* George Tho. Terry, Rector, Full Sutton, nr Stamford Bridge, York. [516/18]

LOW CATTON (Township (Catton), Population 176)

145 All Saints, Low Catton, built of Stone with a Good Tower of the same material. *Consecrated* before 1800 an old Church. *Endowment* Land & Moduses £415 Fees £7. *Sittings* Free 80 Other 200. *On 30 March* Morning GC 150 SS 25 [&]15 from Kexby. *Average* Morning GC 150 SS 25 Evening GC 30 without Sunday Scholars. *Remarks* The reason the attendance in the Evening is so small arises from the width of the Parish & the smallness of the village in which the Church is situated. On Sunday the 30th March 15 Scholars from Kexby. The Kexby Scholars avaraging from 15 to 20 attend the Church when the weather permits. *Signed* Thos. Holmes, Curate of Catton, Catton Rectory, Kexby, nr York. [516/19]

146 Wesleyans, Low Catton. *Erected* unknown. Part of a dwelling House ExW. *Sittings* Free 35. *On 23 March* Morning GC X SS X Afternoon GC 25 SS X Evening GC 13 SS X. *Remarks* As no Preaching was held on Sunday Mar. 30th the acct. was taken on 23 Inst. *Signed* Rosetta Kemp, Stewardess, Low Catton, York. [516/20]

HIGH CATTON (Township (Catton), Population 177)

147   Wesleyans, High Catton. *Erected* 1810. Separate ExW. *Sittings* Free 120 Other 30 Free Space 25. *On 30 March* Morning GC X SS X Afternoon GC 53 SS X Evening GC 20 SS X. *Average* not known. *Signed* John Shepherdson, Steward, High Catton, York. [516/21]

148   Primitive Methodists, High Catton. Dwelling House. *Sittings* Free All. *On 30 March* Morning GC X SS X Afternoon GC 30 SS X Evening GC 27 SS X. *Remarks* On March 31st in the Evening there were 60 assembled therefore I should say about 40 is an average number. *Signed* Henry Peacock, Class Leader & Steward, High Catton, nr York. [516/22]

EAST STAMFORD BRIDGE (Township (Catton), Population 407)

149   Wesleyan Methodist Chapel, Stamford Bridge. *Erected* 1828. SEB ExW. *Sittings* Free 150 Other 174. *On 30 March* Morning GC X SS 45 Afternoon GC 100 SS 35 Evening GC 150. *Average* Morning GC X Afternoon GC 100 Evening GC 150. *Signed* Richard Flood, Chapel Steward, Stamford Bridge, nr York. [516/23]

150   Primitive Methodists, Stamford Bridge. *Erected* Before 1800. Dwelling House ExW. *Sittings* Free Space 60. *On 30 March* Morning GC 10 Afternoon GC 12 Evening GC 25. *Average* Morning GC 10 Afternoon GC 40 Evening GC 40. *Remarks* The Meetings are held in a poor Woman's dwelling house of only one ground Floor. *Signed* Israel Wake for Jane Wake, Stamford Bridge, nr York. [516/24]

FANGFOSS (Parish, Population 188)

151   [St Martin], Fangfoss. The Parish Church is supposed to be the site of a British Church, then rebuilt by the Saxons of wh. we have Saxon remains, burnt by the Danes at the time of the battle of Stamford Bridge from wh. it is distant 3 miles, rebuilt in the time of William Rufus and again built in 1850 – I suppose it to be dedicated to St Mary or St Mary Magdalene but cannot be certain of the dedication. *Consecrated* before 1800. The Church was rebuilt and opened in the year 1850. *Erected* Through the exertions of the Vicar and churchwardens assisted by the Incorporated Soc. for Building Churches grant £80, £200 borrowed on the rates and the contributions of the landed proprietors. *Cost* Parochial Rate £200 Private Benefacton etc £663. *Endowment* Land £48.6.0 Tithe £11.10.0 Pew Rents none Fees/Dues/Other Sources £6.10.0 Easter Offerings not collected. *Sittings* Free 158 Other 23. The old Church accommodated 84. Increase by rebuilding (1850) 97. *On 30 March* Afternoon GC 50 SS 25. *Remarks* There is only one service on Sunday. Fangfoss Vicarage is united to Barmby Moor Vicarage. The Rectory is in the hands of the Ecclesiastical Commissioners. The Rectory was alienated A. D. 1252. *Signed* Robert Taylor, Vicar, Barmby Moor, nr Pocklington. [516/25]

152   Parish School and Wesleyan (Methodist) Chapel, Fangfoss. *Erected* 1837. SEB Sunday and Day school and Wesleyn Chapel. *Sittings* Free 70. *On 30 March*

Evening 60. *Average during 12 months* Morning [sic] Total 50. *Signed* Samuel Rowe, Minister, Pocklington. [516/26]

153 <u>Primitive Methodist, Fangfoss</u>. *Erected* 1840. Dwelling house. *Sittings* Free 30. *On 30 March* Evening GC 12. *Signed* Robt. Gilbank, P[rimitive] M[ethodist] Local Preacher, Fangfoss. [516/27]

WILBERFOSS (Township (P), Population 367)

154 <u>St John the Baptist, Wilberfoss</u>, built partly of Stone having a good Stone Tower. *Consecrated* An old Church when consecrated unknown by me. *Endowment* Land £43.10.0 OPE £10.7.4 Fees £4. *Sittings* Free 100 Other 150. *On 30 March* Afternoon GC 150 SS 27. *Average* Afternoon GC 120 to 150 sometimes more. *Signed* Thos. Holmes, Incumbent, Wilberfoss, nr York. [516/28]

155 <u>Wesleyan (Methodist) Chapel, Wilberfoss</u>. *Erected* 1841. SEB ExW. *Sittings* Free 60 Other 78. *On 30 March* Morning X Afternoon X Evening GC 86. *Average during 12 months* Evening GC 80. *Signed* Richard Agar, A Trustee, Wilberfoss. [516/29]

156 <u>Primitive Methodist Chapel, Wilberfoss</u>. *Erected* 1824. SEB ExW. *Sittings* Free 35 Other 35. *On 30 March* Evening GC 36. *Average during 12 months* Evening GC 40. *Signed* Robert Dickinson, Chapel Steward, Wilberfoss. [516/30]

NEWTON UPON DERWENT (Township (Wilberfoss), Population 235)

157 <u>Wesleyan (Methodist) Chapel, Newton on Derwent</u>. *Erected* About 1817. SEB ExW. *Sittings* Free 60 Other 64 Free Space none. *On 30 March* Morning GC 35 SS 38 Evening GC 37. *Average during 12 months* Morning GC 45 SS 40 Evening GC 45. *Signed* Robert Whitaker, Steward, Newton upon Derwent. [516/31]

SUTTON UPON DERWENT (Township (P), Population 325)

158 <u>St Michael's, Sutton on Derwent</u>. An ancient Parish Church. *Consecrated* before 1800. *Sittings* Free 142 Other 48. *Remarks* Unable to count the congregation on Sunday. *Signed* Geo. Rudston Read, Rector, Sutton upon Derwent, York. [516/32]

159 <u>Wesleyans, Sutton on Derwent</u>. *Erected* 1838. ExW. *Sittings* Free 60. *On 30 March* Morning X Afternoon GC 36 Evening X. *Average* SS none Morning X Afternoon GC 30 Evening X. *Remarks* Voluntarily <u>Statement</u>. *Signed* Charles Bedford, Class Leader, Farmer, Sutton on Derwent. [516/33]

Pocklington Subdistrict[4]

EAST COTTINGWITH (Township (Aughton), Population 318)

160   [St Mary], East Cottingwith. Chapel of Ease. *Sittings* Free 55 Other 121. *On 30 March* Morning X Afternoon GC 40 Evening X. *Remarks* Chapel repewed in 1846 part by Parliamentary Grant and part by Subscription. *Signed* John Gell, Chapel-warden, Chapel of Ease, East Cottingwith, Sutton on Derwent, York. [516/34]

161   Wesleyan, East Cottingwith. Has no particular name. *Erected* before 1800. SEB ExW. *Sittings* Free 84 Other 71 Free Space None. *On 30 March* Morning GC X SS 31 Afternoon GC 80 SS 38 Evening GC 92 SS X. *Dated* 1 April. *Signed* Henry Martin, Chapel Steward, East Cottingwith, Sutton on Derwent, York. [516/35]

162   Meeting House of the Society of Friends, East Cottingwith. *Erected* Before 1800. SEB ExW. *Space* Floor 570 ft. no galleries *Estimated Seating* 125 people. *On 30 March* Morning 11. *Signed* Jonathan Burtt, Gunby, nr Selby. [516/36]

THORNTON (Township (P), Population 194)

163   St Michael, Thornton. Ancient Parish Church. Vicarage. *Consecrated* before 1800. *Endowment* Tithe £92 Glebe £40 Other Sources £9. *Sittings* Free 120 Other 50. *On 30 March* Morning GC 40 SS 30 Afternoon X Evening X. *Remarks* There is but one Service in the Church on Sunday which is alternate Morning or Evening. *Signed* Christopher Rawlins, Vicar, Allerthorpe Vicarage, Pocklington. [516/37]

164   Wesleyan, Thornton. School Room. *Erected* Before 1800. SEB Sunday and Day School. *Sittings* Benches. *On 30 March* Morning X Afternoon GC 40 SS 19 Evening X. *Signed* Robert Gibson, Society Steward, Thornton, Pocklington. [516/38]

STORTHWAITE (Township (Thornton), Population 87)

165   Small Wesleyan Chapel, Storthwood. Entire [No answer on whether exclusively for worship]. *Sittings* Free 50. *On 30 March* Morning GC 22 Evening GC 18. *Average* Morning GC About 20. *Signed* Robert Kirkburn. [516/39]

MELBOURNE (Township (Thornton), Population 535)

166   Wesleyan Methodist Chapel, Melbourne. *Erected* 1811. Entire ExW. *Sittings* Free 60 Other 46 Free Space none. *On 30 March* Morning X Afternoon X Evening [?] GC 40. *Average during 6 months* Morning GC 70 SS 51. *Signed* Robert Atkinson, Local Minister, Melbourn, Pocklington. [516/40]

---

[4]   No returns for the township of Ousthorpe (population 13) in the parish of Pocklington, for the township of Bolton (population 129) – where a Wesleyan Chapel had been built in 1819 (D. and S. Neave, op. cit., p. 47) – in the parish of Bishop Wilton, and the township of Crimthorpe (population 14) in the parish of Great Givendale.

167 Primitive Methodist Chapel, Melbourne. *Erected* 1821. SEB ExW. *Sittings* Free 75 Other 44. *On 30 March* Morning 40 Evening 20. *Average during 12 months* Evening 70. *Signed* Robinson Cheeseman, Minister, Chapman Gate, Pocklington. [516/41]

ALLERTHORPE (Township (P), Population 164)

168 Allerthorpe Church [St Botolph]. Church of an ancient Chapelry. *Consecrated* before 1800. *Endowment* Tithe £73.15.8 Glebe £1.10.0. *Sittings* Free 80 Other 30. *On 30 March* Morning X Afternoon GC 48 SS 22 Evening X. *Remarks* There is but one Service in the Church each Sunday: which is alternately Morning & Evening. *Signed* Christopher Rawlin, Perpetual Curate, Allerthorpe Vicarage, Pocklington. [516/42]

169 Wesleyan, Allerthorpe. *On 30 March* Morning X Afternoon X Evening GC 28. *Remarks* It is a private house in which the services are held. *Dated* 4 April. *Signed* Rob. Sanderson, Society Steward, Allerthorpe, Pocklington. [516/43]

BARMBY ON THE MOOR (Parish, Population 486)

170 The Parish Church of Barmby Moor, St Catharine V[irgin] and M[artyr]. There are remains showing it to be a Saxon Church. It was taken down in 1850 being dilapidated and a new Nave & Chancel is being built to the old Tower & Spire wh. remain. *Consecrated* before 1800. *Erected* Re-erected in 1851. By grant of £120 from Incorporated Society £400 borrowed on the rates and the Contribution of the landed properties this the exertions of the Vicar. *Cost* Parochial Rate £400 Private Benefaction etc £500. *Endowment* Land £16.10.0 Glebe in lieu of Tithes £30 Pew Rents none Fees £2.1.2. *Sittings* The church is rebuilt & when opened Free 285 Other 15. In old church Free 149 Other 15. Increase of accommodation 136 by rebuilding in 1851. *On 30 March* Morning GC 60 SS 35 only one service each Sunday in the Licensed School room, the Church rebuilding. *Average* Before the Church was pulled down there wd. have been in Summer 200 in the Afternoon including 40 Sunday Scholars. *Remarks* The Church is being rebuilt. The service is performed in the National School Licensed by His Grace the Archbishop of York. Had the Church been open the number present wd. have been larger – the number 95 fills the School. The Rectory in the hands of the Eccl. Comrs. The Rectory alienated A. D. 1252. *Signed* Robert Taylor, Vicar, Barmby Moor, nr Pocklington. [516/44]

171 Wesleyan Methodist Chapel, Barmby Moor. *Erected* About 1805. SEB ExW. *Sittings* Free 40 Other 40. *On 30 March* Evening GC 40. *Average* Morning [sic] GC 60. *Signed* George Blanshard, Chapel Steward, Barmby Moor, nr Pocklington. [516/45]

172 Primitive Methodist Chapel, Barmby Moor. *Erected* 1836. SEB ExW. *Sittings* Free 50 Other 52. *On 30 March* Morning 55 Afternoon X Evening 71. *Average during 12 months* Morning GC 50 Afternoon GC X Evening GC 82. *Signed* Henry Quarton, Trustee, Barmby Moor. [516/46]

POCKLINGTON (Township (P), Population 2546)

173 Parish Church of Pocklington [All Saints] in the Deanery of York. *Consecrated* Before 1800. *Endowment* Land £35.12.0 Tithe £28 OPE £23 Fees £2 Easter Offerings £4 Other categories none. *Sittings* Total 500. *On 30 March* SS none at present Morning GC 165 Afternoon none Evening GC 190. *Average* SS none at present Morning GC 170 Afternoon none Evening GC 180. *Remarks* The church is sufficiently large for the Parish but there is a want of free sittings appropriated to the use of the Poor. *Signed* Revd J. F. Ellis, Pocklington. [516/47]

174 Ebenezer Chapel (Independent), Pocklington. *Erected* 1807. SEB ExW. *Sittings* Free 100 Other 400. *Usual Number of Attendants* Morning GC 60 SS 15 Afternoon GC 30 SS 20 Evening GC 100. *Signed* W. Hagyard, Pocklington. [516/48 Simplified]

175 Wesleyan (Methodist) Chapel, Pocklington. *Erected* About 1801 Enlarged in 1813. SEB ExW. *Sittings* Free 104 Other 243. *On 30 March* Morning GC 100 SS 85 Afternoon GC 90 Evening GC 160 SS 20. *Average during 12 months* Morning GC 100 SS 85 Afternoon GC 45 Evening GC 170 SS 20. *Signed* Samuel Rowe, Minister, Pocklington. [516/49]

176 Providence Chapel (Primitive Methodist), Chapman Gate, Pocklington. *Erected* 1821. SEB ExW. *Sittings* Free 150 Other 240. *On 30 March* Afternoon GC 130 Evening GC 190. *Average during 12 months* Afternoon GC 150 Evening GC 200. *Signed* William Newton, Minister, Pocklington. [516/50]

177 St Mary's [Roman] Catholic Chapel, Pocklington. *Erected* Before 1800. SEB ExW. *Sittings* Free 80 Other none Free Space 20. *On 30 March* Morning GC 50 Afternoon X Evening GC 60. *Average during 12 months* Morning GC about 70 Evening GC 80. *Remarks* This Place is Served from the Priory Everingham. The Rev Samuel Walsh attends on Sundays and other days of Devotion but is Home present. The nearest Post is Hayton. No Resident Priest. *Signed* Patrick Keary, Steward, Pocklington. [516/51]

YAPHAM (Township (Pocklington), Population 151)

178 [St Martin], Yapham. Chapel of Ease. *Consecrated* Before 1800. *Endowment* Tithe £43 Fees £0.12.0 Other categories none. *Sittings* All Free Total 100. *On 30 March* Morning SS 20 Afternoon GC 32 SS 24. *Average* Afternoon GC 32 SS 25. *Signed* Ralph Green, Church Warden, Meltonby, Pocklington. [516/52]

179 Yapham School-House (Wesleyan Methodist). SEB. *Sittings* Free All. *On 30 March* Morning GC 33 SS 23 Afternoon X Evening GC 12. *Remarks* The number on Sunday Evenings in general larger. *Dated* 1 April. *Signed* John Walker, Class Leader of the Society, [...] Hall, Yapham, nr Pocklington. [516/53]

180 Primitive Methodist, Yapham. *Sittings* Free All. *On 30 March* Morning X Afternoon X Evening GC 16. *Signed* George Martindale senr, Manager, Yapham, nr Pocklington. [516/54]

MELTONBY (Township (Pocklington), Population 51)

181 Primitive Methodist, Meltonby. *Sittings* Free 30 Other none. *On 30 March* Morning X Afternoon GC 14 Evening X. *Signed* Thomas Richardson, Manager, Meltonby, nr Pocklington. [516/55]

182 Wesleyan (Methodist) Chapel, Bolton. *Erected* About 1819. SEB ExW. *Sittings* Free 60 Other 40. *On 30 March* No service held this afternoon. *Average during 12 months* Afternoon GC 60. *Signed* William Leak, Society Steward, Bolton, nr Pocklington. [516/56]

GREAT GIVENDALE (Township (P), Population 61)

183 Great Givendale Parish Church [St Ethelburga]. An ancient Church recently rebuilt. *Consecrated* before 1800. *Endowment* Land £150 Tithe £20.10.0 Glebe £18. *Sittings* Free 25 Other 39. There has been more than 150 in the Church. *On 30 March* SS none Morning GC X Afternoon GC 36 Evening GC X. *Average during 12 months* SS none Morning GC 15 Afternoon GC 20 Evening X. *Remarks* The Parish of Great Givendale is a very small one with 3 scattered Farm House. The Service alternates with Millington – the average congregation is about 15 or 20. *Signed* W. R. Griesbach, Vicar, Millington Vicarage, Pocklington. [516/57]

MILLINGTON (Parish, Population 289)

184 Parish Church, Millington. No name known. *Consecrated* before 1800. *Endowment* Tithe £23 Glebe £52 OPE £5.16.0. *Sittings* Free 56 Other 56. *On 30 March* Morning GC 36 SS 33 Afternoon GC X Evening GC X. *Average during 12 months* Morning GC 45 SS 33 Afternoon GC 50 SS 33 Evening GC X SS X. *Signed* W. R. Griesbach, MA, Vicar, Millington Vicarage, nr Pocklington. [516/58]

185 Wesleyan (Methodist) Chapel, Millington. *Erected* About 1812. SEB ExW. *Sittings* Free 100 Other 25. *On 30 March* Afternoon GC 45. *Average during 12 months* Afternoon GC 45. *Dated* 4 April. *Signed* Saml. Rowe, Minister, Pocklington. [516/59]

186 Primitive Methodists, Millington. Schoolroom. *Erected* Before 1800. Contiguous to a Dwelling House. Day School. *On 30 March* Evening GC 18. *Average during 12 months* Evening GC 27. *Remarks* Particulars respecting the School Room will be found in Wm. Clark's (Schoolmaster) return. The School Room is occupied Mornings & Afternoons on the Sabbaths, by the Sunday Scholars and service is always in the Evenings by the Prim. Methodists. *Signed* Thomas Oxtoby, Society Steward, Millington, Pocklington. [516/60]

HUGGATE (Parish, Population 547)

187 St Mary's, Huggate. Nave, Side Aisles, Chancel, Vestry, Tower, Spire and Porch. *Consecrated* AD 1220. *Erected* Ralph Pagnell. *Endowment* Land £230 Glebe £35 OPE £236.0.2 Fees £1.4.0 The net value of the Living is £429. *Sittings* Free 88 Other 62. *On 30 March* Morning GC 63 SS 44 Part of the Alternate attendance of

Husband and Wife. *Average* Morning GC 60 SS 42 Part of the alternate attendance of Husband and wife. *Remarks* N. B. The full Rent of the Land is mentioned, without deducting the per Centage allowed for the depressed state of Agriculture – The Fees according to the past year per Mar[riages], Christ[enings] and Burials. The No. 60 in the average attendance is only part of the attendance. The congregation is always changing as husbands and wives come alternately. *Signed* Thomas Rankin, Curate, Huggate, Pocklington. [516/61]

188   Huggate Chapel (Wesleyan Methodist). *Erected* 1837. SEB ExW. *Sittings* Free 60 Other 60. *On 30 March* Morning SS 28 Afternoon GC 34 Evening GC 38. *Average during 12 months* Morning [sic] GC 50 SS 28. *Signed* Thomas Ouston, Steward, Blanch, Pocklington. [516/62]

189   Primitive Methodist Chapel, Huggate. *Erected* 1849. SEB ExW. *Sittings* Free 100 Other 100. *On 30 March* Afternoon GC 65 Evening GC 88. *Average during 12 months* Afternoon GC 80 Evening GC 120. *Signed* William Fewster, Chapel Steward, Huggate, Pocklington. [516/63]

WARTER (Parish, Population 488)

190   St James, Warter. Ancient Parish Church. *Consecrated* before 1800. *Endowment* Money Payment from the Impropriator & Queen Anne's Bounty & Parliamentary Grant Amounting to per Ann. £100. *Sittings* Free 400 Total 400. *On 30 March* Morning GC 80 SS 25. *Average during 3 months* Morning GC 40 SS 30 Afternoon GC 90 SS 30. *Remarks* One alternate Service in Warter Church every Sunday. Above Average when Service is in Morning – Taken [?] in the Afternoon. Half of the above numbers will attend the Wesleyan Chapel the remaining part of the Sunday. *Signed* Saml. Wilson, Vicar, Bloomsbury Hall, Pocklington. [516/64]

191   Wesleyan Methodist Chapel, Warter. *Erected* About 1800. SEB ExW. *Sittings* Free 70 Other 60 Free Space 20. *On 30 March* Morning GC 20 Afternoon GC 70 Evening GC 50. *Average during 6 months* Afternoon GC 90. *Signed* John Harrison, Society Steward, Warter. [516/65]

192   Primitive Methodists, Warter. Dwelling House. *On 30 March* Evening GC 66. *Signed* Thomas Vaux, Warter, Shipton, York. [516/66]

KILNWICK PERCY (Parish, Population 93)

193   St Helen's, Kilnwick Percy. An ancient Parish church. *Sittings* Free 10 Other 70. *On 30 March* Afternoon GC 50 SS 4. *Average* Morning GC 70 SS 6 Afternoon GC 65 SS 6. *Signed* M. A. Lawton, Vicar, Kilnwick Percy, Pocklington, York. [516/67]

NUNBURNHOLME (Township (P), Population 229)

194   Wesleyan (Methodist) Chapel, Nunburnholme. *Erected* 1828. Entire building ExW. *Sittings* Free 50 Other 20 Free Space 20. *On 30 March* Morning GC X Afternoon GC X Evening GC 80. *Average during 12 months* Morning GC X

Afternoon GC X Evening GC 40. *Dated* 5 April. *Signed* John Overind, Steward, Nunburnholme. [516/68]

195   St James, Nunburnholme. An Ancient Parish Church. *Endowment* Tithe £172 Glebe £158. *Sittings* Other 100 Total 100. *On 30 March* Morning GC 9 SS 24 Afternoon GC 27 SS 20. *Average during 12 months* Morning GC 18 to 20 SS 24 Afternoon GC 30 to 35 SS 25. *Signed* H. B. Boothby, Rector, Nunburnholme, York. [516/69]

BURNBY (Parish, Population 129)

196   St Giles, Burnby. *Erected* before 1700. *Sittings* Free 28 Appropriated 80. *Usual Number of Attendants* Morning GC 40 SS 14 Afternoon GC 30 SS 14 Evening no service. *Signed* Chas. Weddall. [516/70 Simplified]

Market Weighton Subdistrict[5]

HAYTON (Township (P), Population 220)

197   Hayton Ancient Parish Church dedicated to St Martin. *Endowment* by Queen Ann's Bounty Land £20 Tithe £80 Glebe 146 acres; OPE £26 for tithe in Burnby; Fees £4 Other categories 0. *Sittings* Free Gallery and long Bench; Other 14 Pews attached to Houses [and] 2 Pews for inhabitants of Burnby and Bielby. *On 30 March* Morning GC 13 Afternoon No service Evening No service. *Average during 12 months* Morning GC 20 SS 20 Afternoon GC 30 SS 20. *Signed* Charles Pyves Graham, Vicar, Hayton, York. [516/71]

198   Primitive Methodist Chapel, Hayton. *Erected* Rebuilt in 1850. SEB ExW. *Sittings* Free 30 Other 40 Free Space 20. *On 30 March* Morning GC none Afternoon GC none Evening GC 45. *Average during 7 months* Morning [sic] GC 30 SS none. *Signed* Thomas Glazier, Steward, Hayton, Pocklington. [516/72]

199   Wesleyan Methodist, Hayton. Dwelling House. *Sittings* Free 35. *On 30 March* Morning X Afternoon X Evening GC 32. *Average during 12 months* Evening GC 25. *Signed* Samuel Rowe, Minister, Pocklington. [516/73]

BIELBY (Township (Hayton), Population 305)

200   Bielby Chapel dedicated to St Peter. Ancient Chapel of Ease to Hayton Mother Church. *Endowment* included in Endowment of Hayton Church. *Sittings* Free Seats near Altar; Other 18 Pews attached to Houses. *On 30 March* Morning No service. *Average during 12 months* Morning GC 25. *Dated* 1 April. *Signed* C. P. Graham, Vicar, Hayton, York. [516/74]

201   Wesleyan Methodist Chapel, Bielby. *Erected* 1837. Separate ExW. *Sittings* Free 50 Other 56. *On 30 March* Morning (Class Meeting) 8 Afternoon GC 52

---

5   No returns for the township of Thorpe-le-Street (population 24) in the parish of Nunburnholme or for the township of North Cliffe (population 81) in the parish of Sancton.

Evening (Prayer meeting) 25. *Average during 12 months* Morning GC X Afternoon GC 52 Evening GC 60. *Signed* William Smith, Steward, Bielby, nr Pocklington. [516/75]

EVERINGHAM (Parish, Population 297)

202 Everingham Church dedicated to St Mary – commonly known by St Emeldis [St Everlilda]. An ancient church built some centuries. *Consecrated* before 1800. *Endowment* Land 120 acres Tithe £80 Glebe 4 acres. *On 30 March* Morning 30. *Average* Morning GC 40 SS none. *Remarks* This is a peculiar parish as the squire of the Place has built a R. C. Chapel, consequently the church is not so well attended. *Signed* J. W. K. Lockwood, Rector, Everingham, Hayton, York. [516/76]

203 St Mary's R[oman] Catholic Church, Everingham. *Erected* Before 1800. SEB ExW. *Sittings* Free accommodation for about 350 or 400. *On 30 March* Morning GC 226 Afternoon GC 179. *Average during 12 months* Morning GC 170 Children 80 Afternoon GC 140 Children 60 Evening none. *Dated* 25 March. *Signed* Ambrose Camburini, Catholic priest, Everingham, nr Hayton. [516/77]

SEATON ROSS (Parish, Population 568)

204 [St Edmund], Seaton Ross. Ancient Parish Church. The Church of a distinct & separate Parish. *Consecrated* before 1800. *Endowment* Glebe £41.19.0 OPE Stipendary Payments £37 Houses £9.10.0 Aggregate anl. amt. £88.9.0. *Sittings* Free 200 Total 200. *On 30 March* Morning GC X Afternoon GC 69 SS 30 Evening GC X. *Remarks* There is a full service at the Church Morning & afternoon Each Sunday alternately. Besides this regular instruction the Children are addressed each Sunday in the Sunday School by the Clergyman & the Children are at liberty to attend either church or Chapels. *Signed* Thos. Hughes Terry, Minister, Seaton Ross, Pocklington. [516/78]

205 Methodist or Wesleyan Chapel, Seaton Ross. *Erected* 1822. Separate. *Sittings* Free 80 Other 70. *On 30 March* Morning GC 64. *Signed* Robert Crouch, Wesleyan Local Preacher, Market Weighton. [516/79]

206 Primitive Methodist Chapel, Seaton Ross. *Erected* 1821. Seperate ExW. *Sittings* Free 60 Other 39. *On 30 March* Afternoon 72. *Signed* William Douthwaite, Steward, Seaton Ross, Pocklington. [516/80]

HARSWELL (Parish, Population 81)

207 Harswell Church, dedicated to St Peter. An old Church. Built some centuries ago. *Consecrated* before 1800. *Sittings* Free 20 Other 25. *Remarks* Average Number of attendants – 30. Service alternately – morning & afternoon. *Signed* William Johnson, Enumerator, Everingham (Rev Henry Milton, Rector). [516/81]

LONDESBOROUGH (Parish, Population 293)

208 All Saints Church, Londesborough. An Ancient Parish Church. *Consecrated* before 1800. *Endowment* Glebe £70 OPE (a Rent Charge) £725. *Sittings* Free 121

Other 132. *On 30 March* Morning Total 64 Afternoon Total 22 Evening X. *Average during 12 months* Morning Total 70 Afternoon Total 35 Evening X. *Remarks* The Services in this Church are, a full service with a Sermon throughout the year <u>in the morning</u>, In the <u>afternoon</u> (except during Summer) <u>only Prayers</u>. *Signed* John Blow, Minister, Rectory, Londesborough, York. [516/82]

GOODMANHAM (Parish, Population 325)

209   <u>All Saints, Goodmanham</u>, an Ancient Parish Church. *Consecrated* before 1800. *Sittings* Free 40 Other 80. *On 30 March* Morning GC 58 Afternoon GC 15. *Average during 12 months* Morning GC 70 Afternoon GC 20. *Signed* William Blow, Minister, Goodmanham, nr Market Weighton. [516/83]

210   <u>Wesleyan (Methodist) Chapel, Goodmanham</u>. *Erected* 1828. SEB ExW. *Sittings* Free 60 Other 50. *Average* Morning GC 80. *Signed* William Foster, Steward, Goodmanham. [516/84]

211   <u>Primitive Methodist, Goodmanham</u>. *Erected* About 1815. A Preaching house and Dwelling house. *Sittings* Free 30 Other none Free Space 6. *On 30 March* SS none Evening GC 26. *Average* SS none Evening GC 20. *Signed* William Mantle, Steward, Goodmanham. [516/85]

MARKET WEIGHTON AND ARRAS (Township (Market Weighton), Population 2001)

212   [All Saints] <u>Market Weighton</u>. An Ancient Parish Church. *Consecrated* before 1800. *Endowment* Tithe £65 Glebe £46 OPE £20 Fees/Dues £5 Easter Offerings £2.10.0. *Sittings* Free 138 Other 470. *On 30 March* Morning GC 186 SS 124 Afternoon X Evening X. *Signed* R. Spofforth, Vicar, Market Weighton. [516/86]

213   <u>Primitive Methodist Chapel, Market Weighton</u>. *Erected* 1828. SEB ExW. *Sittings* Free 32 Other 118. *On 30 March* Afternoon 87 Evening 113. *Average during 12 months* Evening 140. *Remarks* I have given you the Average of our Congregation for every Sunday for the last twelve months afternoon and evening 140 each service that is as near as I can tell. *Signed* Joseph Thompson, Steward, Cordwainer, South Gate, Market Weighton. [516/87]

214   <u>Sion Chapel (Independent or Congregational), Market Weighton</u>. *Erected* 1809. SEB ExW. *Sittings* Free 50 Other 200 Free Space not any. *On 30 March* Morning GC 85 SS 52 Afternoon (Prayer meeting) GC 24 Evening GC 150. *Average during 12 months* Morning GC 100 SS 60 Afternoon (Prayer meeting) GC 25 Evening GC 200. *Signed* John George, Minister, Market Weighton. [516/88]

215   <u>Wesleyan Methodist Chapel, Market Weighton</u>. *Erected* 1787. SEB ExW. *Sittings* Free 85 Other 260 Free Space 80. *On 30 March* SS none Afternoon GC 180 Evening GC 150. *Average during 12 months* SS none Afternoon GC 180 Evening GC 160. *Dated* 2 April. *Signed* Joseph Smith, Society Steward, Market Weighton. [516/89]

SHIPTON[THORPE] (Township (Market Weighton), Population 426)

216 [All Saints] Shipton. The Church of an Ancient Chapelry. *Consecrated* before 1800. *Endowment* Tithe £14 Glebe £22 Fees £1.10.0 Easter Offerings £1.5.0. *Sittings* Free 113 Other 31. *On 30 March* Morning X Afternoon GC 82 Evening X. *Signed* R. Spofforth, Vicar, Market Weighton. [516/90]

217 Wesleyan Methodist, Shipton. *Erected* 1833. SEB ExW. *Sittings* Free 72 Other 60 Free Space None. *On 30 March* Morning GC 56 SS 46 Afternoon No service Evening GC 9. *Average during 12 months* Morning GC 60 SS 46 Afternoon No service Evening GC 16. *Remarks* We only have prayer meetings on a Sunday night, and most of the Members lives some distance from the village so they do not get to the night meeting. *Signed* Thomas West, Chapel Steward, Shipton. [516/91]

218 Primitive Methodist Chappel, Shipton. *Erected* 1834. SEB ExW. *Sittings* Free 41 Other 50. *On 30 March* Evening 100. *Average* Morning GC 80 Evening Total 100. *Signed* John Brigham, Class Leader, Shipton. [516/92]

SANCTON AND HOUGHTON (Township (Sancton), Population 438)

219 All Saints, Sancton. An ancient Parish Church. *Consecrated* before 1800. *Endowment* Land/Tithe/Glebe small allotments of Glebe lands; OPE (money payment) £6.13.4 Pew Rents none; Fees surplice about £1.10.0; Easter offerings none. *Sittings* Free All (120). *On 30 March* Morning GC 35. *Average during 12 months* Morning GC 20 Afternoon GC 20. *Signed* Thos. Mitchell, Minister, Market Weighton. [516/93]

220 Wesleyan Methodist, Sancton. *Erected* more than 40 years ago. SEB ExW. *Sittings* Free 96 Other 74 Free Space 170. *On 30 March* Morning X Afternoon GC 94 SS 40 Evening GC 40. *Average during 12 months* Afternoon GC 94 SS 40. *Signed* William Marshall, Steward & Leader, Sancton, nr Market Weighton. [516/94]

221 The Holy Trinity (Roman Catholic) Houghton. *Erected* Present one opened on 1828 in lieu of one before 1800. SEB ExW. *Sittings* Free 193 Other 20 in the Tribune. *On 30 March* SS X Morning GC 160 Afternoon GC 80 Evening X. *Average during 12 months* SS X Morning GC 150 Afternoon GC 90 Evening X. *Signed* John Glover, Roman Catholic Priest, Houghton, Market Weighton. [516/95]

222 Independent or Congregational, Sancton. Home Mission Preaching Room in connection with Zion Chapel, Market Weighton. *Erected* Before 1800. SEB ExW. *Sittings* Free 40 Free Space 40. *On 30 March* Afternoon GC 32. *Average during 12 months* Afternoon GC 50. *Signed* John George, Minister, Market Weighton. [516/96]

SOUTH CLIFFE (Township (North Cave), Population 86)

223 South Cliffe Chapel [St Leonard]. The Church of an Antient Chapelry. *Consecrated* Henry 7th. *Sittings* Free 70. *On 30 March* Morning GC 25. *Average during 6 months* Morning GC 30 Afternoon GC 35. *Remarks* South Cliffe is a chapelry in the Parish of North Cave, it is united with it for all Ecclesiastical purposes & has no separate endowment – only a house & field for the repairs of the Chapel let at £8 per ann. *Signed* John Jarratt, Vicar, North Cave, nr Howden. [516/97]

HOWDEN DISTRICT (HO 129/517)

Holme-on-Spalding-Moor Subdistrict and Parish
(Population 1713)

224   All Saints, Holme-upon-Spalding-Moor (Sometimes said to be dedicated to St John, Bapt.). An ancient Parish Church. *Consecrated* before 1800. *Sittings* Free 60 Other 268. *On 30 March* Morning GC 45 SS 55 Afternoon GC 62 SS 47. *Average during 12 months* Morning GC 60 SS 40 Afternoon GC 100 SS 40. *Remarks* In consequence of the remote position of the Church the general congregation consists of entirely different persons, with few exceptions, Morning & Afternoon. *Signed* Charles Yate, Minister, Vicarage, Holme-upon-Spalding-Moor, Hayton, nr York. [517/2]

225   Wesleyan Methodists, Bursea. *Erected* Before 1800. A private dwelling House. *Sittings* Free Space 60. *On 30 March* Morning 55 Afternoon X Evening X. *Average* SS none Morning GC 40. *Remarks* The Dwelling House has had Divine Worship about 3 years. *Signed* John Smith, Class Leader, Residing at Spaldington, in the township of Bubwith, Howden Circuit. [517/3]

226   Holme [Roman] Catholic Chapel. *Erected* Before 1800. SEB ExW. *Sittings* Free About 200. *On 30 March* Morning GC 100 Children 40 Afternoon The same. *Average during 12 months* Believe Morning GC 100 Children 40 Afternoon GC 110. *Signed* Thomas Cockshoot, Catholic Priest, Holme, Hayton. [517/4]

227   Holme Wesleyan (Methodist) Chapel. *Erected* 1827 in lieu of a smaller one which had been erected some 50 years or more. SEB ExW. *Sittings* Free 156 Other 132 Free Space 50 may stand. There is no space set apart for standing. *On 30 March* Afternoon GC 130 SS 66 Evening GC 89. *Signed* John Hare, Steward, Holme, Hayton. [517/5]

228   Primitive Methodist Chapel, Holme. *Erected* 1830. SEB ExW. *Sittings* Free 90 Other 62 Free Space 30 may stand. There is no space set apart for standing. *On 30 March* Afternoon 70 Evening 93. *Signed* Robinson Cheeseman, Primitive Methodist Minister, Chapman Gate, Pocklington. [517/6]

Bubwith Subdistrict[1]

ELLERTON PRIORY (Parish, Population 342)

229   St Mary's, Ellerton. *Erected* rebuilt 1848. *Sittings* Free 179 Appropriated 48. *Usual Number of Attendants* Morning GC 70 Afternoon GC 120. *Signed* Wm. Geo. Wilkinson. [517/7 Simplified]

---

[1]   No returns for the townships of Harlthorpe (population 78), Gribthorpe (population 52) and Willitoft (population 33), all in the parish of Bubwith.

230 <u>Wesleyan (Methodist) Chapel, Ellerton Priory</u>. *Erected* 1811. SEB ExW. *Sittings* Free 50 Other 72. *On 30 March* Morning GC 44 SS 23 Evening GC 47. *Signed* George Wake, Steward, Ellerton, nr Bubwith. [517/8]

231 <u>Latter Day Saints, Ellerton</u>. *On 30 March* Morning X Afternoon GC 14 Evening GC 23. *Average during 4 months* 20. *Signed* Robert Young, Presiding Elder, Ellerton. [517/9]

AUGHTON (Township (P), Population 225)

232 <u>All Saints, Aughton</u>. *Erected* about 1300. *Sittings* Free 100 Appropriated 200. *Usual Number of Attendants* Morning GC 50 SS 30 Afternoon GC 80 SS 30. *Signed* Geo. Mower Webb, BA, Curate. [517/10 Simplified]

233 <u>Wesleyan Chapel, Aughton</u>. *Erected* 1844. A separate building ExW. *Sittings* Free 50 Other 50. *On 30 March* Afternoon GC 54. *Signed* Geo. Drewry, Steward, Aughton, nr Bubwith. [517/11]

[517/12: Mis-filed return relating to Aughton near Rotherham: see West Riding (South) **2318**]

LAYTHAM (Township (Aughton), Population 111)

234 <u>Laytham School Room (Wesleyan)</u>. Formerly a dwelling house. Used as a place of Worship and School. *Sittings* Free 55 Other None Free Space 6. *On 30 March* Morning GC 42 SS 23 Afternoon GC X SS 20 Evening GC 50. *Average during 12 months* Morning GC 45 SS 23 Afternoon GC X SS 20 Evening GC 48. *Signed* John Lowther, Society Steward, Laytham, Bubwith, Selby. [517/13]

BUBWITH (Township (P), Population 583)

235 <u>All Saints, Bubwith</u>. *Erected* about 1200. *Sittings* Free 100 Appropriated 350. *Usual Number of Attendants* Morning (alternate Sundays) GC 100 SS 26 Afternoon (alternate Sundays) GC 250 SS 26 Evening (alternate Sundays) GC 120. *Signed* Wm. Geo. Wilkinson. [517/14 Simplified]

236 <u>(Wesleyan) Methodist Chapel, Bubwith</u>. *Erected* before 1800. SEB ExW. *Sittings* Free 100 Other 104. *On 30 March* Morning GC 36 Afternoon GC 129 SS 35 Evening GC 112. *Average during 12 months* SS once a day about forty; Morning GC 120 [or] 40 Afternoon GC 40 [or] 120 Evening GC 180 [or] 60. These show the avarage two Sundays as the services vary, one Sunday 2 preaching 1 prayer next Sunday 1 preaching 2 prayer. *Signed* John Stubbins, Steward, Bubwith, nr Selby. [517/15]

FOGGATHORPE (Township (Bubwith), Population 99)

237 <u>Foggathorpe Wesleyan Methodist Chapel</u>. Separate ExW. *Sittings* Free 50 Other 60 Free Space 28. *On 30 March* SS None Morning GC 20 Afternoon GC 100 Evening GC 32. *Average* SS None Morning GC 18 Afternoon GC 105 Evening GC 30. *Signed* Robert Lightfoot, Chapel Steward, Foggathorpe, Bubwith. [517/16]

BREIGHTON CUM GUNBY (Township (Bubwith), Population 193)

238   Wesleyan Methodists, Breighton. A Room ExW. *Sittings* Free the whole. *On 30 March* Morning GC 32 SS 16 Afternoon GC 48 Evening GC 50. *Signed* Jas. Middlebrook, Manager, Breighton, Selby. [517/17]

SPALDINGTON (Township (Bubwith), Population 323)

239   Wesleyan (Methodist) Chapel, Spaldington. *Erected* 1820. SEB this Building is also used as a Day School. *Sittings* Free 115 Other 52. *On 30 March* Morning GC 52 SS 15 Afternoon X Evening GC 25 SS 5. *Average during 12 months* Morning GC 90 SS 26 Afternoon X Evening GC 50 SS 10. *Signed* Richard Dawson, Member in Society, Spaldington, Howden. [517/18]

Howden Subdistrict[2]

WRESSLE (Hamlet (P), Population 167)

240   St John Parish Church, Wressle, the church of a distinct separate Parish. *Consecrated* This Church was rebuilt in the year 1799 at the Expense of the Patron, the late Lord Egremont, and the Parishioners, on the site of the old Parish Church. Col. Wyndham is the present Patron & the owner of the whole Parish. *Endowment* Land £42 Tithe £141.18.6 Fees £1. *Sittings* Free none Other 264 appropriated to the different Tenants & Labourers. *On 30 March* Morning X Afternoon GC 63 SS 31 Evening X. *Average during 12 months* Morning GC 25 SS 26 Afternoon GC 75 SS 26 Evening X. *Signed* Thos. Guy, Curate, Howden. [517/20]

241   Primitive Methodist, Wressle. *Erected* Before 1800. *Sittings* Free 28. *On 30 March* Morning GC X SS X Afternoon GC X SS X Evening GC 20 SS X. *Average during 6 months* Morning GC X SS X Afternoon GC 15 SS X Evening GC 20 SS X. *Remarks* Our Publick religious services at this place are conducted in a Cottage occupied by Mr. George Peckett. *Signed* William Harwood, Minister, Penfold Street, Howden. [517/21]

242   Wesleyan, Wressle. In a dwelling House. *On 30 March* Afternoon GC 30. *Dated* 28 March. *Signed* William Ingram, Wesleyan Minister, Howden. [517/22]

HEMINGBROUGH (Township (P), Population 528)

243   St Marys', Hemingbrough. An ancient Parish Church. *Endowment* Land £51.16.6 Tithe (In lieu of) £20 Fees Surplice £8.3.6. *Sittings* Free 80 Other 315. On

---

2   No returns for the hamlets of Loftsome (population 20), Newsholme (population 138) and Brind (population 53) in the parish of Wressle; for the townships of Menthorpe with Bowthorpe (population 77) and Brackenholme with Woodall (population 71) in the parish of Hemingbrough; for the extra-parochial area of Brindleys (population 6); nor for the townships of Knedlington (population 178), Kilpin (population 385), Saltmarsh (population 144), Cotness (population 28), Metham (population 60), Balkholme (population 220), Belby (population 40) and Thorpe (population 36), all in the parish of Howden.

30 March Morning GC 76 SS 70 Afternoon GC 93 SS 70. *Average during 12 months* Morning GC From 90 to 150 SS 75 Total 195 Afternoon GC From 90 to 200 SS 75 Total 220. *Remarks* The reason of the discrepancy of the numbers of the Congregation attending the Church on the 30 March & the average number of those attending during the year is this: During the Summer months & in fine Weather, the Congregation comes from the Villages in the Parish who can scarcely be expected to attend during the Winter Months on Acct. of distance from the Church & bad roads to travel on. *Signed* John Ion, Vicar, Hemingbrough, Howden. [517/23]

244 Wesleyan (Methodist) Chapel, Hemingbrough. *Erected* 1848. Entire Building ExW. *Sittings* Free 100 Other 90. On 30 March Afternoon 111 Evening 147. *Signed* William Kilby, Chapel Steward, Brackenholme, nr Howden. [517/24]

245 Primitive Methodists, Hemingbrough. On 30 March Morning GC 10 Evening GC 14. *Signed* Samuel Marshall, Steward, Hemingbrough, Howden. [517/25]

BARMBY ON THE MARSH (Township (Howden), Population 500)

246 St Helen, Barmby on the Marsh, an ancient chapelry in the Parish of Howden. *Consecrated* I understand about one hundred & fifty years ago but I have no distinct date. *Endowment* Land £22.15.0 OPE (from the Trustees of Garlethorpe's Charity) £26 Fees £1.10.0 All other categories None. *Sittings* Free 70 Other 180. On 30 March Morning GC 57 SS 72 Evening X. *Average during 12 months* Morning GC 40 SS 70 Afternoon GC 90 SS 70 Evening X. *Signed* Henry Atkinson, Incumbent, Drax, Selby. [517/26]

247 Wesleyan (Methodist) Chapel, Barmby. *Erected* about 1812. SEB ExW. *Sittings* Free 72 Other 68 The Chapel is 30 feet long by 20 feet broad & will seat 140 persons. On 30 March no school Afternoon GC 71 Evening GC 35. *Signed* Josh. Good, Steward, Barmby, nr Howden. [517/27]

248 Primitive Methodist Chappel, Barmby on the Marsh. *Erected* 1838. House, joining Place of worship. *Sittings* Free 40 Other 80. On 30 March Afternoon 35 Evening 75. *Average* 440 [sic]. *Remarks* The Chappel is 28 feet Long by 18 Broad and will Seat 140 persons. *Signed* Thomas Bickerton, Class Leader, Barmby Marsh, Howden. [517/28]

ASSELBY (Township (Howden), Population 296)

249 Wesleyan Chapel, Asselby. *Erected* 1810. All the Building. Chapel & School. *Sittings* Free 70 Other 48 Free Space 20. On 30 March Morning GC 85 SS 41 Afternoon GC 30 SS 35 Evening GC 55. *Average* Morning GC 85 SS 41. *Signed* James Barker, Class Leader, Asselby, Howden. [517/29]

250 Perimitry [Primitive?] Wesleans,[3] Asselby. *Erected* 1850. *Sittings* Free 60 Other 74. On 30 March Afternoon 60 Evening 73. *Signed* Isac. Haresine. [517/30]

---

[3]   Other variants of spelling on this return are 'Primite Weslians' and 'Primative Wesaloms'.

HOWDEN (Township (P), Population 2491)

251   St Peter & St Cuthbert [Howden Minster]. An ancient Parish Church, the Church of a distinct & separate Parish, & formerly a Collegiate Church. *Consecrated* At the latter part of the 12th century or the beginning of the 13th. *Endowment* Land £71.4.0 OPE (From the Exchequer) £31.2.8 Fees £20 Other Sources £24.15.0. *Sittings* Free (Scholars) 60 Other 650 Other categories none. The other sittings are appropriated to the different houses in the Town & Parish, but many have no sittings. *On 30 March* Morning GC 153 SS 97 Afternoon set apart for Baptism Evening GC 220 SS 35. *Average during 12 months* Morning GC 250 SS 70 Afternoon X Evening GC 200 SS 40. *Signed* Thos. Guy, Vicar, Howden. [517/31]

252   Independent Chapel, Bridgegate, Howden. *Erected* Before 1800 Enlarged since 1800. SEB ExW. *Sittings* Free 100 Other 350. *On 30 March* Morning GC 200 SS 59 Afternoon GC 80 SS 59 Evening GC 330. *Dated* 1 April. *Signed* Geo. Richards, Pastor, Howden. [517/32]

253   Primitive Methodist Chapel, Saint John's Street, Howden. *Erected* 1837. SEB ExW. *Sittings* Free 36 Other 124. *On 30 March* Morning GC X SS X Afternoon GC 70 SS 30 Evening GC 65 SS X. *Average during 12 months* Morning GC X SS X Afternoon GC 70 SS 45 Evening GC 60 SS X. *Signed* Revd William Marwood, Minister, Pinfold Street, Howden. [517/33]

254   R[oman] Catholic, Howden. ExW. *Sittings* Free 120 Other none Free Space none. *On 30 March* Morning GC 63 SS 22 Afternoon no service Evening GC 61. *Average during 12 months* Morning GC 65 SS 25 Evening GC 110. *Signed* Rev Ambrose Camburini, Catholic Priest, Everingham, nr Hayton. [517/34]

255   Wesleyan Methodist Chapel, Howden. *Erected* 1787 re-erected 1832. SEB ExW. *Sittings* Free 180 Other 420 Free Space 100. *On 30 March* Morning GC 231 SS 67 Afternoon GC 221 Evening GC 366. *Remarks* The Chapel has been enlarged from time to time. *Signed* William Ingram, Minister, Wesley Place, Howden. [517/35]

SKELTON (Township (Howden), Population 262)

256   Wesleyan (Methodist) Chapel, Skelton. *Erected* 1842. SEB ExW. *Sittings* Free 60 Other 52. *On 30 March* Afternoon GC 60. *Signed* pro Robt. Harrison [?], Trustee, Skelton, Howden. [517/36]

YORKFLEET (Township (Howden), Population 206)

257   Weslin [Wesleyan?] Chapel, Prodeston [Protestant?]. *Erected* 1821. Entire ExW. *On 30 March* Morning GC 24 Afternoon GC 38 [?] Evening GC 15. *Signed* Thos. Blanshard, Manager, Yorkfleet. [517/37]

LAXTON (Township (Howden), Population 332)

258   Chapelry of Laxton [St Peter] founded and erected in the 1st year of Charles

1st's reign. *Consecrated* In 1st year of Charles 1st. *Erected* by Anne, Elizabeth and Grace Dorey [?], three maiden Sisters. *Endowment* Land £32.10.0 OPE (Interest on £200 from Queen Anne's Bounty) £6.10.0 Fees £2 Other Sources (For preaching six anniversary sermons on particular days) £3 Total £44. *Sittings* Free 50 Other 250. *On 30 March* Morning GC 55 SS 40 Afternoon X Evening X. *Average during 12 months* Afternoon GC 70 SS 40 Evening X. *Remarks* Service is performed once every Sunday (morning & afternoon alternately). *Signed* Wm. Hutchinson, Perpetual Curate, Howden. [517/38]

259   Wesley (Methodist) Chapel, Laxton. *Erected* 1848. SEB ExW. *Sittings* Free 80 Other 74. *On 30 March* Morning GC no servis Afternoon GC no servis Evening 140. *Average* Morning 100 Afternoon 120 Evening 120. *Signed* John Margrave Hill, Trustee, Laxton. [517/39]

EASTRINGTON (Township (P), Population 386)

260   [St Michael], Eastrington, an ancient parish Church. *Consecrated* It is ancient. I have no knowledge when. *Sittings* Free 162 Other 126. *On 30 March* Morning GC 23 SS 26 Afternoon 59 SS 27 Evening GC X. *Average* Evening GC X. *Remarks* I can make no difference to that on the return of the Liber Ecclesiasticus viz £202 per Annum with a house. I am at present draining part of the Glebe & then shall have a valuation. *Signed* C. Hamerton, Vicar, Eastrington, nr Howden. [517/40]

261   Wesleyan (Methodist) Chapel, Eastrington. *Erected* 1827. SEB ExW. *Sittings* Free 100 Other 72. *On 30 March* Morning 64 Afternoon 74. *Signed* Robert Fielden, Steward, Grocer, Draper, Eastrington. [517/41]

262   Primitive Methodists, Eastrington. *Erected* Before 1800. *Sittings* Free 40. *On 30 March* Evening GC 46. *Average during 12 months* Morning GC 20 Afternoon GC 30 Evening GC 30. *Signed* John Lazenby, Leader, Eastrington, Howden. [517/42]

PORTINGTON AND CAVIL (Township (Eastrington), Population 386)

263   Wesleyan (Methodist) Chapel, Portington. *Erected* Before 1800. SEB ExW. *Sittings* Free 70. *On 30 March* Morning GC 5 (a class meeting) Afternoon GC X Evening GC 27. *Average during 12 months* Evening GC 35. *Signed* Mary Ann Bell, Stewardis, Portington Hall, Howden. [517/43]

Newport Subdistrict[4]

NEWPORT-WALLINGFEN (Township (Eastrington), Population 373)

264   Wesleyan Chapel, Newport. *Erected* 1812. SEB ExW. *Sittings* Free 130 Other

---

[4]   No returns for the townships of Bellasize (population 276) in the parish of Eastrington or the township of Drewton with Everthorpe (population 153) in the parish of North Cave.

266. On *30 March* Afternoon GC 119 SS 147 Evening GC 127. *Signed* Joseph Brellaim [?], Chapel Steward, Newport, nr Howden. [517/45]

GILBERDYKE (Township (Eastrington), Population 721)

265 Primitive Methodist Chapel, Gilberdike. *Erected* 1846. Separate Building ExW. *Sittings* Free 40 Other 90. *On 30 March* Morning GC 50 Afternoon X Evening X. *Average during 12 months* Morning GC 90 SS X Afternoon X Evening X. *Signed* John Brookes, Trustee, Greenock, nr Howden. [517/46]

266 Gilberdike Wesleyan Chapel. *Erected* 1846. Separate ExW. *Sittings* Free 80 Other 60. *On 30 March* Morning X Afternoon GC 94 SS 60 Evening GC 95. *Average during 12 months* Morning X Afternoon GC 75 SS 55. *Remarks* The Chapel is built upon an allotment of Ground formerly allotted to the Township of Bellasize upon a Common called Bishopsoil, but as it is a Mile from Bellasize and close adjoining Gilberdike it is considered as Gilberdike Chapel. *Signed* Edwd. Oliver, Steward, Gilberdyke, nr Howden. [517/47]

HOTHAM (Parish, Population 336)

267 [St Oswald], Hotham. *Consecrated* 1500. *Sittings* Appropriated 200. *Usual Number of Attendants* Morning GC 80 SS 30 Afternoon GC 80 SS 30. *Signed* H. J. Baines [517/48 Simplified]

BLACKTOFT (Township (P), Population 377)

268 Without any particular name – but, simply, Blacktoft Church [Holy Trinity] – formerly an appendage to Brantingham, but separated from that parish by a Deed of the Patrons in 1784 and is now a separate Parish. *Consecrated* before 1800. The present Church is entirely new – rebuilt upon the old site in 1841. Date of original consecration not known. *Erected* Rebuilt – partly by sale of the old lead – partly by private Subscriptions, especially from the late Amaziah Empson Esqr. Lord of the Manor, & Mrs Sarah Empson: partly by a Parish rate & partly by a Grant from Ch. Building Society. *Cost* By Ch. Build. So. Grant £150 Parochial Rate £130 Old Material raised £160 Private Benefaction etc £1200. *Endowment* Land £47 Glebe £10.10.0 OPE £150 Fees £3 Dues £1 Other categories 0. *Sittings* Free 132 Other 150. *On 30 March* Afternoon GC about 160. *Average over 12 months* Morning GC 130 SS 0 Afternoon GC 240 SS 20. *Remarks* [mainly on separate sheets] The mention of a Sunday School requires some explanation, as well as that of only time of Divine service on a Sunday in the Church. The children in the immediate vicinity of the Church are in the hands of the Wesleyans, who have a daily school and a Sunday School. The children are never brought to Church on a Sunday morning – but only once a fortnight when the Service is in the afternoon. I have made every effort, since I came to reside in 1842, to raise & establish a School in connexion with the church, but hitherto have failed. It was when the old Church was taken down in 1839 that the Wesleyans gathered the children under their superintendence – & there being no resident clergyman from time immemorial, until I came to reside in 1842: &

though I have done every thing in my power to procure a School on the principles of the Church, I cannot succeed.

A large number of my parishioners are located three, four, & five miles from their parish Church, & the same distance from any other Church. I have for the space of nearly nine years performed Divine Service on a Sunday in a Room hired for that purpose under the sanction of the late Archbishop of York, with the design of having a Chapel of Ease for that part of my Parish; providing I could first obtain some endowment upon it to secure the perpetuity of the Service. For their endowment I have applied in various quarters, but in vain. The Township of Scalby, and its immediate vicinity I have thus striven to serve, without any encouragement but that of trying to do my duty in the Parish, as the appointed Minister thereof. *Signed* Edward Ward, Minister, Howden. [517/49-51]

269 (Wesleyan Methodist) Chapel, Blacktoft. *Erected* 1839. SEB ExW. *Sittings* Free 60 Other 90. *On 30 March* Morning GC 50 SS 20. *Average during 12 months* GC 100 SS 20. *Remarks* Service is performed Morning & Afternoon alternatively. The Afternoon congregations are much larger than the Morning. The Chapel is generally full. *Signed* John Overend, Steward, Blacktoft, Howden. [517/52]

SCALBY (Township (Blacktoft), Population 145) and
CHEAPSIDES (Extra Parochial (Blacktoft), Population 39)

270 [Anglican], Cheapside [old place name]. A Room formerly a Warehouse – separate from any other building. [Used] With the full concurrence of his Grace the late Lord Archbishop of York, who was made acquainted with the whole case. *Sittings* Free 90 Total 90. *Average* Morning GC 30 Afternoon GC 60. *Remarks* This place is used as a Chapel of Ease for the Township of Scalby, & its immediate vicinity, and tho' not exactly in my parish, is the only place we can get. It is rented, and the congregation help to pay the rent. *Signed* Edward Ward, Minister, Howden. [517/53]

FAXFLEET (Township (South Cave), Population 312)

271 (Wesleyan) Methodist Chapel, Faxfleet. *Erected* 1843. SEB ExW. *Sittings* Free 60 Other 60 Free Space none. *On 30 March* Morning 75 Evening 96. *Average* Morning GC 100 SS None. *Signed* J. Scholfield, Society Steward, Faxfleet, Howden. [517/54]

272 Primitive Methodist, Faxfleet. *Erected* Rebuilt in 1850. Separate ExW. *Sittings* Free 64 Free Space 20. *On 30 March* Morning GC 11 Evening GC 11. *Average* Morning GC 25 Evening GC 20. *Signed* John Miner [?], Steward, Bramfleet, Limiting Newport. [517/55]

BROOMFLEET (Township (South Cave), Population 172)

273 (Wesleyan) Methodist Chapel, Broomfleet. *Erected* 1822. Separate ExW. *Sittings* Free 30 Other 40. *On 30 March* Morning 18 Afternoon 70. *Average* Total 88. *Signed* Wm. Purdon, Chapel Steward, Broomfleet, nr South Cave. [517/56]

NEW VILLAGE (Extra Parochial, Population 146)

274 Primitive Methodist Chapel, New Village [old place name]. *Erected* 1827. SEB ExW. *Sittings* Free 60 Other 86. *On 30 March* Morning GC X. *Average during 12 months* Morning X Afternoon GC 120 Evening GC 146. *Signed* Henry Armatage, Secretary, New Village, nr Howden. [517/57]

NORTH CAVE (Township (P), Population 899)

275 All Saints, North Cave. An Antient Parish Church. *Consecrated* before 1800. *Endowment* Tithe £197.10.0 Glebe £48.10.0 Fees £9. *Sittings* Free 138 Other 258. *On 30 March* Morning GC 85 SS 90 Afternoon GC 100 SS 81. *Average during 6 months* Morning GC 100 SS 90 Afternoon GC 120 SS 90. *Remarks* No deduction is made in this Return for a Curate to whom £110 p. Ann. are paid. A Curate is necessary there being two Churches, one at North Cave, the other at South Cliffe; & three full services every Sunday. *Signed* John Jarratt, Vicar, North Cave, nr Howden. [517/58]

276 Wesleyan Methodist Centenary Chapel, North Cave. *Erected* 1839. SEB ExW. *Sittings* Free 100 Other 180. *On 30 March* Morning GC 80 SS 44 Afternoon GC X Evening GC 131. *Signed* John Stather Petch, Steward, North Cave, nr Howden. [517/59]

277 (Primitive Methodist) Chapel, Church Street, North Cave. *Erected* 1819. SEB ExW. *Sittings* Free 60 Other 177. *On 30 March* Morning X Afternoon 100 Evening 200. *Average during 12 months* Has above Stated. *Signed* Francis Newmarch, Trustee; James Stather, R. W. Simpson, Grocers; North Cave. [517/60]

278 Meeting House of the Society of Friends, North Cave. *Erected* About 1793 on the site of an old one. SEB ExW. *Space* Floor 646 ft Galleries 221 ft. *Estimated Seating* 150. *On 30 March* Morning 8 Afternoon X Evening X. *Signed* Jo. Collinson jun., North Cave, Howden. [517/61]

BEVERLEY DISTRICT (HO 129/518)

South Cave Subdistrict[1]

NORTH NEWBALD (Township (Newbald), Population 665)

279 <u>St Nicholas, Newbald</u>. Old Parish Church. *Consecrated* before 1800. *Endowment* Land £154 Tithe £26.10.0 OPE £55 Fees £5. *Sittings* Free 400 Total 400. *Signed* G. B. Blyth, Vicar, Newbald Vicarage, nr North Cave. [518/3]

280 <u>Borough Gate Chapel (Wesleyan Methodists), North Newbald</u>. *Erected* About 1805. Separate Building ExW. *Sittings* Free 40 Other 140 Free Space Not any. On 30 March Morning GC 74 SS 16 Afternoon GC X Evening GC 65. *Average during 12 months* GC 98 SS 22. *Signed* William Wilson, Steward, North Newbald, North Cave. [518/4]

281 <u>Home Mission Station (in connection with Sion Chapel, Market Weighton, Independent or Congregational), Newbald</u>. A room in a private house ExW. *Sittings* Free 45 Free Space Not any. *Average* Week Evenings only GC 35. *Signed* John George, Minister, Market Weighton. [518/5]

282 <u>Primitive Methodist Ebenezer, North Newbald</u>. *Erected* 1839. SEB ExW. *Sittings* Free 38 Other 108. *On 30 March* Afternoon GC 120 SS 10 Evening GC 109. *Signed* John Hornsey, Chapel Steward, Miller, South Newbald. [518/6]

SOUTH CAVE (Township (South Cave), Population 937)

283 <u>All Saints Parish Church, South Cave</u>. *Consecrated* long before 1800. *Endowment* Tithe Vicarial & commuted to rent charge Glebe about 58 Acres Fees about £8 per annum. *Sittings* Total 250. *On 30 March* Morning GC 110 SS Boys 30 Girls 40 Afternoon GC 108 SS The same as morning Evening GC X. *Remarks* On a separate paper. [undated] *Signed* Edward William Stillingfleet, Vicar of South Cave. [518/8]

Covering letter from Stillingfleet to the Registrar General:

Sir, If these remarks should fall into the hands of Mr. Graham, I beg leave (as a Clergyman) to tender him my thanks for the kind consideration shown in the first paragraph of his Circular. I am quite desirous, that any information which I can give, should be both "full & correct". And it is, because I have thought I could only make misleading & ex parte statements, instead of supplying "accurate knowledge", that I answer as I have done. Question I, II, III, & IV are very easily answered by me. Not so Question V. I have stated the number of Acres of Glebe attached to the Living of South Cave, but the rental of that Glebe must be altogether uncertain in

---

[1]   No returns for the township of South Newbald (population 243) in the parish of Newbald or the township of Thorpe Brantingham (population 58) in the parish of Brantingham.

these times, returns are now being made to the respective tenants, and if free trade measures continue, it is quite impossible to state the degree of depreciation, which must lower produce and rentals. Similar observations apply to Rent Charge in lieu of Tythe, that has already fallen some Five per cent, and I have seen stated, on demi-official authority, that in about five years, the averages will be fallen some Twenty Five per cent. Therefore, for any future calculations, present receipts would only mislead. "Error instead of truth would be disseminated". On Question VI I beg to add what space in the paper did not allow. That, I knew of only Faculty Pew in South Cave Church, & that belonged to a person now dead, who has left no family to represent him. What sittings in South Cave Church are appropriated to families are so by prescription. The larger moiety of the sittings, is free.

On question VII, may I be permitted to remark, that Congregations are very frequently over-rated; & that Congregations are, by no means, a test of Membership. Many persons, who say they are "of the Church", attend Divine Worship with sad infrequency; and many will attend one Service of the day at some Meeting House, who still profess to be members of the Established Church. Our Summer Congregations are larger than our winter ones: & at this time of the year they are smaller than at any other, excepting during harvest. As to Schools, I would just observe, that in South Cave, all is voluntary in support of the Church Schools beyond some £7.10.0 per annm; & that (as it arises from the rental of land) will, most probably, decrease with falling times.

As a general observation, may I be allowed to add, that, in very many agricultural parishes, "means of instruction" ought to "keep pace" with extent of surface, quite as much as with "population", and that District parishes are imperatively required for any efficient "instruction". The Parish of South Cave is formed by a population scattered over Ten Miles in length. It is therefore, obviously, of quite an unmanageable extent for any efficient "instruction", as it now is. [518/7]

284   Wesleyan, South Cave. *Erected* 1816. SEB ExW. *Sittings* Free 70 Other 160. *Usual Number of Attendants* Afternoon GC 120 Evening GC 100 No Sunday School. *Signed* John Hill, Registrar, South Cave. [518/9 Simplified]

285   Primitive Methodist Chapel, South Cave. *Erected* 1837. SEB ExW. *Sittings* Free 30 Other 82. *On 30 March* SS none Afternoon GC 35 SS None Evening GC 45. *Average during 12 months* SS none Afternoon GC 50 Evening GC 50. *Dated* 1 April. *Signed* Thomas Wilkinson, Steward, South Cave. [518/10]

286   West End Chapel (Independent), South Cave. *Erected* 1662. SEB ExW. *Sittings* Free 60 Other 200. *On 30 March* Morning GC 50 SS 15 Afternoon GC 30 SS 21 Evening GC X. *Average during 12 months* Morning GC 70 SS 25 Afternoon GC 30 SS 26 Evening GC X. *Remarks* That is the general congregation for the Sabbath morning & afternoon 100 Scholars 56. *Signed* Thomas Roberts, Minister, South Cave, Howden. [518/11]

ELLERKER (Township (Brantingham), Population 323)

287   St Ann's Chapel, Ellerker. *Consecrated* August 23 1843 In lieu of an old or previously existing Chapel by which 125 additional seats were obtained. *On 30 March* Morning GC 85 SS 50 Afternoon GC 95 SS 50. *Average* Morning GC 85 SS 50 Afternoon GC 95 SS 50. *Remarks* Service only alternate Sundays in Morning and afternoon respectively so that one column only must be added up. *Dated* 26 March. *Signed* George Fyler Townsend, Vicar, Brantingham, Howden. [518/13]

BRANTINGHAM (Township (P), Population 166)

288   All Saints Church, Brantingham. *Consecrated* From time Immemorial. *On 30 March* Morning GC 85 SS 50 Afternoon GC 100 SS 50. *Average* Morning GC 85 SS 50 Afternoon GC 100 SS 50 Evening GC In Summer 120. *Remarks* The Service is held morning and afternoon on alternate Sundays, so that only one column is to be added. *Dated* 26 March. *Signed* George Fyler Townsend, Vicar, Brantingham, Howden. [518/12]

ELLOUGHTON CUM BROUGH (Township (Elloughton), Population 506)

289   St Mary, Elloughton. Ancient Parish Church. Body & Chancel rebuilt in 1844 at a cost of about £650: £246 raised by rate, the remainder by Mrs Raikes of Welton. The old Tower remains. *Consecrated* before 1800. *Endowment*[2] Land £56 Tithe £65 Glebe £13.6.0 OPE ([Ecclesiasti]cal Commissioners)£17 Fees £3 Dues Copyhold house & 3 acres of land £14 Total £155.13.6. *Sittings* Free 220 Total 220. *On 30 March* Afternoon GC 85. The average number of attendants during the Winter is about 60, in summer 120. *Signed* Thos. Williams, Vicar of Elloughton, South Cave. [518/14]

290   Wesleyan Methodists, Elloughton. SEB ExW. *Sittings* Free All. *Usual Number of Attendants* Morning GC 30 No Sunday School. *Signed* John Hill, Registrar, South Cave. [518/15 Simplified]

291   Indep[endent], Elloughton. *Sittings* Free 50 Other 60. *Dated* 23 August 1852. *Signed* John Hill, Registrar. [518/16 Registrar's Enquiry]

292   Primitive (Methodist) Chapple [Brough?]. *Erected* 1830. An Entire Building for the worship of Almighty God. No School. *Sittings* Free 56 Other 100. *On 30 March* Morning 120 Afternoon X Evening 90. *Signed* William Laverack, Steward, Brough. [518/17]

ROWLEY (Part Parish, Population 384)

293   St Peter's, Rowley, an Ancient Parish Church. *Endowment* Tithe £1101 Glebe £250. *Sittings* Free 90 Other 110. *On 30 March* Morning GC 60 SS 22 Afternoon GC 24 SS 22. *Average* Morning GC 80 SS 20 Afternoon GC 25 SS 30. *Signed* Levett E. Thoroton, Rector of Rowley, Beverley. [518/18]

---

2   Further details of endowments were noticed on the form, but are incomprehensible because the edge of the document has been torn.

294   (Wesleyan) Methodist Chapel, Little Weighton. *Erected* About 1825. Entire ExW. *Sittings* Free 70 Other 64. *On 30 March* Morning GC X Afternoon GC X Evening GC 58. *Average during 12 months* Morning GC X Afternoon GC X Evening GC 80. *Signed* Rich. Brough, Steward, Hunsley, Beverley. [518/19]

295   Wesleyan Methodist, [Riplingham?]. *Erected* about 1806. *Sittings* Free 60. *On 30 March* Morning GC X Afternoon GC 30 Evening GC X. *Average during 12 months* Morning GC X Afternoon GC 40 Evening GC X. *Signed* John Johnson, Steward, Riplingham, South Cave. [518/20]

Beverley Subdistrict[3]

SKIDBY WITH SKIDBY-CARR (Parish, Population 361)

296   Skidby Parish Church [St Michael]. Ancient Parish Church. *Consecrated* Previous to AD 1400. *Endowment* There is no endowment for Skidby separate from Cottingham. It is a separate Parish, but time out of mind has been held together with Cottingham. Fees Abt. £1. *Sittings* Free 65 Other 185. *On 30 March* Morning X Afternoon GC 41 SS 29. *Average* Morning GC 50 SS 35 Afternoon X Evening X. *Remarks* Generally a Morning Service. *Signed* Charles Overton, Vicar of Cottingham & Incumbent of Skidby, nr Hull. [518/21]

297   Baptist Chapel, Skidby. *Erected* 1819. Separate ExW. *Sittings* Free 20 Other 70 Free Space 20. *On 30 March* Morning GC X Afternoon GC 40 SS 12 Evening X. *Average during 12 months* Afternoon GC 50 SS 20. *Signed* Reuben Jefferson, Deacon, Skidby, Beverley. [518/22]

298   Wesleyan (Methodist) Chapel, Skidby. *Erected* 1826. Entier Building ExW. *Sittings* Free 25 Other 52 Free Space 25. *On 30 March* Evening GC 50. *Average* Evening GC 58. *Signed* John Ringrate, Overlooker, Skidby. [518/23]

PROVOSTS FEE (Manor (Walkington), Population 266)

299   All Saints Church, Walkington. *Consecrated* Before 1800. *Endowment* Dues £5.6.0. *Sittings* Free 173 Other 42. *On 30 March* Morning GC 12 SS 23 Afternoon GC 91 SS 26. *Average* Morning GC 15 SS 35 Afternoon 150. *Remarks* As to the fees they are uncertain. As I occupy the Glebe I am not able, from the very low price of Agricultural produce to state, what my income will amount to till the years end. *Signed* Danl. Ferguson, Rector, Walkington, nr Beverley. [518/24]

HOWDEN FEE (Manor (Walkington), Population 433)

300   (Primitive Methodist) Chapple, Walkington. *Erected* 1837. Separate ExW. *Sittings* Free 50 Other 40. *On 30 March* Morning GC X SS 53 Afternoon GC 74

---

3   No returns for the hamlets of Bentley (population 62) and Risby (population 52) in the parish of Rowley, or the townships of Thearne (population 99), Eske (population 45),

Evening GC 63. *Average during 3 months* 1224 [sic] Morning GC 70 SS 53 Evening Total 123. *Signed* James Boothby, Chapple Steward, Walkington, nr Beverley. [518/25]

301 Wesley Chapel (Wesleyan), Walkington. *Erected* 1822. SEB ExW. *Sittings* Free 70 Other 66. *On 30 March* Morning GC X SS not any Afternoon GC 40 Evening GC 70. *Remarks* We have no standing room or open space in this Chapel only a aile up the Middle 3 feet whide as a passage. *Signed* James Robinson, Chapel Steward. [518/26]

WOODMANSEY WITH BEVERLEY PARK (Township (St John Beverley), Population 441)

302 Woodmansey [Anglican] Chapel. Not consecrated or licensed. *Erected* by Anthony Atkinson Esquire. No Income Not Endowed. *On 30 March* Evening GC 40. *Average during 6 months* Evening GC 50. *Signed* John Cambage Thompson, Curate, Beverley. [518/27]

WEEL (Township (St John Beverley), Population 135)

303 [Anglican], Weel. Service in Farm House. *Average* Evening GC 40. *Remarks* There is no Church or Chapel here at Weel, but there is a Service in the Kitchen of a Farm House. *Signed* John Cambage Thompson, Curate, Beverley. [518/28]

TICKTON WITH HULL BRIDGE (Township (St John Beverley), Population 274)

304 Saint Paul's Church, Tickton. *Consecrated* Nov. 13 1845. *Erected* By private Subscription. *Cost* Total £1000. *Endowment* Pew Rents £11. *Sittings* Free 130 Other 30. *On 30 March* Morning GC 27 SS 43 Afternoon GC 77 SS 45. *Average during 6 months* Morning GC 29 SS 45 Afternoon GC 75 SS 45. *Remarks* Tickton has no income for the Minister. The Ecclesiastical Comrs ought to grant an Income here. *Signed* John Cambage Thompson, Curate, Beverley. [518/29]

305 Wesleyan, Tickton. *Erected* 1828. SEB ExW. *Sittings* Free 20 Other 48. *On 30 March* Morning GC X Afternoon GC X Evening GC 58. *Signed* John Platts, Steward, Hull Bridge, nr Beverley. [518/30]

BEVERLEY ST MARY (Parish (Beverley Borough), Population 3682)

306 St Mary's Church. It is an ancient Parish Church, date when built & consecrated not known. It is common to the United Parishes of St Mary & St Nicholas in Beverley: united 1667. *Consecrated* Not known, probably in the 12th Century. *Endowment* Land £15 Tithe £290 Glebe & House £50 OPE (Crown Rent) £3 Fees £20 Easter Offerings £20. *Sittings* Free 87 Sunday School Sittings 250 Other 838. *On 30 March* Morning GC 500 SS 238 Afternoon GC 110 Evening GC 350. *Average* Morning GC 500 to 600 Afternoon GC 80 to 120 Evening GC 500 to 600. *Remarks* The Congregations are at present smaller & the Schools thinner than usual from the Parishes, being severley visited by Influenza. The Children were not numbered in the Afternoon. *Signed* Wm. Francis Sandys, Vicar, The Vicarage, Beverley. [518/31]

307 St John's Chapel ([Roman] Catholic). *Erected* 6 years. ExW. *Sittings* Space available for 200 Free 63 all free Other No other Sittings. *Usual Number of Attendants* Morning GC from 60 to 90 SS 30 Evening GC the same. *Signed* Bernard Branigan, North Bar Without, [Beverley]. [518/32 Simplified]

308 Wesley Chapel (Wesleyan Methodists). *Erected* 1833. SEB ExW. *Sittings* Free 200 Other 600. *On 30 March* Morning GC 300 SS 120 Evening 500. *Average during 12 months* Morning [sic] GC 600 SS 120. *Dated* 3 April. *Signed* Thomas Llewellyn, Minister, 80 Lister St, Hull. [518/33]

309 Wesleyan Chapel, Walkergate. *Erected* 1804 Enlarged 1837. SEB ExW. *Sittings* Free 400 Other 600 Free Space Ailes only. *On 30 March* Morning GC 600 SS 145 Afternoon GC 100 Evening GC 800. *Signed* N. J. Wreghill, Chapel Steward, No Bar Street, Beverley. [518/34]

310 Scotch Baptist Chapel. *Erected* 1808. Separate Building ExW. *Sittings* Free All 250. *On 30 March* Morning GC 50 Afternoon GC 20 Evening GC 50. *Signed* James Everson, Minister, Wednesday Market, Beverley. [518/35]

BEVERLEY ST MARTIN (Parish (Beverley Borough), Population 3917)

311 St John's Chapel. *Consecrated* By the late Archbishop of York in Oct. 1841 As an additional Church but without cure of souls. *Erected* By private subscription. *Cost* Private Benefaction etc £4,000. *Endowment* Pew Rents £120 Other Sources £3.5.0. *Sittings* Free 300 Other 550. *On 30 March* Morning GC 300 SS 90 Evening GC 400. *Average during 12 months* Morning GC 300 SS 100 Evening GC 450. [undated] *Signed* Anthony Thomas Carr, Incumbent, St John's Parsonage, Beverley. [518/36]

312 St John's Church, Beverley, or the late Collegiate Church of St John or Beverley Minster. The Parish Church for the Parish of St John with St Martins annexed. *Consecrated* At or before 692 1st a Parish church 2d A Monastery & Collegiate Church 3 From the Reign of Queen Elizth a Parish Church. *Endowment* Land £50 Glebe House £35 OPE £125 Fees £28. *Sittings* Free 1000 Total 1000. *On 30 March* Morning GC 386 SS 213 Afternoon GC 492 SS 236 Evening X. *Remarks* The numbers taken on the 30 of March will be about the average. *Signed* John B. Birtwhistle, Incumbent Curate, Beverley. [518/37]

313 Independent Chapel, Lairgate. *Erected* Before 1800. SEB ExW. *Sittings* Free 126 Other 462. *On 30 March* Morning SS 110 Afternoon GC X SS 120 Evening SS X. *Average during 12 months* Morning GC 180 SS 100 Afternoon GC X SS 115 Evening GC 220 SS X. *Remarks* There is a School room open to the Chapel available for public worship which will hold about 200 Children. *Signed* William Young, Minister, Beverley. [518/38]

314 Primitive Methodist Chapel, Wednesday Market. *Erected* 1825. SEB ExW. *Sittings* Free 144 Other 279 Free Space None. *On 30 March* Morning GC 257 SS 71 Afternoon GC 197 Evening GC 400. *Average during 6 months* Morning GC 257 SS

71 Afternoon GC 60 Evening GC 400. *Signed* George Wood, Minister, Albert Terrace, Beverley. [518/39]

315 (Particular) Baptist Chapel, Well Lane. *Erected* 1834. SEB ExW. *Sittings* Free 100 Other 400 Free Space None. *On 30 March* Morning GC 143 SS 45 Afternoon GC 110 SS 60 Evening GC 238. *Signed* Robert Johnston, Minister, Flemingate, Beverley. [518/40]

BEVERLEY ST NICHOLAS (Parish (Beverley Borough), Population 1316)

316 Beckside Chapel and Schoolhouse (Wesleyan Methodist). *Erected* 1825. SEB ExW. *Sittings* Free 110 Other 30. *On 30 March* Afternoon GC 29 SS 92 Evening GC 65. *Signed* William Watson, Steward, Joiner & Grocer, Beckside, Beverley. [518/41]

BISHOP BURTON (Parish, Population 566)

317 All Saints, Bishop Burton. An ancient Parish Church, the nave of which was rebuilt and enlarged about twenty seven years since. *Consecrated* Before 1800. *Endowment* Land £80 Tithe (rent charge) £13.6.8 Glebe and house £15 OPE (Augmentation) £16 Fees (average) £2.5.0 Other Sources £2. *Sittings* Free about 60 Other about 200. *On 30 March* Morning GC X SS 45 Afternoon GC 67 SS 45 Evening GC X. *Remarks* The Incumbent begs leave to state that in Country Villages as in this the number of attendants at the Parish Church varies considerably. In this Village many of the Inhabitants attend public worship in the chapels, one part of the day, [...] in the morning at one dissenting Chapel, in the Evening at the Wesleyan Chapel & in the afternoon at the church. *Signed* William Procter, Vicar, Vicarage, Bishop Burton, nr Beverley. [518/42]

318 Bishop Burton Chapel, Wesleyan Methodists. *Erected* 1840. SEB ExW. *Sittings* Free 70 Other 90. *On 30 March* Evening 116. *Average during 12 months* Evening GC 120. *Signed* Robert Lonsbrough, Debuty Steward & Leader, Bishop Burton, Beverley. [518/43]

319 Baptist Chapel, Bishop Burton. *Erected* before 1800. Separate ExW. *Sittings* Free 80 Other 170. *On 30 March* Morning GC 65 SS 18 Afternoon GC 125 Evening GC 30 SS 20. *Signed* John Jefferson, Minister, Bishop Burton, nr Beverley. [518/44]

CHERRY BURTON (Parish, Population 496)

320 St Michael's Church, Cherry Burton. A very old Church perhaps built about the 12th Century. *Endowment* Tithe £1050 Glebe 25 a(cres) 1 r[od] 30 p[erches] Fees £2. *Sittings* Free 60 Other 96. *On 30 March* Morning GC 99 SS 44 Afternoon GC 49 SS 44 Evening GC 31 SS 7. *Average* Morning Total 143 Afternoon Total 93 Evening Total 40. *Remarks* From the sixth of April to the sixth of October there is no afternoon service and a greater number of persons attend in the evening. *Signed* John Thomas Forbes Hicks, Curate, Cherry Burton, Beverley. [518/45]

321   Wesleyan Methodist, Cherry Burton. *Erected* 1825. SEB ExW. *Sittings* Free 60 Other 62. *On 30 March* Evening GC 93. *Average during 12 months* Morning [sic] GC 95. *Signed* David Pickering, Chappel Steward, Cherry Burton, Beverley. [518/46]

322   Primitive Methodist, Cherry Burton. *Erected* 1844. *Sittings* Free 55 Other 55 Free Space 20. *On 30 March* Afternoon GC 70. *Average during 12 months* Afternoon GC 50. [Undated, unsigned] [518/47]

Lockington Subdistrict

ETTON (Parish, Population 498)

323   St Mary, Commonly called Etton Parish Church. Ancient Parish Church. *Consecrated* before 1800. *Endowment* Pew Rents None; Fees I don't take them; Dues None; Easter Offerings None. *Sittings* All free Total 250. *On 30 March* Morning GC 118 SS 41 aut circa [or thereabouts] Afternoon GC very few. *Average* Morning GC 100 SS 41 Afternoon GC few SS 41 aut circa. *Remarks* In the absence of the Rector who resides at Bishopthorpe[4] I do not consider that I am warranted to make a return of his income from Etton. *Signed* Rob. Machell, Curate, Etton Parsonage, nr Beverley. [518/48]

324   (Primitive Methodist) Chapel, Etton. *Erected* 1825. SEB ExW. *Sittings* Free 26 Other 60. *On 30 March* Morning GC X Afternoon GC 40 Evening GC 68. *Signed* Rev J. Ratcliffe; Richard Witty, Steward, Etton, Beverley. [518/49]

SOUTH DALTON (Parish, Population 299)

325   St Mary's, South Dalton. An ancient Parish Church. *Endowment* Tithe £319.14.2 Glebe £72 Fees £1.16.8. *Sittings* Free 150. *On 30 March* Morning GC 52 SS 39 Afternoon GC 40 SS 32. *Signed* Edwin Hotham, Rector, South Dalton, Beverley. [518/50]

326   Wesleyan, South Dalton. *Erected* 1824. SEB ExW. *Sittings* Free 50 Other 60 Free Space None. *On 30 March* SS None Morning GC X Afternoon GC 30 Evening GC 60. *Signed* Robert Leak Wilson, Steward, South Dalton, Beverley. [518/51]

HOLME ON THE WOLDS (Parish, Population 153)

327   Saint Peter, Holme on the Wolds. An ancient Parish Church. *Consecrated* before 1800. *Endowment* Land small; allotments of Glebe lands; OPE £6.13.4 (money payment) Annual Value fifty pounds. *Sittings* Free All free neatly pewed Total 110. *On 30 March* Service Once on the Sabbath Day, No Scholars, 44 Persons. *Average during 12 months* About fifty Persons, No Sunday School. *Signed* Thos. Mitchell, Minister, Market Weighton. [518/52]

---

4   W. H. Dixon, also Canon Residentiary of York and Vicar of Bishopthorpe.

328 <u>Wesleyan, Holme on the Wolds</u>. Part of a dwelling House. *Sittings* Free All. *Usual Number of Attendants* Afternoon GC 35. *Signed* X The Mark of Fanny Clark, Holme on the Wolds, Beverley. [518/53 Simplified]

LUND (Parish, Population 503)

329 <u>All Saints, Lund</u>. *Erected* Ancient Church, Chancel Built about 1400. *Sittings* Free All Total 262. *Usual Number of Attendants* 100 Morning GC 60 SS 40 Afternoon GC 100 SS 40. *Signed* The Information was furnished by John Robinson, the Parish Clerk of Lund. Geo Theakstone. [518/54 Simplified]

330 <u>Wesleyan Chapel, Main Street, Lund</u>. *Erected* 1835. SEB ExW. *Sittings* Free 40 Other 75. *Usual Number of Attendants* Morning GC 40 Afternoon GC 50. *Signed* Robert Robson, Lund, Beverley. [518/55 Simplified]

331 <u>Primitive Methodist Chapel, Lund</u>. *Erected* 1839. SEB ExW. *Sittings* Free 30 Other 80 Free Space 20. *On 30 March* Morning GC X Afternoon GC X Evening GC 80. *Average* Morning [sic] GC 90. *Signed* David Hodsfield, Society Steward, Taylor & Draper, Lund. [518/56]

KILNWICK (Township (P), Population 264)

332 <u>All Saints, Kilnwick</u>. *Erected* about 1200. *Sittings* Free 150 Appropriated 20 ['all free' also written]. *Usual Number of Attendants* about 100 Morning GC 50 SS 40 Afternoon GC 100 SS 40. *Signed* Francis Lundy, Incumbent. [518/58 Simplified]

BESWICK (Township (Kilnwick), Population 224)

333 <u>Chapel of Beswick [St Margaret]</u>. *Consecrated* Unknown. Licensed by the Archbishop of York. *Endowment* Land £42 Tithe £75 Total £117. *Sittings* Free 130 Total 130. *On 30 March* Morning GC 37. *Average* Morning GC 40 Afternoon GC 50. *Signed* Joseph Rigby, Perpetual Curate of Beswick, Hutton, nr Driffield. [518/57]

334 <u>Baptist, Beswick</u>. Part of a House. *Sittings* Free All Other None. *Usual Number of Attendants* Evening GC 30. *Signed* Willm. Duggleby, Beswick, Beverley. [518/62 Simplified]

LOCKINGTON (Township (Kilnwick/Lockington), Population 523)

335 <u>St Mary, Lockington</u>. *Erected* about 1000. *Sittings* Free 200 Appropriated 16 ['all free' also written]. *Usual Number of Attendants* from 100 to 150 Morning GC 50 SS from 30 to 40 Afternoon GC 100 SS do. [ie from 30 to 40]. *Signed* Francis Lundy, Rector. [518/64 Simplified]

336 <u>Primative Methodist Chapell, Lockington</u>. *Erected* 1825. Entire Exclusively. *Sittings* Free 30 Other 60 Free Space 20. *On 30 March* Morning GC X Afternoon GC X Evening GC 90. *Average during 3 months* Evening GC 80. *Signed* James Gunton, Steward, Lockington. [518/59]

337   Wesleyan Methodist Chappel, Lockington. *Erected* 1812. SEB ExW. *Sittings* Free 60 Other 84 Free Space None. *On 30 March* SS None Morning GC X Afternoon GC 100 Evening GC X. *Average* Morning [sic] GC 90 SS None. *Signed* Robert Fox, Steward, Farmer, Lockington, Beverley. [518/60]

AIKE (Township (Lockington/St John Beverley), Population 108)

338   Aike Chapel. Not consecrated or Licensed. *Erected* by Lord Hotham. *Endowment* not endowed no Income. *Sittings* Free 60 Total 60. *Average during 6 months* Morning GC 20 SS 15. *Remarks* There is only Service here once a Fortnight & there was no Service on the 30th March. *Signed* John Cambage Thompson, Officiating Minister, Beverley. [518/66]

339   Primative Methodist, Aike. *Erected* Used for divine Service Since 1845. Dwelling House. *Sittings* Free 30. *On 30 March* Afternoon GC 15. *Average during 6 months* Evening GC 20. *Signed* Nicholas Milner his X Mark, Leader, Scorborough, Beverley. [518/61]

SCORBOROUGH (Parish, Population 90)

340   Parish Church [St Leonard], Scorborough. Consecrated. *Endowment* Tithes Commuted. *Sittings* Free 100 Other 50. *On 30 March* Varies. *Average* Varies. *Dated* [?] 6 April. *Signed* H. Jennings, Curate. [518/65]

LECKONFIELD WITH ARRAM (Parish, Population 362)

341   St Catherine, commonly known by the name of Leckonfield Church. Ancient Parish Church. *Consecrated* before 1800. *Endowment* Fees I never take any; Other Sources No; Other Categories None. *Sittings* Free All Total 200. *On 30 March* Afternoon GC 40 SS 15. *Remarks* The Endowment of the Church is from Land granted by Queen Anns bounty, and Nine pounds per Annum from Colonel Wyndham. Total Net Yearly amount £40, and No House of Residence. *Signed* Rob. Machell, Perpetual Curate, Etton, nr Beverley. [518/67]

342   Wesleyan, Leckonfield. Part of a dwelling House. *Sittings* Free All. *Usual Number of Attendants* Evening GC 35. *Signed* William Sissons, Leckonfield, Beverley. [518/68 Simplified]

343   Wesleyan, Arram. Part of dwelling House. *Sittings* Free All. *Usual Number of Attendants* Afternoon GC 15 Evening GC 15. *Signed* The Information furnished by William Sissons, of Leckonfield. G. Theakstone. [518/63 Simplified]

Leven Subdistrict

LEVEN (Township (P), Population 876)

344   Holy Trinity, Leven. *Erected* 1845. *Sittings* Free 330 Appropriated 30. *Usual Number of Attendants* Morning GC 130 SS 63 Afternoon GC 150 SS 63 Evening GC

None. *Signed* George Derbyshire 8 oclock P.M., 9 Dec. 1851, have only Just received this Paper from the Revd G. Wray and partly fill up from his Information. [518/69 Simplified]

345   Wesleyan Methodist Chapel, Leven. *Erected* 1816. SEB ExW. *Sittings* Free 72 Other 107. *On 30 March* Morning GC X SS 67 Afternoon GC 61 SS 71 Evening GC 132. *Signed* Robinson Pool, Chapel Steward, Leven. [518/70]

346   Primitive Methodist Chapel, Leven. *Erected* 1836. SEB ExW. *Sittings* Free 34 Free Space 30. *On 30 March* Morning GC 20 Afternoon X Evening GC 40. *Average during 12 months* Morning GC 20 Afternoon GC X Evening GC 40. *Dated* 27 March. *Signed* John Crow, Minister; to William Dearing, Chapel Steward, Leven, nr Beverley. [518/71]

ROUTH (Parish, Population 172)

347   All Saints, Routh. An ancient parish church. *Consecrated* Before 1800. *Sittings* Free All. *On 30 March* Morning GC 29 SS 19 Afternoon GC 30 SS 19. *Average* Morning GC 40 SS 19 Afternoon GC 45 SS 19. *Signed* Henry Maister, Curate, Routh, Beverley. [518/72]

MEAUX (Township (Wawne), Population 89)

348   Meaux Chapel (Independent). *Erected* 1823. Entire ExW. *Sittings* Free 20 Other 45. *On 30 March* Afternoon GC 30. *Average during 6 months* Morning GC 20 Afternoon GC 30 Evening GC X. *Remarks* Divine service is held on the Forenoon and Afternoons Alternately. Kept as a Preaching Station of the East Riding Home Missionary Society. *Signed* William Meldrum, Preacher, Beverley. [518/73]

WAWNE (Township (P), Population 258)

349   St Peter, Wawne. An ancient Parish Church. *Consecrated* Before 1800. *Sittings* Free 300 Total 300. *On 30 March* Morning GC 50 SS 24 Afternoon GC 45 SS 24 Evening X. *Average during 12 months* Morning GC 65 SS 28 Afternoon GC 100 SS 28 Evening X. *Remarks* This Living is endowed with £200 from Land, Tithes & Queen Anne's Bounty, not time to get particulars from the Vicar. *Signed* Charles Kipling, Curate, Waghen, nr Beverley. [518/74]

Sutton-on-Hull Subdistrict

SUTTON (Parish (with Stoneferry), Population 7473)

350 St James' Church, Sutton, an ancient Parish Church. *Consecrated* before 1800. *Endowment* Tithe £49 OPE £35 Fees £20 Other Sources £15. *Sittings* Free 353 Total 353. *On 30 March* Morning GC 160 SS 80 Afternoon GC 142 SS 88 Evening X. *Average during 12 months* Morning GC 200 SS 85 Afternoon GC 150 SS 85 Evening X. *Remarks* The space available for public worship is only sufficient for 75 families in consequence of the very objectionable arrangement of pews. *Signed* John Adams Eldridge, MA, Minister, Sutton, nr Hull. [519/1]

351 St Marks, Sutton. *Sittings* Free 600 Other 535. *Dated* 21 August 1852. *Signed* Joseph Darby. [520/3 Registrar's Enquiry[1]]

352 Holborn Street Chapel (Independent), Witham. *Erected* 1830. SEB ExW. *Sittings* Free 198 Other 432. *On 30 March* Morning GC 90 SS 80 Afternoon SS 90 Evening SS [sic] 150. *Remarks* Influenza and other diseases are at present very prevalent in the neighbourhood – absent from the Sabbath School in the afternoon about 60 and from the congregation in the Evening about 40. *Signed* Rev Ebenezer Morley, Minister, Hull. [519/2]

353 Kingston Chapel (Wesleyan Methodists), Witham. *Erected* 1840. SEB ExW. *Sittings* Free 500 Other 1496. *On 30 March* Morning GC 550 SS 264 Afternoon No Service; Evening GC 700 SS 60. *Average during 12 months* Morning GC 650 SS 290 Evening GC 800 SS 60. *Signed* Willm. Davison, Minister, 12 Pemberton Street, Hull. [519/3]

354 Wesleyan Chapel, Sutton. *Erected* About 1812. SEB ExW. *Sittings* Free 36 Other 122. *On 30 March* Morning GC X SS X Afternoon GC 71 SS 55 Evening GC 100. *Average during 12 months* Morning GC X SS X Afternoon GC 65 SS 50 Evening GC 90. *Signed* George Cowl, Steward, Sutton, Hull. [519/4]

355 Primitive Methodist, Sutton. *Erected* 1832. SEB ExW. *Sittings* Free 12 Other 76. *On 30 March* Morning X Afternoon X Evening 52. *Average* Morning X Afternoon X Evening X [sic]. *Signed* James Carrick, Leader, Sutton. [519/5]

STONEFERRY (Parish (with Sutton), Population 310)

356 Wesleyan (Methodist) Chapel, Stoneferry. *Erected* 1839. SEB ExW. *Sittings*

---

[1] This return has been located here in this edition on the basis of the document itself which gives the superintendent registrar's district as Sculcoates and the the registrar's district as Sutton. St Mark's was, however, in a part of the old parish of Sutton known as the Groves, a built-up area on the edge of Hull, under which district it is filed in the PRO sequence.

Free 44 Other 44. *On 30 March* Morning GC 22 SS None Afternoon GC X SS X Evening GC 35 SS None. *Average during 12 months* Morning GC 30 Afternoon GC X Evening GC 50. *Signed* Willm. Davison, Minister, 12 Pemberton Street, Hull. [519/6]

Cottingham Subdistrict

COTTINGHAM (Parish, Population 2854)

357   St John's Church, Newland. *Consecrated* Sept. 1833 as a Chapel of Ease to Cottingham. *Erected* By Subscription including 3 1/2 acres of land. *Cost* By Parliamentary Grant £240 Private Benefaction etc £1370 Total £1610. *Endowment* Land £9 Glebe 3 acres; Pew Rents £20 and 30 Other Sources Voluntary. *Sittings* Free 250 Other 250. *On 30 March* Afternoon GC 110 SS 30. *Average* Afternoon GC 100 SS 35. *Signed* Charles Overton, Vicar of Cottingham, Cottingham, nr Hull. [519/7]

358   Cottingham Parish Church, St Mary's, Ancient Parish Church. *Consecrated* Previous to 1400. *Endowment* Land Rent charge upon Rectory £200 Glebe £15 Crown [?] rent £4.12.6 Q. A. Bounty – deducting payment under Gilbert Act £5.4.6 Fees £19 Total £243.17.0. *Sittings* Free 500 Other 600. *On 30 March* Morning GC 223 SS 70 Evening GC 320. *Average* Morning GC 300 SS 100 Evening GC 400. *Remarks* The Vicar of Cottingham has always to keep a Curate having, in addition to the Parish Church of Cottingham, to provide for Skidby Church – attached to Cottingham, & also for St John's Church Newland, in the Parish of Cottingham. *Signed* Charles Overton, Vicar, Cottingham, nr Hull. [519/8]

359   Bethel (Methodist New Connexion), Dunswell. *Erected* About 1814. SEB ExW. *Sittings* Free 40 Other 40. *Usual Number of Attendants* Morning GC None Afternoon GC 45 Evening GC 45. *Signed* John Wilkinson, Dunswell, nr [...], Beverley. [519/9 Simplified]

360   Newland Wesleyan Chapel. *Erected* Before 1800. SEB ExW. *Sittings* 60. *On 30 March* SS None Evening GC 55. *Signed* George Waddington, Steward, Newland, nr Hull. [519/10]

361   Wesleyan Methodist Chapel, Northgate, Cottingham. *Erected* 1803 Rebuilt & enlarged 1814. SEB ExW. *Sittings* Free 160 Other 250 Free Space None. *On 30 March* Morning GC 120 SS 80 Afternoon No service Evening GC 150. *Average during 12 months* Morning GC 160 SS 88 Afternoon GC No service Evening GC 250. *Signed* James Alsop, for the Steward, Cottingham, nr Hull. [519/11]

362   Primitive Methodist Chapel, Cottingham. *Erected* 1828. Entire Building ExW. *Sittings* Free 32 Other 116. *On 30 March* No Sunday School Afternoon GC 57 Evening GC 58. *Average* Afternoon GC 100 Evening GC 100. *Signed* Thomas Clark, Steward, Thwaite, Cottingham, nr Hull. [519/12]

363   Zion Chapel, (Independent or Congregational), Cottingham. *Erected* 1819

In lieu of one which Existed before 1800. SEB ExW. *Sittings* Free 218 Other 386. *On 30 March* Morning GC 60 SS 44 Afternoon GC 86 SS 47. *Signed* William Penton [?], Manager, Cottingham. [519/13]

WILLERBY (Township (Kirk Ella), Population 214)

364   Primitive Methodist Chapel, Willerby. *Erected* 1850. Entire ExW. *Sittings* Free 30 Other 85 Free Space 30. *On 30 March* Afternoon 70 Evening 100. *Signed* Jane Dodsworth, Stewardess, Willerby, nr Hull. [519/14]

Ferriby Subdistrict[2]

WELTON (Township (P), Population 682)

365   St Helen's, Parish Church of Welton cum Melton. Founded in the reign of William Rufus. *Endowment* Tithe £51 Glebe 333 acres Fees £10 Other Sources a small manor. *Sittings* Free 100 Other 360. *On 30 March* Morning GC 210 SS 106 Afternoon GC 145 SS 100 Evening X. *Remarks* The congregation rather below the average in the morning. Many of the unoccupied sittings are in pews attached to the principal houses in the parish, whose present inhabitants are not sufficient to fill them. Persons frequently complain to me that tho' they are church people they are obliged to attend Chapel beacuse there is no room for them in the Church. *Signed* Thomas Bradley Paget, Vicar, Melton Grange, Howden. [519/15]

366   Independent. *Erected* 1814. Separate ExW. *Sittings* Free 90 Other 75 Free Space 0. *Signed* John Gildward, Deacon, Welton. [519/16]

367   Forester's Lodge (Primitive Methodists), Welton. *Erected* 1840. Room. *Sittings* Free 30 Other 40. *On 30 March* Evening GC 19. *Average during 12 months* Evening GC 28. *Signed* John Rudd, Class Leader, Welton, Hull. [519/17]

368   Unitarian, Welton. A Day School being also taught in it. *Sittings* Free All Free 30. *On 30 March* Evening GC 13. *Average during 12 months* Evening GC 15. *Signed* Thomas Simpson, Minister, 6 Sovereign Place, William Street, Hull. [519/18]

369   Wesleyan, Welton. *Erected* 1815. SEB ExW. *Sittings* Free 70 Other 170. *On 30 March* Morning GC X Afternoon GC 68 Evening GC 172. *Average during 6 months* Morning [sic] GC 200. *Signed* John Hudson, Chapel Steward, Welton, nr Hull. [519/19]

NORTH FERRIBY (Township (P), Population 472)

370   All Saints Church, North Ferriby. An Ancient Parish Church. *Consecrated* July 1848 when the Ancient Parish Church was taken down and rebuilt. *Endowment* Land £86.16.0 Glebe £3.10.0 OPE £40.14.0 Fees £5 Total £136 [sic]. *Sittings* Free

---

2   No returns for the township of Wauldby (population 49) in the parish of Elloughton, nor for the township of Melton (population 174) in the parish of Welton.

116 Other 292. *On 30 March* Morning GC 76 SS 42 Afternoon GC 95 SS 42. *Signed* Chas. N. Wawn, Vicar, North Ferriby, Hull. [519/20]

371 <u>Primitive Methodist, Ferriby</u>. *Erected* 1828. SEB ExW. *Sittings* Free 48 Other 84. *On 30 March* Morning GC X Afternoon GC X Evening GC 115. *Average during 12 months* Morning [sic] GC 110. *Signed* William Hunter, Steward, Melton, nr Ferriby, Howden. [519/21]

SWANLAND (Township (North Ferriby), Population 457)

372 <u>Independent Chapel, Swanland</u>. *Erected* 1651. Entire ExW. *Sittings* Free 80 Other 320. *On 30 March* Morning GC 200 SS 23 Afternoon GC 180. *Average during 12 months* Morning GC 200 SS 27. *Remarks* Not having had a stated minister for the last two years, the number of attendants has rather decreased. *Signed* John Smith, Deacon, North Ferriby, nr Hull. [519/22]

373 <u>Wesleyan Methodist, Swanland</u>. SEB. *Sittings* Free 60. *On 30 March* Evening GC 43. *Average during 12 months* Evening GC 40. *Remarks* This place of Worship is a "Hired Room" and the appointment of preachers is with The Rev'd Charles Prest 11 Storey Street Hull. *Signed* Wm. Hy. Walmsley, Tenant. [519/23]

374 <u>Swanland Primitive Methodist</u>. *Erected* 1828. SEB ExW. *Sittings* Free 30 Other 70. *On 30 March* Evening GC 45. *Average during 12 months* GC 45. *Signed* Edward Harper, Local Preacher, Swanland, nr Hull. [519/24]

Hessle Subdistrict

KIRK ELLA (Township (P), Population 306)

375 <u>Ancient St Andrew's Parish Church of Kirk Ella</u>. *Consecrated* before 1800. *Endowment* Land £212.15.0 Glebe £30 OPE £14.13.9 Fees £13.2.1 Easter Offerings £3.2.8. *Sittings* Free All Total 300. *On 30 March* Morning GC 150 SS 39 Afternoon GC 80 SS 37 Evening X. Average during 12 months Morning GC 200 SS 50 Afternoon GC 100 SS 50 Evening X. *Signed* Joseph Thompson, Vicar, Kirk Ella, Hull. [519/25]

WEST ELLA (Township (Kirk Ella), Population 137)

376 <u>Wesleyan Methodist, West Ella</u>. Private House. *Sittings* Free 35. *On 30 March* Evening GC 19. *Average during 12 months* Evening GC 30. *Signed* Charles Prest, Wesleyan Minister, 11 Story St, Hull. [519/26]

ANLABY (Township (Kirk Ella), Population 500)

377 <u>Anlaby Wesleyan (Methodist) Chapel</u>. *Erected* About 1809. SEB ExW. *Sittings* Free 34 Other 56. *On 30 March* Afternoon GC 52 SS 34 Evening GC 51. *Signed* William Ashton, Steward, Willoughby [Willerby], nr Hull. [519/28]

HESSLE (Parish, Population 1576)

378 All Saints, Hessle, an Ancient Parish Church. *Consecrated* Before 1800. *Endowment* Land & Glebe £300 OPE £8 Fees £5 Dues/Tithes/Easter Offerings £35. *Sittings* Free 200 Other 300. *On 30 March* Morning GC 289 SS 61 Afternoon GC 239 SS 61. *Signed* Henry Newmarch, Vicar, Hessle, nr Hull. [519/27]

379 Hessle Wesleyan (Methodist) Chapel. *Erected* 1813. SEB ExW. *Sittings* Free 51 Other 170. *On 30 March* Afternoon GC 80 SS 55 Evening GC 160. *Signed* David Coulson, Steward, Grocer, Hessle, nr Hull. [519/29]

380 [duplicate] Wesleyan (Methodist) Chapel, Hessle. *Erected* 1813. SEB ExW. *Sittings* Free 51 Other 170 Free Space 70. *On 30 March* Afternoon GC 72 Evening GC 165. *Signed* James Watson, Chapel Steward, Hessle, Hull. [519/31]

381 Primitive Methodist, Hessle. *Erected* 1827. SEB ExW. *Sittings* Free 36 Other 105. *On 30 March* Morning GC X Afternoon GC 46 SS 48 Evening GC 110. *Signed* William Markin Hare, Chapel Steward, Bricklayer, Hessle. [519/30]

Hedon Subdistrict

HEDON (Parish, Population 1029)

382 St Augustine's, Hedon. Ancient Parish Church. *Consecrated* Before 1800. *Endowment* Land £6.10.0 Tithe £63 Fees £4.10.0 Gross amount £74. *Sittings* Free 115 Other 526. *On 30 March* Morning GC X Afternoon GC 246 SS 80 Evening GC X. *Signed* Revd James Hare Wake, Minister, Hedon, Hull. [519/33]

383 (Roman) Catholic Chapel, Hedon. *Erected* 1810. Entire ExW. *Sittings* Free All. *Usual Number of Attendants* Morning GC 60 Evening GC 25. *Signed* John Day, Registrar, Hedon, nr Hull. [519/34 Simplified]

384 Primitive Methodist Chapel, Hedon. *Erected* 1800. SEB ExW. *Sittings* Free 30 Other 90. *On 30 March* Morning GC 40 SS 42 Evening GC 60 SS 10. *Average* GC 50 SS 42. *Signed* James R. Parkinson, Minister, No. 3, Norfolk Place, Beverley Road, Hull. [519/35]

385 Wesleyan Methodist Chapel, Hedon. *Erected* 1818. SEB ExW. *Sittings* Free 70 Other 90. *On 30 March* Morning GC 50 SS 23 Afternoon GC X SS 26 Evening GC 64. *Average* Morning SS 26. *Remarks* Every alternate Sunday the Service is in the afternoon and evening. *Signed* George Thorp, Chapel Steward, Hedon, nr Hull. [519/36]

PRESTON (Township (P), Population 887)

386 All Saints, Preston. Ancient Parish Church. *Consecrated* Before 1800. *Endowment* Land £28 Tithe £50 Fees £5 Other Sources £16 Total £99. *Sittings* Free 30 Other 370. *On 30 March* Morning GC 80 SS 65 Afternoon X Evening 78. *Average*

Morning GC 120 SS 65 Afternoon GC 190 SS 65 Evening GC 90. *Signed* James Hare Wake, Minister of Preston, Hedon, Hull. [519/37]

387   Primitive Methodist Chapel, Preston. *Erected* 1822. Separate Building ExW. *Sittings* Free 85 Other 72. *On 30 March* Morning SS None Afternoon GC 50 Evening GC 70. *Signed* James R. Parkinson, Minister, 3 Norfolk Place, Beverley Road, Hull. [519/38]

388   Wesleyan Methodist Chapel, Preston. *Erected* 1812. SEB ExW. *Sittings* Free 82 Other 160. *On 30 March* Morning 140 Afternoon 101 Evening 67. *Average during 12 months* Morning [sic] GC 84 SS 60. *Remarks* 84 is considered the avarage (exclusive of Scholars) attending <u>Twice</u> every Sunday. 60 is considered the avarage (of Scholars) attending <u>once</u> every Sunday. *Signed* Robert Teasdale, Steward, Preston, Hull. [519/39]

389   Latter Day Saints. *Remarks* 10 is considered the avarage congregation but service is not conducted regularly. The preachers come from Hull but the people to [sic] know nothing more about it. There was no service on Sunday March 30 1851. [undated, unsigned] [519/40]

MARFLEET (Parish, Population 193)

390   St Egedius, Marfleet. An Ancient Parish Church. *Consecrated* before 1800. *Sittings* Free 125 Total 125. *On 30 March* Afternoon GC 91. *Remarks* There is a Sunday School held in the Church, conducted & the expence defrayed by the Clergyman, assisted by 3 Teachers, attendance very uniform, may be stated at 46, I mention it here, not having received a School Return. *Signed* J. Robinson, Incumbent, Marfleet, nr Hull. [519/32]

391   Wesleyan Chapel, Marfleet. *Erected* 1815. Seperate ExW. *Sittings* Free 20 Other 10. *Usual Number of Attendants* Morning GC 18 Afternoon GC 20. *Signed* John Day, Registrar, Hedon, nr Hull. [519/41 Simplified]

KINGSTON-UPON-HULL BOROUGH

SCULCOATES DISTRICT HO129/519 (PART)

Drypool Subdistrict, Parish and Township
(Population 2748)

392   St Peter's, Drypool, an ancient Parish Church. *Consecrated* in 14th Century. Rebuilt in 1823, by Private Benefaction but not consecrated again. *Endowment* Land £29 Glebe £36 OPE £10 Pew Rents £90 Fees £64 Easter Offerings £23. *Sittings* Free 722. *On 30 March* Morning GC 800 SS 110 Afternoon X Evening GC 400. *Dated* 1 April. *Signed* Thomas Morton, Minister, Drypool, Hull. [519/42]

East Sculcoates Subdistrict (Sculcoates Parish)
(Population 11414)

393   Charter House Chapel, Charter House Lane, Hull, a private Chapel for the use of the inmates in the house. *Consecrated* before 1800. *Sittings* Total None [See Remarks]. *On 30 March* Morning GC X Evening GC X. *Remarks* This Chapel is entirely & exclusively for the use of the Inmates of the Hospital; it has therefore no space available for Public worship. *Signed* Fredk. Willm. Bromley, Assist. to the Master, Charter House, Hull. [519/43]

394   St Mary's Church, Sculcoates. An Ancient Parish Church. *Consecrated* Before 1800. *Endowment* Land £26 Glebe £5 Pew Rents £22 Fees £220 Easter Offerings £20. *Sittings* Free 350 Other 560. *On 30 March* Morning GC 200 SS 109 Evening GC 150 SS 50. *Average* Morning GC 177 SS 150 Evening GC 128 SS 60. *Signed* Thomas Scott Bonnin, Curate of St Mary's, 18 Wellington Place, Hull. [519/44]

395   Bethell (Methodist New Connexion), Sculcoates. *Erected* 1799. SEB ExW. *Sittings* Free 165 Other 760 Free Space None. *On 30 March* Morning GC 350 SS 119 Evening GC 300. *Average* Morning GC 300 Evening GC 350. *Remarks* The average attendance is put down 350 but it is estimated that not less than 650 persons identify themselves as attending this place of worship, many attend in the morning that are not present in the evening, & vice versa many in the evening that are not present in the morning. *Signed* George Page, Society Steward, 32 Waterworks Street, Hull. [519/45]

396   Mason Street Primitive Methodist Chapel. *Erected* Bought by us in 1841. Seperate Building ExW. *Sittings* Free 150 Other 380 Free Space 170. *On 30 March* Morning GC 400 SS 100 Afternoon SS X Evening GC 750. *Average during 12 months* Morning GC 400 SS 100 Afternoon GC X Evening GC 650. *Signed* Richard

Dodsworth, Steward; John Bywater, Primitive Methodist Minister, 13 Spencer Street, Hull. [519/46]

397   Tabernacle (Wesleyan Methodist Association), Sykes Street. *Erected* 1826. SEB ExW. *Sittings* Free 100 Other 620. *On 30 March* Morning GC 173 SS 61 Evening GC 230. *Signed* Robert Rutherford, Minister, Neville Street, Hull. [519/47]

398   Wesleyan Methodist Chapel, Scott St., [Hull]. *Erected* 1804. SEB ExW. *Sittings* Free 132 Other 394. *On 30 March* Morning GC 350 SS 45 Afternoon No Service Evening GC 400. *Average* Morning GC 400 SS 45 Evening GC 500. *Signed* John S. Richardson, Chapel Steward, Merchant, Hull. [519/48]

399   Primitive Methodist, Church Street. *Erected* 1847. SEB ExW. *Sittings* Free 150 Other 650 Free Space 100. *On 30 March* Morning GC 400 SS 288 Evening GC 500. *Average during 12 months* Morning GC 380 SS 204 Evening GC 500. *Remarks* [...] Many Strangers very often at the Evening Service which causes the Chapel to be full very often. *Signed* Forster Thompson, Steward, 64 Lowgate [Hull]. [519/49]

West Sculcoates Subdistrict (Sculcoates Parish)
(Population 10911)

400   St Pauls, Sculcoates. A new Parish Church for Sculcoates under 6 & 7 Vic. C. 37. *Consecrated* Oct. 27, 1847 As a New Church provided for the New Parish formed under the above act. *Erected* By private Subscription assisted by Grants from the Church building Commissioners & Incorporated Society. *Cost* Private Benefaction etc about £4000 expended without the ground but left still unfinished for want of funds. *Endowment* OPE £150 Pew Rents this source uncertain; Fees also uncertain; Dues/Easter Offerings a very small proportion collected. *Sittings* Free 600 Other 600. *On 30 March* Morning GC about 400 SS 102 Afternoon X Evening about 500. *Remarks* The Easter offerings wd. amount to a considerable sum but, the Minister feels unwilling to enforce the payment from such as oppose the payment of Easter Dues. *Signed* R. Kemp Bailey MA, Perpetual Curate, Sculcoates, Hull. [519/50]

401   Christ Church, Sculcoates. *Consecrated* Sept. 26th 1822 by the Archbishop of York. *Erected* By private benefactions & subscriptions only. *Cost* Private Benefaction etc abt. £9000 Total £9000. *Endowment* Pew Rents £180 Fees £5. *Sittings* Free 500 Other 940. *On 30 March* Morning GC 703 SS 170 Evening GC 720. *Average* Morning GC 680 SS 120 Evening GC 700. *Remarks* The slight increase of attendance above the average may be accounted for by the fineness of the weather on the 30th of March. *Signed* John King, Incumbent, Sculcoates, Hull. [519/51]

402   Stepney Chapel (Methodist New Connexion), Beverley Road, Sculcoates. *Erected* 1849. SEB ExW. *Sittings* Free 40 Other 115. *On 30 March* Morning GC 60 Evening GC 80. *Signed* Francis Oliver, Steward, 94 Portland Street, West End, Hull. [519/52]

403 Reformed Baptist Evangelizing Church, Charles Street, Hull. SEB ExW. *Sittings* 34 x 18 ft all free. *On 30 March* As the place has just been opened the numbers attending cannot well be reported. *Signed* John L. Milton, Minister, 24 Silvester Street, Hull. [519/53]

404 Baker Street Chapel (Independent). *Erected* In the year 1844. SEB ExW. *Sittings* Free 330. *On 30 March* Morning GC 150 Evening GC 300. *Remarks* Though this chapel is returned as "Independent", it is not what is commonly so called, or connected with the Congregational body. The chapel is the property of the Minister. *Signed* Andrew John Jukes, BA of Trin. Coll. Cambridge (Late Curate of St John's Church, Hull), Minister, 7 Albert Street, Spring Bank, Hull. [519/54]

405 Albion Chapel (Independent), [Hull]. *Erected* 1842. SEB ExW. *Sittings* Free 456 Other 1030 Free Space 250. *On 30 March* Morning GC 947 SS 344 Evening GC 1303. *Average during 12 months* Morning GC 950 SS 350 Evening GC 1400. *Signed* Newman Hall, Minister, Hull. [519/55]

406 St Charles Borromeo (Roman Catholic), Jarrat Street, [Hull]. *Erected* September 1829. SEB ExW. *Sittings* Free 448 Other 200 (All free in the Evening) Free Space 150 Space for boys in & round the Sanctuary 50 or 60. *On 30 March* Morning GC 1050 [total of two services] SS 150 Afternoon GC X SS X Evening GC 600 SS 250. *Average during 12 months* Morning GC 1050 or 1100 SS 150 Afternoon GC X SS X Evening GC 600 SS 250. *Remarks* The services at St Charles are 3: two in the morning and one in the Eveg. The morning services are attended by two distinct congregations. The Eveng. comprises many who attended in the morning as well as others who did not attend either Morning Services. N.B. The church is generally as full as stated, often much fuller. *Signed* Michael Trappers, R. Catholic Rector, Jarratt Street, Hull. [519/56]

407 Saloon of Mechanics Institute (Wesleyan Methodist Reformers), George St, Hull. *Erected* 1841. *Sittings* Free About 500 Other About 500 Free Space an additional 4 to 500. *On 30 March* No Service. *Average during 3 months* Morning GC 650 Evening GC 1000. *Remarks* The Saloon being Shut up on the 30th from a previous arrangement we had a Service in a Room in the Morning where there were 200 Persons, in the afternoon we had South St Chapel there were 500 Persons present and in the evening from 900 to 1000 Persons at the same place. *Signed* William Foule, Treasurer, 17 Spring Bank, Hull. [519/57]

408 Long Room of the Mechanics' Institute (Baptist), George Street, [Hull]. *On 30 March* Morning GC 50 Afternoon GC X Evening GC 60. *Average during 12 months* Morning GC 70 Afternoon GC X Evening GC 100. *Signed* William Boards, Deacon, 34 Lowgate, Hull. [519/58]

409 George St Chapel (Baptist), [Hull]. *Erected* 1796. SEB ExW. *Sittings* Free 90 Other 500 Free Space None. *On 30 March* Morning GC 175 SS 70 Afternoon SS 101 Evening GC 191. *Signed* William Joseph Stuart, Minister, 20 Windsor Street, Hull. [519/59]

410 Disciples of Christ, No. 8 Vincent Street, Hull. *Erected* About 10 Yrs. ExW. *Sittings* Free 34 All free. *On 30 March* Morning 10 adults 9 children Afternoon 6 adults Evening 7 adults. *Average during 12 months* Morning/Afternoon/Evening GC 12 adults. *Remarks* No denominational name being agreed upon by this society the number of the Society cannot be determined by the Name. But sometimes take the designations of Bn. of the Reformation, Christian Reformers, disciples of Jesus or the new American denomination. [undated] *Signed* Thomas Wilkinson, Elder, 26 Little Queen Street, Hull. [519/60]

HULL DISTRICT[1] (HO 129/520)

Humber Subdistrict
(Wards of Humber (population 4363), Austin (population 2598), Trinity (population 2576) and Whitefriars (population 2371))

411 Holy Trinity Church. Antiently a Chapel of Ease to the Parish Church of the adjoining Parish of Hessle, but constituted a distinct & separate Parish Church by Act. 13. Ch. 2d. *Consecrated* Supposed to have been consecrated 1312. *Endowment* Tithe £4 Glebe £45 OPE £52.10.0 Pew Rents £136 not paid to the Minister; Fees £190 Easter Offerings £50 voluntarily paid; Other Sources £267. *Sittings* Free 500 Other 480. *On 30 March* Morning GC 511 SS 215 Afternoon GC 217 SS 133 Evening GC 461. *Remarks* The Pew Rents are received by the Churchwardens & applied by them to the use of the Church. The Easter Offerings, if the payment were enforced according to Law, would amount to at least three hundred pounds per annum. *Signed* Thomas Feetam, Churchwarden, Upholsterer, Hull. [520/1A]

412 The Mariner's Church. Chapel of Ease, especially for the accomodation of seamen. *Consecrated* The original Buildg. licensed in the beginning of 1828. The new church on the same site, opened on 15th of June 1834. Licensed as a church for the benefit especially of Mariners' frequenting the Port. *Erected* By private benefactions & subscriptions. *Cost* Private Benefaction etc £1800 Total £1800. *Endowment* Pew Rents £196 Other Sources £220. *Sittings* Free about 400 Other about 530 Total 930 The number published in the old Reports is 1077, but I think this is above the real accommodation. *On 30 March* Morning GC about 430 SS 120 Evening GC about 650. *Remarks* This church is held on a Lease which expires in about 60 or 70 yrs from this time, at an annual rent of £65. The lease is made to the Trustees of the Mar. church Society & when it expires, the church, which was built by subscription on the site of a dissenting chapel, will belong to the Lessor unless funds can be raised to purchase it. *Signed* Chas. Cook, Incumbent, 6 Coltman St, Kingston upon Hull. [520/2]

[520/3: Registrar's enquiry relating to St Mark's, Sutton: see **351** and note.]

---

[1]   The Hull District constituting only the central area of the town was made up of the united parishes of Holy Trinity and St Mary.

413   Trinity House Chapel. *Erected* 1840. *Sittings* Free about 400 Total 400. *Usual Number of Attendants* Morning GC about 300 SS None Afternoon SS Nil Evening GC Nil SS Nil. *Signed* John Wreghill. [520/4 Simplified]

414   Wesley Chapel (Wesleyan Methodists). *Erected* 1833. SEB ExW. *Sittings* Free 200 Other 600. *Usual Number of Attendants* Morning GC 300 SS 120 Evening 500. *Signed* James Thompson, Chapel Steward, 10 Ingtongate, Hull. [520/5 Simplified]

415   Hull Synagaogue (Jews), Robinson Row. *Erected* 1825. SEB ExW. *Sittings* Free 35 Other 60. *On Saturday 29 March* Morning GC 74 Afternoon GC 17 Evening GC 21. *Average during 12 months* Morning GC 40 Afternoon GC 15 Evening GC 25. *Dated* George Alexander, President; Bethel Jacobs, Hony. Secretary, 7 Whitefriargate, Hull. [520/6]

416   Bethel Chapel (United Presbyterian), Prince Street. *Erected* Before 1800. SEB ExW. *Sittings* Free 470 Other 130. *On 30 March* Morning GC 117 Evening GC 89. *Average* Morning GC 100. *Signed* George Wallace, Elder & Manager, 12 Brook Street, Hull. [520/7]

St Mary Subdistrict
(Ward of St Mary North, population 6200)

417   St Mary's. Ancient Parish Church. *Consecrated* Before 1800. *Endowment* Land £49 OPE £150 Pew Rents £15 Fees £30 Dues £4.4.0 Easter Offerings £15. *Sittings* Free 250 Other 750. *On 30 March* Morning GC 389 SS 120 Afternoon X Evening GC 450. *Remarks* 477 Sittings are let in the Church, the revenue from which goes to the Parish. *Signed* John Scott, Incumbent of St Mary's, Hull. [520/8]

418   Meeting House of the Society of Friends. *Erected* before 1800. SEB ExW. *Space* Floor 1100 ft Galleries 444 ft. *Estimated Seating* 386. *On 30 March* Morning GC 111 Afternoon GC 61. *Remarks* attendance 30th of 3 month below the usual amount. *Signed* John Clernethan, Spring [?] Street, Hull. [520/9]

419   George Yard Chapel (Wesleyan Methodists). *Erected* Before 1800. SEB ExW. *Sittings* Free 280 Other 784. *On 30 March* Morning GC 382 SS 130 Afternoon X Evening 481. *Average during 12 months* Morning GC 482 SS 140 Evening GC 630 SS None. *Signed* Henry Davies, Wesleyan Minister, 19 Trinity House Lane. [520/10]

420   Bowlalley Lane Chapel (Unitarian). *Erected* Before 1800. SEB ExW. *Sittings* Free 90 Other 400 Free Space None. *On 30 March* Morning GC 155 SS 65 Afternoon GC X Evening GC 130. *Signed* John Shannon, Minister, 7 Canton Place, Hull. [520/11]

421   Salthouse Lane Chapel (Baptist). *Erected* Before 1800. SEB ExW. *Sittings* Free 50 Other 500. *Average during 12 months* Morning GC 200 SS 80 Evening GC 250 SS 20. *Signed* D. M. N. Thomson, Minister, 24 Caroline Street, Hull. [520/12]

Myton Subdistrict

(Wards of North Myton (population 12639) and South Myton (population 19923))

422   St John's Proprietary Church, St John's Street. *Consecrated* Before 1800. *Endowment* Pew Rents £236.1.0. *Sittings* Free 250 Other 1250. *On 30 March* Morning GC 656 SS 91 Afternoon GC 300 Evening GC 406. *Average* Morning GC 640 SS 90 Afternoon GC 350 Evening GC 420. *Signed* Edwin Thompson, Curate, 29 Neville Street, Hull. [520/13]

423   St Stephen's Church. A Chapel of Ease to the Holy Trinity Church. *Consecrated* Licensed Apr. 11 1844 Consecrated Sep. 22 1845 As an additional Church. *Erected* By Private Benefactions & Subscr. & a Grant of £500 from Incorporated Soc. for Building Churches, & £1500 from the Eccles. Commissioners for England. *Cost* By 2 Society Grants £1000 Private Benefaction etc £6000 Total £7000. *Endowment* Pew Rents £246 Fees £15. *Sittings* Free 600 Other 600. *On 30 March* Morning GC 450 SS 209 Evening GC 577. *Average during 6 months* Morning GC 450 SS 210 Afternoon GC X SS X Evening GC 580 SS X. *Signed* John Deck, MA, Incumbent, Belgrave Terrace, Hull. [520/14]

424   Gaol [Anglican Chapel], Kingston Street. Within the Precincts of the Gaol. *Licensed* in 1824 For the use of the Prisoners. *Erected* By the Borough of Hull. *Cost* By the Borough of Hull. Cost cannot be told as it was erected with the other Buildings of the Gaol. *Endowment* No Endowment. *Sittings* Free about 200 Other 12. *On 30 March* Morning GC 162 Afternoon GC 161 Evening GC X. *Average* Generally between 140 to 150 Evening GC X. *Signed* James Selkirk, Chaplain, Gaol, Hull. [520/15]

425   St James, intended to be a District Church (Holy Trinity parish) but District not yet assigned. *Consecrated* August 27 1831 As an additional Church. *Erected* By parliamentary Grant and private Subscriptions. *Cost* Parliamentary Grant £3500 Private Benefaction etc £2100 Total £5600. *Endowment* Pew Rents £260 Fees £54. *Sittings* Free 600 Other 601. *On 30 March* Morning GC 610 SS 200 Afternoon GC X Evening GC 800. *Signed* William Knight, Incumbent, Hull. [520/16]

426   Providence Chapel (Independent), Hope Street. *Erected* Before 1800. SEB ExW. *Sittings* Other 1150. *On 30 March* No Service Repairing. *Average during 6 months* Morning GC 150 SS 25 Evening GC 150. *Remarks* The undersigned has been Minister of the Chapel Six Months. *Signed* George Gladstone, Minister, 8 Norfolk Street, Hull. [520/17]

427   Latter Day Saints, Paragon Street. *Erected* Since 1800. Lower flat in Publick Hall. Upper flat Exclusive. *Sittings* Free 500 all free. *On 30 March* Morning 50 Total 70 [sic] Afternoon 90 Evening 150. *Dated* 1 April. *Signed* Hugh Findley, Minister, 17 Manchester Place, Pattery, Hull. [520/18]

428   Waltham Street Chapel (Wesleyan Methodists). *Erected* 1813. SEB ExW. *Sittings* Free 300 Other 1200 Free Space 300. *On 30 March* Morning GC 745 SS 110

Evening GC 862. *Average during 12 months* Morning GC 850 SS 110 Evening GC about 1000. *Signed* Geo. Wilkinson, a Trustee & Secretary to the Trustees, 29 Bourne Street, Hull. [520/19]

429 South St Church. No denomination. The religion of Christ is the universal religion, & Such we seek to cultivate & diffuse. Saving faith (with us) consists not in opinions, but in a truthful, Christlike life. All sects are evils & names tyrants. *Erected* 1842. SEB The School room used also for Temperance meetings. *Sittings* Free 383 Other 327. *On 30 March* Morning GC 300 SS About 80 Afternoon GC 400 Evening GC 800. *Average during 12 months* Morning GC 300 SS 80 Evening GC 350. *Signed* John Pulsford, Minister, Hull. [520/20]

430 West Street Chapel (Primitive Methodist). *Erected* 1819. SEB ExW. *Sittings* Free 200 Other 595. *On 30 March* Morning 1000 Afternoon none Evening 600. *Average during 12 months* Morning GC 500 SS 70 Evening GC 750. *Signed* John Lipson [?], Class Leader [further illegible words]. [520/21]

431 Moxon St Chapel (Independent). *Erected* Don't know, rented. Used as a day school. *Sittings* Free 250 Free Space 50. *On 30 March* Afternoon GC 80. *Average* Afternoon GC 100. *Remarks* This is in connexion with Albion Chapel & under the Supervalence of its Minister. *Signed* Newman Hall, Minister, Hull. [520/22]

432 Salem Chapel, (Independents or Congregationalists), Cogan Street. *Erected* 1832. SEB ExW. *Sittings* Free 250 Other 700 Free Space None. *On 30 March* Morning GC 330 SS 150 Afternoon GC X Evening GC 430. *Average during 12 months* Morning GC 400 SS 210 Afternoon GC X Evening GC 500. *Remarks* Many Captains, Mates and others connected with the Port of Hull, attend this place of worship, and have sittings. At this period of the year the greater portion are out on their voyages. *Signed* The Revd James Sibree [?], Minister, 56 Lister Street, Hull. [520/23]

433 Mile Street Chapel, (Primitive Methodist). Unoccupied. SEB ExW. *Signed* Mary Doyle, owner, 2 Mile Street, Hull. [520/24]

434 Institute Chapel, in connexion with the Port of Hull Society for the Religious Instruction of Seaman (Unsectarian) Waterhouse Lane. *Erected* Society commenced 1821 Present Chapel opened 1842. SEB Used also for the general purposes of a Sailors' Institute. *Sittings* Free 500 (All) Free Space 100. *On 30 March* Morning GC 74 SS 45 Afternoon GC 278 SS 50 Evening GC 130. *Average* The above is a fair representation. *Remarks* It is the custom of the Sunday School for only half the children to attend Service at once; viz: Boys, A. M., Girls, P. M. and vice versa. *Signed* H. Miller, Superintendent, Sailors' Institute, Hull. [520/25]

435 Independent Methodist Chapel. *Erected* 1823 or 1824 occupied by us since 1826. SEB ExW. *Sittings* Free 122 Other 560 Free Space The Aisles and Passages afford Standing room for above 100 more than Returned, and the vestry behind the Chapel is available, by two doors which open into it, on particular occasions, to above 100 more. *On 30 March* Morning GC 450 SS 67 Afternoon GC 350 SS 80

Evening GC 500. *Signed* William Mac Conkey, Minister, 25 Ocean Place, Hull. [520/26]

436   Bethesda Chapel (Independent) Osborne [Street]. *Erected* 1842. SEB ExW. *Sittings* Free X Other 500 Free Space none. *On 30 March* Morning (German Lutheran Church) GC about 200 SS X Afternoon X Evening (Independent) GC about 200 SS X. *Average* None. *Signed* Samuel Lane, Minister, 79 Osborne St, Hull. [520/27]

437   Primitive Methodist, Great Thornton Street. *Erected* 1849. SEB ExW. *Sittings* Free 120 Other 505. *On 30 March* Morning GC 380 SS 146 Evening GC 880. *Average during 12 months* Morning GC 420 SS 120 Evening GC 580. *Remarks* The cause of the large congregation was a Funeral Sermon being preached and all the Aisles were full. *Signed* William Holliday, Chapel Steward, Ebor Place, Porter Street, Hull. [520/28]

438   Wesleyan, Great Thornton Street. *Erected* 1842. SEB ExW. *Sittings* Free 300 Other 1000. *On 30 March* Morning GC 700 SS 193 Afternoon No Service Evening GC 750. *Average during 12 months* Morning GC 800 Evening GC 900. *Signed* William Jackson, Minister, 33 Lister Street. [520/29]

PAULL (Township (P), Population 606)

439   Paull Parish Church, dedicated to St Andrew and St Mary. *Consecrated* Cannot tell on account of its antiquity. *Endowment* From various sources, at present £160 net. *Sittings* Free 20 Other 230. *On 30 March* Morning GC 62 SS 27. *Average during 12 months* Morning GC 150 SS 50 Total 200 on Sunday. *Remarks* The Church is situated 1/2 a mile from the Village. The pews are appropriated to the chief houses and the poor are shut out. *Signed* J. S. Jones, Vicar, Paull, nr Hull. [521/1]

440   Wesleyan (Methodist) Chappil, Paull. *Erected* About 1810. SEB ExW. *Sittings* Free 80 Other 40. *On 30 March* Afternoon GC 96. *Average during 12 months* Afternoon GC 60 Evening GC 60. *Signed* Wm. Eastwood, Steward, Paull, nr Hull. [521/2]

441   Primitive Methodist, Paull. Separate ExW. *Sittings* Free All. *On 30 March* Morning GC X Afternoon GC X Evening GC 57. *Average during 12 months* Morning GC 35. *Signed* Robert Walker, Steward, Paull, nr Hull. [521/3]

THORNGUMBALD (Township (Paull), Population 278)

442   Independent Chaple, Thorngumbald. *Erected* Before 1800. SEB ExW. *Sittings* Free 100 Other 30. *On 30 March* Morning GC 25 SS 21 Evening GC 30. *Average during 12 months* Morning GC 30 SS 20 Evening GC 40. *Signed* Revd Wm. J Bettinson, Minister, Thorngumbald, Hull. [521/4]

443   Wesleyan Methodists, Thorngumbald. *Erected* 1840. Seperate ExW. *Sittings* Free 40 Other 40 Free Space None. *On 30 March* Evening GC 39. *Average during 12 months* Afternoon GC 40 Evening GC 40. *Signed* Thomas Smith, Steward, Thorngumbald, nr Hull. [521/5]

444   Thorngumbald Chapel of Ease (St Mary's). *Consecrated* perhaps, nearly 1000 years ago. No one can tell on account of its great antiquity. *Erected* Unknown. *Endowment* Served gratis by the Vicar with many thanks. *Sittings* Free 20 Other 40. *On 30 March* Morning GC 42. *Remarks* In the summer, there may be fifty persons as a Congregation and ten or twelve Sunday Scholars. *Signed* J. S. Jones, Minister, of the Chapel of Ease, Paull, nr Hull. [521/6]

BURSTWICK WITH SKECKLING (Township (Burstwick), Population 509)

445   All Saints Parish Church, Skeckling. *Consecrated* before 1800. *Endowment* Land £170 Tithe £7 Glebe £3 OPE House & Land £30 Fees £8 Easter Offerings £0.10.0. *Sittings* Free 25 Other 375. *On 30 March* Morning GC 90 SS 30 Afternoon

---

[1]   The Patrington district was not divided into subdistricts. There are no returns for the hamlet of Camerton (population 20) in the parish of Burstwick, for the township of Out-Newton (population 58) in the parish of Easington, for the townships of Waxholme (population 106) and South Frodingham (population 56) in the parish of Owthorne, or for the township of Owstwick (population 103) in the parishes of Roos and Garton.

X Evening GC 25. *Average* Morning GC 70 SS 30 Afternoon GC X Evening GC 30. *Remarks* The first Columns were filled by mistake for the average. *Signed* F. B. King, MA, Curate of the Parish, Burstwick. [521/7]

446 Primitive Methodist Chapel, Burstwick. *Erected* 1848. SEB ExW. *Sittings* Free 32 Other 94 Free Space none. *On 30 March* Morning SS No Sunday School Afternoon GC 94 Evening GC 86. *Signed* Richard Andrew, Trustee and Manager, Burstwick, Holderness. [521/8]

447 Wesleyan Methodist Chapel, Burstwick. *Erected* 1847. SEB ExW. *Sittings* Free 24 Other 76. *On 30 March* Afternoon GC 37 Evening GC 12. *Average during 12 months* Afternoon GC 45 Evening GC 25. *Signed* Richard Smailes, Minister, Burstwick, Hull. [521/11]

RYHILL (Township (Burstwick), Population 216)

448 Primitive Methodist, Ryhill. *On 30 March* Evening GC 27. *Signed* Sarah Ambler, Ryhill, nr Hull. [521/9]

449 Wesleyan Methodist Chapel, Ryehill. *Erected* 1822. SEB ExW. *Sittings* Free 36 Other 90. *On 30 March* Morning GC 37 Afternoon GC 20 Evening GC X. *Signed* Wm. Perritt, Steward, Ryehill. [521/10]

KEYINGHAM (Parish, Population 746)

450 St Nicholas, Keyingham. An ancient Church. *Consecrated* before 1800. *Endowment* Land £58 OPE £20 Fees £3. *Sittings* Free 140 Other 224. *On 30 March* Afternoon GC 190 SS 59. *Average during 12 months* Morning GC 80 SS 70 Afternoon GC 170 SS 70. *Remarks* Divine service is celebrated alternately morning & afternoon. Income greatly reduced by Free Trade. *Signed* James Potter, Curate of Keyingham, nr Hull. [521/12]

451 Primitive Methodist Chapel, Keyingham. *Erected* 1846. SEB ExW. *Sittings* Free 48 Other 126 Free Space none. *On 30 March* Morning GC 45 No Sunday School; Afternoon No public service in the afternoon on the 30th; Evening GC 114. *Average during 12 months* Morning GC 45 No Sunday School Afternoon GC 55 Evening GC 120. *Remarks* Services alternately morning and afternoon. *Signed* Richard Hudson, Trustee and Steward, Keyingham, Holderness. [521/13]

452 Wesleyan Methodist Chapel, Keyingham. *Erected* 1848. SEB ExW. *Sittings* Free 40 Other 109 Free Space none. *On 30 March* Morning X Afternoon X Evening 78. *Average during 12 months* Morning GC X Afternoon GC 80 Evening GC 70. *Remarks* Erected in Lieu of a previous Chapel built in 1807 but not on the same site. *Signed* R. B. Clough, Chapel Steward, Post Master, Keyingham. [521/14]

OTTRINGHAM (Parish, Population 663)

453 St Wilfred's, Ottringham, an ancient Parish Church. *Endowment* Land £15.10.7 Tithe 0 Glebe 0 OPE £59.11.0 Pew Rents 0 Fees about £4 Dues 0. *Sittings*

Free 228 Other 239. *On 30 March* Morning GC 76 to 80 SS 45. *Average* Morning GC 100 SS 55 Afternoon GC 150 SS 55. *Remarks* In the above return of the annual value of the Benefice no deduction is made for the rent of a house, which if the Incumbent were resident would reduce the income to the extent of from £12 to £15 per annum. *Signed* Miles Mackereth, Perpetual Curate of Ottringham, nr Keyingham, Holderness. [521/15]

454 Wesleyan (Methodist) Chapel, Ottringham. *Erected* 1815. SEB ExW. *Sittings* Free 40 Other 117. *On 30 March* Afternoon GC 94 Evening GC 130. *Signed* Thomas Brown, Minister, Patrington, Holderness. [521/16]

WINESTEAD (Parish, Population 131)

455 St Germain, Winestead. Gothic church. *Consecrated* before 1800. *Endowment* Land £300. *Sittings* Other 20 pews. *On 30 March* Afternoon GC 60 SS 6. *Average during 12 months* Morning from 50 to 60 Evening from 50 to 60. *Signed* Henry C. J. Hildyard, Rector, Winestead Rectory, Hull. [521/17]

SUNK ISLAND (Parish, Population 310)

456 The Parish Church of Sunk Island [Holy Trinity] Wm. 4. C. 59. s. 21. *Licensed* Dec. 1830. *Consecrated* 24 Sep. 1833 Large additions having been made to the Sunk Island in the years 1800 by the embankment of warplands from the River Humber, a church was built in 1801 which was not endowed before 23 July 1830. *Erected* Lessees of the house & their Tenants. *Cost* Private Benefaction etc £300 There was provision in the Lease for building a Church. *Endowment* OPE £250 Fees 10s. *Sittings* Free 60 Other 110. *On 30 March* Morning GC 49 Afternoon GC Nil Evening GC Nil. *Average during 12 months* Morning GC 80 Afternoon GC 85 Evening GC Nil Total [ie Morning and Afternoon] alternately. *Remarks* The whole of Sunk Island is the property of the Crown. By the Act 1st. Wm. 4th c. 59. sec. 20. 21. 22. 23. 24. etc. it is provided that Sunk Island shall become a parish etc and the Church endowed by investment in the funds etc. *Dated* 5 April. *Signed* Robert Metcalf, Incumbent Minister of Sunk Island, Patrington, Hull. [521/18]

457 Wesleyan (Methodist) Chapel, Sunk Island. *Erected* 1847 in lieu of one erected in 1810. SEB ExW. *Sittings* Free 30 Other 68. *On 30 March* Afternoon GC 60 Evening GC 36. *Signed* William Richardson, Steward, Sunk Island, Patrington. [521/19]

PATRINGTON (Parish, Population 1827)

458 St Patrick's, Patrington, the ancient Parish Church. *Consecrated* Before 1800. *Endowment* Land, Tithe and Glebe £600 Fees £2 Other categories none. *Sittings* Free 190 Other 450. *On 30 March* Morning GC 135 SS 53 Afternoon GC 150 SS 53. *Average* Morning GC 230 SS 55 Afternoon GC 250 SS 55. *Remarks* The weather being unfavourable on the 30th March the congregation, both parts of the day, was less than usual. *Dated* 5 April. *Signed* R. H. Kitchingman, Rector, Patrington Rectory, Hull. [521/20]

459   Primitive Methodist Chapel, Patrington. *Erected* 1841. SEB ExW. *Sittings* Free 80 Other 160 Free Space none except aisles. *On 30 March* Morning No Public service in the morning No Sunday School Afternoon GC 227 Evening GC 241. *Signed* William Luddington, Minister, Patrington, Holderness. [521/21]

460   Wesleyan (Methodist) Chapel, Patrington. *Erected* 1811. SEB ExW. *Sittings* Free 86 Other 188. *On 30 March* Morning GC 42 SS 40 Evening GC 102. *Signed* Thomas Brown, Minister, Patrington, Holderness. [521/22]

WELWICK (Parish, Population 468)

461   Welwick Church dedicated to St Mary, a very ancient Gothic structure. *Consecrated* Before 1800. *Endowment* Land £52 Tithe £26 Fees 10s. *Sittings* Free 80 Other 360. *On 30 March* Morning X Afternoon GC 130 SS 29. *Average* GC about 130 SS from 25 to 30. *Remarks* Having two Churches I have one full service at each church morning & afternoon alternately. *Dated* 4 April. *Signed* John Watson, Vicar of the Parish, Holmpton, Patrington, Hull. [521/23]

462   Primitive Methodist Chapel, Welwick. *Erected* 1848. SEB ExW. *Sittings* Free 20 Other 90 Free Space None but the ile. *On 30 March* Morning X Afternoon X Evening 64. *Signed* John Marshall, Minister, Patrington, Holderness. [521/24]

463   Wesleyan (Methodist) Chapel, Welwick. *Erected* 1849. SEB ExW. *Sittings* Free 30 Other 96 Free Space None but the ile. *On 30 March* Morning GC X Afternoon GC X Evening 76. *Average during 12 months* Evening GC 120. *Signed* Wm. Wright, Chapel Steward, Welwick Row, nr Patrington. [521/25]

SKEFFLING (Parish, Population 212)

464   St Helens, Skeffling. An ancient Parish Church. *Endowment* Land £50 OPE (Money payment) £10 Cottage & Garden £8 Total £68. *Sittings* Pews amply sufficient for the parish Total 218. *Average during 12 months* Morning GC 30 Afternoon GC 50 SS 10. *Signed* Geo. Inman, Incumbent, Skeffling, nr Patrington. [521/26]

465   Providindence Chapel (Wesleyan Methodist), Skeffling. *Erected* 1822. SEB ExW. *Sittings* Free 40 Other 62. *On 30 March* Afternoon GC 40 Evening GC 25. *Average during 12 months* Afternoon GC 40 Evening GC 50. *Signed* Christopher Atkinson, Steward, Skeffling, Patrington. [521/27]

KILNSEA (Parish, Population 157)

466   [Anglican] Kilnsea. [Church] lost by the encroachment of the Sea. *Consecrated* The duty now performed in a Cottage, by permission of the Archbishop of York, containing about 30 persons. *Endowment* Land £33 Tithe £56 OPE £14 arising from cottages. *Sittings* All free Total 30. *On 30 March* Morning 12. *Average* Morning 10 Afternoon 20. *Remarks* The duty is performed on one Sunday in the Morning & on the following in the afternoon and the next omitted. *Signed* Frederick Thomas Wilson, Curate of Kilnsea, Easington, nr Patrington, Hull. [521/28]

EASINGTON (Township (P), Population 567)

467   Primitive Methodist Chapel, Easington. *Erected* 1822. SEB ExW. *Sittings* Free none Other 132 Free Space None but the aisle. *On 30 March* Evening 130. *Average during 12 months* Morning [sic] GC 100 SS 53. *Remarks* We are on the eve of erecting a new Chapel, the old one being insufficient to accomadate our increasing congregations. *Signed* John Marshall, Minister, Patrington, Holderness. [521/29]

468   Wesleyan (Methodist) Chapel, Blackwell Hill, Easington. *Erected* 1851. SEB ExW. *Sittings* Free 32 Other 108 Free Space about 6 feet besides Aisles. *On 30 March* Afternoon GC 71 SS 14 Evening 35. *Average during 2 months* GC 90 one service SS 15. *Remarks* The chapel in an Unfinished state. The seats all let, applications for more. The school only began March 23 1851, not fully organised as yet. *Signed* George Dennison, Steward, Farmer, Easington. [521/30]

HOLMPTON (Parish, Population 92)

469   St Nicholas, Holmpton. An ancient church. *Consecrated* Before 1800. *Endowment* Land £150 Fees 10s. *Sittings* Free 113 Other 70. *On 30 March* Morning GC 97 SS 29 Afternoon X Evening X. *Average* GC 100 SS from 25 to 30. *Remarks* Having two Churches I have one full service in each Church Morning & Afternoon alternately. *Dated* 4 April. *Signed* John Watson, Rector, Holmpton, Patrington, Hull. [521/31]

470   Wesleyan (Methodist) Chapel, Holmpton. *Erected* 1820. SEB ExW. *Sittings* Free 39 Other 36. *On 30 March* Afternoon GC 36. *Average* GC 34. *Signed* James Green, Steward, Plowland Cottage, Holderness. [521/32]

WITHERNSEA (Township (Hollym), Population 109)

471   Primitive Methodist, Withernsea. *Erected* Not known. SEB ExW. *Sittings* Free 50 Other None Free Space None. *On 30 March* Morning GC None Afternoon No service Evening No service. *Average* Morning GC 14 Afternoon GC None. *Remarks* The Chapel was converted into its present use in the year 1849. Before that period it was used as a School previous to that as a Cart Shed. There is no available space for the Accomodation of hearers Benches being set all over the ground floor. *Dated* 1 April. *Signed* Grice Jackson, Steward, Withernsea, nr Patrington. [521/34]

HOLLYM (Township (P), Population 407)

472   Hollym Church [St Nicholas]. *Consecrated* Built in 1814, in lieu, & on the site of the ancient Parish Church, which was in a very dilapidated state. *Endowment* Tithe, Glebe, Fees, Dues, Easter Offerings about £415 -15 = £400. [A lengthy note explains that £15 is paid annually to the Rector of Holmpton in return for him undertaking the pastoral care of 166 Hollym parishioners living nearer to Holmpton church than their own]. *Sittings* Appropriated to the respective occupants of all the houses in the Parish. *On 30 March* Morning GC 20 SS 29 Afternoon GC 70 SS 30 Total 105 [sic] Evening No Divine Service. *Average* Evening No Divine Service. *Remarks*

a. The Congregation is generally the greatest when there is a sermon, which was the case on March 30 p.m. b. Most if not all, of the inhabitants of Withernsea, reside not less than a mile & 1/2 from the Church. The bad state of the weather & of the roads, therefore often makes a material difference in the numbers present. Not knowing that this question [on average] would be asked, I am unable to answer it: on the previous occasion, when the numbers were counted about a month ago, they exceeded 100. *Dated* 7 April. *Signed* Chas. Barker, Vicar, Hollym, nr Patrington. [521/35]

473 Wesleyan (Methodist) Chapel, Hollym. *Erected* 1805. SEB ExW. *Sittings* Free 40 Other 36 Free Space None. *On 30 March* Evening GC 50. *Signed* John Hilton, Steward, Patrington. [521/33]

OWTHORNE (Township (P), Population 163)

474 All Saints, Owthorne. An ancient Parish Church. *Consecrated* before 1800. *Endowment* Land (a money payment out of the Great Tithes) £20 OPE (By Rent of Land purchased with Queen Anne's Bounty less income Tax) £36.8.0 Fees say 9s per annum on an average. *Sittings* Free 60 Other 182. *On 30 March* Morning GC 21 Afternoon GC X Evening GC X. *Signed* Paul Henzell Wilton, Officiating Minister, Owthorne Vicarage, Patrington. [521/36]

475 Wesleyan (Methodist) Chapel, Owthorne. *Erected* 1805. SEB ExW. *Sittings* Free 45 Other 55. *On 30 March* Morning GC 31 Afternoon GC X Evening GC 20. *Average* Afternoon GC 60. *Remarks* The morning congregation from some cause was little more than one half of an average congregation. The service is every alternate Morning and afternoon and every Sunday evening a prayer meeting. I should fix the average of each Sunday's congregation to be Morning and Evening 70 Afternoon & evening 50. *Signed* J. B. Shaker (Steward), Owthorpe, Patrington. [521/37]

RIMSWELL (Township (Owthorne), Population 137)

476 Rimswell Chapel. A modern brick Edifice. *Consecrated* [18]02 In lieu of a Church previously existing. *Endowment* Land £39 Acres; Tithe or Glebe £229 less Income Tax; Fees (annual average) £2. *Sittings* Free 100 Other 180. *On 30 March* Morning X Afternoon GC 77 SS 12 Evening X. *Average* Morning GC 50 SS 10 Afternoon GC 80 SS 10 Evening X. *Remarks* Rinswell Chapel is about Two & a half miles distant from the Village of Owthorne where the Mother Church formerly stood. *Signed* Paul H. Wilton, Vicar, Owthorne Vicarage, Patrington, Hull. [521/38]

477 Primitive Methodist Chapel, Rimswell. *Erected* 38 Years Ago. Separate [Contradictory answers on whether ExW]. *Sittings* Free 25 Other 45 Free Space 20. *On 30 March* Morning GC X Afternoon GC 40 Evening GC 20. *Average* Morning GC 40 SS None. *Signed* Robin Kay; David Tuton. [521/39]

HALSHAM (Parish, Population 264)

478 All Saints, Halsham, an ancient Parish Church. *Consecrated* before 1800

Time not known. *Sittings* Free (including the chancel) about 90 Other 210. *On 30 March* Afternoon GC 65. *Average* Morning Total 70 Afternoon Total 80. *Signed* Miles Mackereth, Curate of Halsham, nr Keyingham, Holderness. [521/40]

ROOS (part of Parish, Population 599)

479   All Saints, Roos, an ancient Parish Church. *Consecrated* before 1800. *Endowment* Land £138? [sic] Tithe £201.10.0 Glebe £262.16.0 OPE £0 Pew rents £0 Other Categories £5 total. *Sittings* Free 150 Other 230. *On 30 March* Morning GC 127 SS 86 Afternoon GC 132 SS 90 Evening X. *Average during 12 months* Morning GC 115 SS 85 Afternoon GC 125 SS 85 Evening X. *Remarks* The two Church Aisles were rebuilt & the Interior refitted & warmed at the expense of the Rector in 1842. [undated] *Signed* Charles Hotham, Rector, Roos, Hull. [521/41]

480   Primitive Methodist Chapel, Roos. *Erected* 1836. SEB ExW. *Sittings* Free 30 Other 110 Free Space None. *On 30 March* Afternoon GC X Evening GC 76. *Average* Morning GC 40 Evening GC 100. *Signed* James Bilton, Steward, Grocer, Roos. [521/42]

481   Wesleyan (Methodist) Chapel, Roos. *Erected* 1808. SEB ExW. *Sittings* Free 20 Other 76 Free Space 30. *On 30 March* Morning X Afternoon 38 Evening 22. *Average during 6 months* Afternoon GC 50. *Signed* John Eshelby, Steward, Roos. [521/43]

BURTON PIDSEA (Parish, Population 394)

482   St Peter's Church, Burton Pidsea, an Ancient Parish Church. *Consecrated* before 1800. *Endowment* Land £11 OPE £31 Fees £3. *Sittings* Free 40 Other 200. *On 30 March* Morning GC 37 SS 36. *Average* Morning GC 40 SS 36 Afternoon GC 60 SS 36. *Remarks* The service is alternate in the morning & afternoon - e.g. one service every Sunday. Income reduced by Free Trade. *Signed* James Potter, Curate of the Parish, Keyingham, nr Hull. [521/44]

483   Wesleyan Methodist Chapel, Burton Pidsea. *Erected* 1847. SEB ExW. *Sittings* Free 38 Other 121. *On 30 March* Afternoon 61 Evening 68. *Average during 12 months* Afternoon GC 60 Evening GC 60. *Signed* Thomas Dugden, Chapel Steward, Burton Pidsea. [521/45]

484   Primitive Methodists, Burton Pidsea. *Erected* 1844. SEB ExW. *Sittings* Free 20 Other 60 Free Space 80. *On 30 March* no service that day SS none. *Average* Morning GC 50 Evening GC 56. *Signed* Richard Hastings, Chapel Steward, Burton Pidsea, nr Hedon. [521/46]

TUNSTALL (Parish, Population 159)

485   Primitive Methodist, Tunstall. Dwelling House. *Sittings* Free about 50. *On 30 March* Morning No public service; No Sunday School; Afternoon GC 22 Evening No public service. *Signed* William Luddington, Minister, Patrington, Holderness. [521/47]

HILSTON (Parish, Population 50)

486 St Margaret's, Hilston. Ancient Parish Church. *Consecrated* Before 1800. *Endowment* Tithe £12.19.0 Glebe £50 Fees 5s Other Categories None. *Sittings* Free 53. *On 30 March* Morning GC X Afternoon GC 31 Evening GC X. *Average during 12 months* Morning GC 25 Afternoon GC 30 Evening GC X. *Remarks* Divine Service is solemnized in the Church <u>once</u> only, on Every Sunday, Good Friday, Christmas Day, & Ash Wednesday. On the <u>first</u> Sunday in the month the service is in the Morning, on every other Sunday in the afternoon. *Signed* Thomas Briarly Browne, Officiating Minister, Roos, nr Hull. [521/48]

SKIRLAUGH DISTRICT (HO 129/522)

Humbleton Subdistrict[1]

GARTON-WITH-GRIMSTON (Township (P), Population 165)

487   St Michael, Garton Parish Church, Vicarage. *Consecrated* before 1800, in very early times. *Endowment* Tithe £120 Total £120. *On 30 March* Afternoon GC 62. *Average during 12 months* Afternoon Total 60. *Remarks* The service is alternately in the morning and afternoon the average for the year is about 60. *Signed* John Jadis, Offc. Minister, Humbleton Vicarage, Sproatley, Hull. [522/1]

488   (Wesleyan) Chapel, Garton. *Erected* 1826. SEB ExW. *Sittings* Free 46 Other 54. *On 30 March* Morning 41 Evening 30. *Average* Morning GC 45. *Signed* Joseph Cheesewright, Wesleyan Minister, Hornsea. [522/2]

ELSTRONWICK (Township (Humbleton), Population 157)

489   St Lawrence, Elstronwick, an old chapel with burial ground attached. *Consecrated* before 1800, in the reign of Henry VIII. *Endowment* not endowed. On 30 March No service. *Average* Between 40 & 50. *Remarks* The service alternately in the morning & afternoon. *Signed* John Jadis, Minister, Humbleton Vicarage, Sproatley, Hull. [522/3]

HUMBLETON (Township (P), Population 145)

490   St Peter, Humbleton. Parish Church, Vicarage. *Consecrated* in very early times before 1800. *Endowment* Land £112 Tithe £152 OPE £12 Total £276. *On 30 March* Morning GC 30. *Average during 12 months* Afternoon GC 80. *Remarks* The service is alternately in the morning & afternoon and the average for the whole year is about 80; general congregation. *Signed* John Jadis, Minister, Humbleton Vicarage, Sproatley, Hull. [522/4]

SPROATLEY (Parish, Population 463)

491   St Swithin, Sproatley. *Erected* 1820. *Sittings* Free 80 Appropriated 120. *Usual Number of Attendants* Morning GC 70 SS about 50 Afternoon GC 100 SS about 50 Evening GC No Service. *Remarks* There is only one service morning and afternoon alternately. *Signed* Charles J. Wall, Curate of Sproatley. [522/5 Simplified]

492   Wesleyan Methodist Chapel, Sproatley. *Erected* About 1810. SEB ExW. *Sittings* Free 64 Other 72. *On 30 March* Morning GC X Afternoon GC X Evening GC 43. *Average during 12 months* Afternoon GC 70 Evening GC 55. *Signed* Robert Evison Clark, Society Steward, Sproatley, nr Hull. [522/6]

---

1   No returns for the townships of Fitling (population 136), Danthorpe (population 41) and Flinton (population 108) in the parish of Humbleton.

LELLEY (Township (Preston), Population 151)

493 [Anglican], Lelley, An unconsecrated Building, in which Public service is performed by permission of the Archbishop. *Erected* By a Committee of Management. *Cost* Subscription £189. *Endowment* No Endowment. *Sittings* Free 58 Other 90. *On 30 March* Afternoon 32. *Average during 12 months* Morning GC 50 SS 20 Afternoon GC 50 SS 20 Evening X. *Signed* Thomas Fussey, Church Warden, Lelley, Sproatley. [522/7]

WYTON (Township (Swine), Population 91)

494 Wesleyan Methodist Chapel, Wyton. *Erected* about 1840. SEB ExW. *Sittings* Free 32 Other 38. *On 30 March* Afternoon GC 41 Evening GC 20. *Average during 12 months* Morning GC 25 Afternoon GC 30 Evening GC 25. *Signed* John Weatherill, Trustee, Wyton, Hull. [522/8]

Skirlaugh Subdistrict[2]

BILTON (Township (Swine), Population 99)

495 St Peter, Bilton. Chapel of Ease, serviced from Swine. *Consecrated* before 1800. *Endowment* Land £45 Glebe £35. *Sittings* Free 40 Other 60. *On 30 March* Morning X Afternoon 30 Evening X. *Average during 12 months* Morning GC 40 alternately [with Afternoon] Evening GC X. *Signed* Robert Smithson, Chapelwarden, Bilton, nr Hull. [522/9]

496 Primitive Methodist, Bilton. *Erected* been used for Religious Public Worship Since the year 1848. Private Dwelling House, Preaching Occasionally. *Sittings* Free All; Other None; Free Space None. *On 30 March* Morning GC X Afternoon GC X Evening GC 20. *Remarks* There are no Pews all Free Sittings. Preaching every Sunday Night. *Signed* William Shields X [his] mark, Occupier (as House), Bilton, Hull. [522/12]

SWINE (Township (P), Population 193)

497 Saint Mary's, Swine. An Ancient Parish Church. *Consecrated* before 1800. *Endowment* Land £40 Tithe compn. £18 Glebe £27 OPE £14.13.8 Pew Rents none Other Sources £0.17.6. *Sittings* (Stalls & Benches) 107 Other (Pews) 350 All the Pews are free but apportioned to the Farms etc. *Average during 12 months* Morning GC 80 SS 25 Afternoon GC 120 SS 25 Evening X. *Remarks* Divine Service is performed in this Church, morning and afternoon, alternately. *Signed* Robert Douthwaite, Churchwarden, Swine, Hull. [522/13]

---

2   No returns for the townships of Thirtleby (population 69), Coniston (population 115), Ganstead (population 81), Benningholme and Grange (population 79) and North Skirlaugh (population 190), all in the parish of Swine, and the hamlet of Arnold (population 194) in the parishes of Swine and Long Riston.

498   Wesleyan Methodist Chapel, Swine. *Erected* 1829. SEB ExW. *Sittings* Free 50 Other 61 Free Space all taken up with Pews & Forms. *On 30 March* Morning GC 56 SS 27 Evening GC 50. *Remarks* The Swine Wesleyan Methodist Chapel was built by voluntary contributions upon Land belonging to Wm. Wilberforce Esqr. for which a small Rent is paid Annually. Service is performed in this Chapel morning, afternoon & Evening alternately, generally two services each Sunday. *Signed* George Taylor, Steward, Swine, nr Hull. [522/10]

499   Primitive Methodist, Swine. *Erected* first used for Public Worship in the year 1846. Dwelling House used Occasionally for Public worship. *Sittings* All free Free Space none. *On 30 March* Morning GC None Afternoon GC None Evening GC 20. *Average during 12 months* Morning GC None Afternoon/Evening alternately GC 30. *Remarks* There are no Pews all are Free Sittings. Observe. This house was first used for public Worship about the year 1800 by the Calvinists, afterwards by the Wesleyan Methodists, but is Now used by the Primitive Methodists. *Signed* Josph Knowles, Occupier, Swine, Hull. [522/11]

ELLERBY (Township (Swine), Population 287)

500   Wesleyan Methodist, Ellerby. *Erected* 1838. SEB ExW. *Sittings* Free 46 Other 46 Free Space 20. *On 30 March* Morning GC 45 SS 44 Afternoon GC 50 SS 44. *Signed* Tim Stockdale, Chapel Keeper, Ellerby, nr Hull. [522/14]

MARTON (Township (Swine), Population 110)

501   Marton [Roman] Catholic Chapel. *Erected* 1789 There was always a chapel even in the worst day's of Protestant Persecution. Adjoining the Priests' dwelling House; used exclusively as a place of worship. *Sittings* Free All. The only real exclusive seats, are those of the Tribune, to which Sir Clifton Constable's family have access through the dwelling of the Chaplain. Height of Chapel 22 ft. Number of sittings in the body of the Chapel 30. Other 60ft by 24. *On 30 March* SS None Morning GC 150 Evening X. *Average* Morning GC about 180 SS None. *Signed* Very Revd Robt. Hogarth, Dean and Vicar Genl., Priest, Burton Constable, Hull. [522/15]

SOUTH SKIRLAUGH (Township (Swine), Population 322)

502   St Augustine, South Skirlaugh. Chapel of Ease. *Consecrated* before 1800. *Endowment* OPE £3 6s 8d. *Sittings* Free 300 Total 300. *On 30 March* Morning GC 45. *Average during 12 months* Morning GC 70 Afternoon GC 150 SS 60. *Signed* Richard Lythe, Vicar of Swine cum Skirlaugh, nr Hull. [522/16]

503   Primitive Methodist Chapel, Skirlaugh. *Erected* Before 1800. SEB ExW. *Sittings* Free 12 Other 44 Free Space 20. *On 30 March* Morning X Afternoon X Evening about 50. *Average during 3 months* Morning X Afternoon X Evening about 55. *Signed* John Crow, Minister, Seaton, nr Hull. [522/17]

504   Wesleyan Chapel, South Skirlaugh. *Erected* 1820. Entire ExW. *Sittings* Free 83 Other 101 Free Space Nothing but Aisles. *On 30 March* Afternoon GC 84 SS 60

Evening GC 60. *Signed* Thomas Barker, Steward, Schoolmaster, North Skirlaugh. [522/47]

LONG RISTON (Township (P), Population 316)

505   St Margaret's, Long Riston. *Erected* AD 1339. *Sittings* Free 160 Appropriated 18 [or] 3 pews Total 163 [sic]. *Usual Number of Attendants* Morning GC 56 to 60 SS 20 Afternoon GC 140 SS 23 Evening GC No Service. *Signed* J. Beaumont Walpole, Clerk, Curate of Riston. [522/18 Simplified]

506   Primitive Methodist Chapel, Riston. *Erected* 1836. SEB ExW. *Sittings* Free 20 Other 60. *Remarks* Average number of Attendants 30. *Signed* George Poster, Manager, Riston, nr Hull. [522/19]

507   Independent Chapel, Riston. *Erected* 1837. Entire ExW. *Sittings* Free 24 Other 80. *On 30 March* Morning GC 20 SS 21 Afternoon GC X SS 20 Evening GC 31. *Average during 6 months* Morning GC 25 SS 20 Afternoon GC 45 SS 25 Evening GC 35. *Remarks* Divine Service is held morning & evening and afternoon & evening on alternate sabbaths. A Station of the "East Riding Home Missionary Society". *Signed* William Meldrum, Preacher, Beverley. [522/20]

RISE (Parish, Population 197)

508   All Saints Parish Church, Rise. *Consecrated* 1845 In lieu of an old Church pulled down. *Erected* Richard Bethell Esq. *Cost* Cost unknown. *Endowment* Tithe (net income) £448 Glebe (net income) £50 Total £498. *Sittings* Free 100 Other 75. *On 30 March* Morning GC 92 SS 10 Afternoon GC 70 SS 10. *Signed* William J. Whately, Minister, Rise Rectory, nr Hull. [522/21]

Aldbrough Subdistrict[3]

WITHERNWICK (Parish, Population 513)

509   The Church of Withernwick, St Alban's. A small gothic Building, patron the prebendary of Holm in York Cathedral. The Revd G. Houldsworth of Boroughbridge Vicar: Revd Wm. Craven of Aldbrough Officiating Minister. *Consecrated* not known. *Erected* not known. *Endowment* Land £120 Tithe £47.16.6 Glebe £5 Pew Rents none Fees/Dues u[n]k[nown] Easter Offerings £0.15.0 Other Sources £9.10.0. *Sittings* All Free the Pews being alloted to the Householders. *On 30 March* Morning GC 20 SS 45. *Remarks* The Officiating Minister not being willing to make a return I have obtained the above Information from the late parish clerk. J. Palmer. *Dated* 11 April. *Signed* Barrington Webster, Enumerator, Withernwick. [522/22]

---

3   No returns for the townships of West Newton (population 239) and East Newton (population 27) in the parish of Aldbrough.

510   Primitive Methodist, Withernwick. *Erected* 1843. SEB ExW. *Sittings* Free 50 Other 80 Free Space 40. *On 30 March* Afternoon 44 Evening 42. *Average during 12 months* Afternoon GC 50 Evening GC 50. *Signed* William Bradshaw, Society Steward, Withernwick. [522/23]

511 [duplicate] Primitive Wesleyan, Withernwick. *Erected* about 8 or 10 yrs ago. Separate ExW. *Sittings* Free About 30 Other About 60. *Usual Number of Attendants* SS not Any Morning GC about 20 Afternoon GC 30 Evening GC 40. *Signed* J. H. Clark, Aldbro', nr Hull. [522/26 Simplified]

512   Wesleyan Methodist, Withernwick. *Erected* 1811. SEB ExW. *Sittings* Free 62 Other 120 Free Space none. *On 30 March* Afternoon GC 94 SS 22. *Average* the above number is abt. an average. *Remarks* In 1843 the Chapel was enlarged when 21 Sittings was added thereto. In 1850 the Chapel was heightened when a gallery was put up containing 54 Sittings. *Signed* Joseph Cheesewright, Wesleyan Minister, Hornsea. [522/24]

513 [duplicate] Wesleyan Chapel, Withernwick. *Erected* 60 or 70 years ago. Separate ExW. *Sittings* Free about 50 Other about 100. *Usual Number of Attendants* SS Cannot tell Morning GC About 60 Afternoon GC About 70 Evening GC About 80. *Signed* J. H. Clark, Aldbro', nr Hull. [522/25 Simplified]

ALDBROUGH (Township (P), Population 834)

514   The Church of Aldbrough, St Bartholomew, is a Large Gothic Building of which the Queen is Patron and the Revd W. Craven is Vicar. *Consecrated* not known. *Erected* In the Church is a circular stone on which is enscribed as translated "Ulf commanded the church to be erected for the souls of Hanum and Gunthard" Ulf here mentioned is supposed the same who gave his estate to the church of York and in this gift was included Aldbrough where he has a castle the foundation of which is now Levelled. *Endowment* Land £134 Tithe £195 Fees £5 Easter Offerings £10. *Sittings* All Free the pewes being alloted to the house holders Total 370. *On 30 March* Afternoon GC 70 SS 50 Evening GC 30. *Average* Morning GC 50 SS 45 Afternoon GC 60 SS 50 Evening GC 30. *Remarks* The Vicar not being willing to make a return I have from the Parish Books obtained the above information. *Dated* 7 April. *Signed* John Kispin [?], Enumerator, Aldbro', nr Hull. [522/27]

515   Primitive Wesleyan, Aldbrough. *Erected* About twelve month ago. Separate ExW. *Sittings* Free about 20 Other about 40. *Usual Number of Attendants* SS Not Any Morning GC 20 Afternoon GC 30 Evening GC 40. *Signed* J. H. Clark, Aldbro', nr Hull. [522/28 Simplified]

516   Wesleyan Chapel, Aldbrough. *Erected* 1803. SEB ExW. *Sittings* Free 80 Other 169. *On 30 March* Afternoon GC 170 SS 30 Evening GC 180. *Average* Afternoon GC 170 SS 30 Evening GC 190. *Signed* Joseph Cheesewright, Wesleyan Minister, Hornsea, nr Hull. [522/29]

GREAT AND LITTLE COWDEN (Township (Mappleton), Population 146)

517   Wesleyan Chapel, Great Cowden. *Erected* 1835. Entire ExW. *Sittings* Free 20 Other 9 Pews. *On 30 March* Afternoon GC 40. *Average* The above about the average Congregation. *Remarks* The only Place of worship in <u>Cowden</u>. *Signed* John Collinson, Steward, Cowden, Hull. [522/30]

Hornsea Subdistrict

MAPPLETON (Township (P), Population 164)

518   All Saints, Mapleton, an ancient Parish Church. *Consecrated* before 1800. *Endowment* Land £14 Tithe £30 Glebe £4 Fees £1 Other Sources £10. *Sittings* Free 200 Other 0. *On 30 March* Morning GC 60 SS 50 Afternoon GC X Evening GC X. *Average during 12 months* Morning GC 70 SS 55 Afternoon GC 150 SS 55. *Signed* Christr. Forge, Minister, Mapleton, nr Hull. [522/31]

519   Wesleyan and Independent Chapell, Mappleton. *Erected* 1838. SEB ExW. *Sittings* Free 20 Other 50. *On 30 March* Morning X Afternoon X Evening 30. *Average during 6 months* Morning [sic] GC 40. *Signed* Robert Bustard, Trustee, Mappleton, Hornsea. [522/32]

GREAT HATFIELD (Township (Mappleton), Population 165) and LITTLE HATFIELD (Township (Sigglesthorne), Population 44)

520   (Wesleyan Methodist) Chapel, Hatfield. *Erected* 1838. Entire. *Sittings* Free 25 Other 53. *On 30 March* Morning 30 Evening 42. *Average during 12 months* Morning GC 20 Evening GC 46. *Signed* Elizabeth Hepper, Stewardess, Hatfield Parva, nr Hornsea. [522/37]

SIGGLESTHORNE (Township (P), Population 210)

521   St Lawrence, Sigglesthorne. *Sittings* Free 327 Other 18. *Dated* 27 Septr. 1852. *Signed* William Henderson. [522/33 Registrar's Enquiry]

SEATON AND WASSAND (Township (Sigglesthorne), Population 360)

522   Primitive Methodist Chapel, Seaton. *Erected* December 1837. SEB ExW. *Sittings* Free 28 Other 94 Free Space 100. *On 30 March* Morning GC X SS X Afternoon GC 47 SS X Evening GC 60 SS 27. *Average during 12 months* Morning GC X SS X Afternoon GC 45 SS X Evening GC 90 SS 31. *Signed* Francis Taylor, Steward, Seaton, Hull. [522/34]

523   Wesleyan Chapel, Seaton. *Erected* 1810. SEB ExW. *Sittings* Free 40 Other 60 Free Space None. *On 30 March* Morning GC X Afternoon GC 30 Evening GC 25. *Average during 12 months* Morning GC 30 SS none. *Signed* George Hardy, Steward, Seaton, nr Hull. [522/35]

GOXHILL (Parish, Population 58)

524   St Giles, Goxhill, an ancient Parish Church. *Consecrated* before 1800. *Endowment* Tithe £175 Glebe £53. *Sittings* Free 60 Other (moveable) 20. *On 30 March* Morning GC X SS 0 Afternoon GC 71 SS 0 Evening GC X. *Signed* Christr. Forge, Minister of Goxhill, Mappleton, nr Hull. [522/36]

HORNSEA WITH BURTON (Parish, Population 945)

525   Antient Parish Church of Hornsea dedicated to St Nicholas. *Consecrated* before 1800. *Endowment* Land £90 Tithe £15 Fees £3 Other Categories £0. *Sittings* Free 650 Other 10 (all are free but the Vicar & Rectors Pews). *On 30 March* Morning GC 100 SS 70 Evening Total X. *Average* Morning GC 150 SS 90 Afternoon GC 200 SS 90. *Remarks* During the Summer Season when Hornsea is visited as a bathing place the Church is usually nearly full. *Signed* W. L. Palmes, Vicar, Hornsea, Hull. [522/38]

526   Bethesda (Independent), Hornsea. *Erected* 1807. SEB ExW. *Sittings* Free 50 Other 300. *On 30 March* Morning GC 70 SS 37 Afternoon X Evening GC 125 SS 15. *Signed* Thomas Poole, Minister, Hornsea, Hull. [522/39]

527   (Wesleyan) Chapel, Hornsea. *Erected* 1814. SEB ExW. *Sittings* Free 80 Other 170. *On 30 March* Morning GC 56 Evening 110. *Signed* Joseph Cheesewright, Wesleyan Minister, Hornsea. [522/40]

528   Primitive Methodist Chapel, Hornsea. *Erected* 1835. SEB ExW. *Sittings* Free 50 Other 106 Free Space None. *On 30 March* Morning SS 18 Afternoon GC 100 SS 18 Evening GC 110 SS 18. *Average during 12 months* Morning SS 18 Afternoon GC 30 SS 18 Evening GC 50. *Signed* Robert Langham, Minister, Hornsea. [522/41]

ATWICK (Parish, Population 324)

529   St Lawrence, Atwick. Ancient Parish Church. *Consecrated* before 1800. *Endowment* Land £30 Tithe £102 Glebe (Q. A. Bounty to pay out of House rent) £20 OPE £15 Fees £1 Glebe-House rented by me and chiefly at my own cost. *Sittings* Free 60 or 65 Other 70. *On 30 March* Morning GC 16 SS 22 Afternoon GC 41 SS 22 Evening X. *Average during 12 months* Morning GC 25 SS 30 Afternoon GC 60 SS 30 Evening X. *Remarks* The Ch. is 1/4 mile from Village. Conventicle in the Village. The Ch. much better attended in the Summer Months. The Situation & road to, very bleak. Ch. damp & cold. Any further information desired will be readily communicated. *Signed* R. G. S. Browne, BA, Vicar, Atwick Vicarage, nr Hull. [522/42]

530 [duplicate] St Lawrence, Atwick. *Erected* before 1800. *Sittings* Free 50 Appropriated 120. *Usual Number of Attendants* Morning GC 22 SS 28 Afternoon GC 70 SS 28. *Signed* V. Knowles, Schoolmaster, Atwick, nr Sigglesthorne, Hull. [522/43 Simplified]

531 (Wesleyan Methodist) Chapel, Atwick. *Erected* 1821. SEB ExW. *Sittings* Free 62 Other 66. *On 30 March* Morning GC 36 Evening GC 73. *Signed* William Wilson, Society Steward, Atwick, Sigglethorne, Hull. [522/44]

532 Primitive Methodist, Atwick. Room. Not erected as a place of Worship. Not separate ExW. *Sittings* Free 12 Other 19 Free Space none. *On 30 March* Afternoon GC 32. *Average during 12 months* SS X Morning GC 20 Afternoon GC 20 Evening GC 25. *Signed* James [...] Garton, Leader, Atwick, nr Sigglesthorne, Hull. [522/45]

Brandesburton Subdistrict[4]

NUNKEELING WITH BEWHOLME (Parish, Population 269)

533 [St Helena], Nunkeeling. *Consecrated* Before 1800. *Endowment* Land £23 OPE £32.5.0. *Sittings* All free except one for the lay Rector: Total 120. *On 30 March* Morning GC 20 SS 8 Afternoon GC X Evening GC X. *Average during 12 months* Morning GC 30 SS 12 Afternoon X Evening X. *Signed* Ralph Otterburn, Incumbent, Frodingham, Driffield. [522/46]

NUNKEELING WITH BEWHOLME (Parish, Population 269)

534 Wesleyan Methodist Chapel, Bewholme. *Erected* 1831. SEB ExW. *Sittings* Free 25 Other 60. *On 30 March* Afternoon GC 20. *Average* Morning GC 35 Afternoon GC 20 Evening GC 35. *Remarks* This Chapel is Private property and is not given up to the Methodist Conference. *Signed* William Brankley, Steward, Bewholme, Sigglesthorne. [522/48]

535 Primitive Methodist Chapel, Bewholme. *Erected* 1839. SEB ExW. *Sittings* Free 20 Other 58. *On 30 March* Morning GC X Afternoon GC X Evening GC 40. *Average during 6 months* Afternoon GC 35 SS 30 Evening GC 45 SS 12. *Signed* James Thompson, Steward, Bewholme, nr Hornsea. [522/49]

CATWICK (Parish, Population 206)

536 [St Michael], Catwick. *Erected* about AD 1000. *Sittings* Free 400 Appropriated none. *Usual Number of Attendants* SS See the Schoolmistress' return Morning GC 60 Afternoon GC 30 Evening GC No evening Service. [Signature illegible] [522/50 Simplified]

537 (Wesleyan) Chapel, Catwick. *Erected* 1855. SEB ExW. *Sittings* Free 20 Other 44. *On 30 March* Afternoon GC 30 Evening GC 30. *Signed* Joseph Cheesewright, Wesleyan Minister, Hornsea. [522/51]

---

4   No returns for the township of Bonwick (population 25) in the parish of Skipsea, for the township of Moor Town (population 28) in the parish of Brandesburton, for the township of Hempholme (population 117) in the parish of Leven, for the township of Dunnington (population 69) in the parish of Beeford, and for the township of Catfoss (population 39) in the parish of Sigglesthorne.

538 Primitive Methodist Chapel, Catwick. *Erected* 1839. SEB ExW. *Sittings* Free 19 Other 61 Free Space None. *On 30 March* Morning GC 26 Afternoon GC X Evening GC 24. *Average during 12 months* Morning GC 22 Afternoon GC X Evening GC 16. *Signed* Richard Lyon, Leader, Catfoss, Brandsburton, nr Beverley. [522/52]

BRANDESBURTON (Township (P), Population 751)

539 St Mary, Brandesburton. *Erected* about 1100. *Sittings* Free 700 Appropriated none. *Usual Number of Attendants* SS See Schoolmasters and Schoolmistresses Returns Morning GC 200 Afternoon GC 100 Evening GC No Evening Service. [Signature illegible, but same as **536**] [522/53]

540 Independent, Brandsburton. *Erected* 1809 Rebuilt 1842. SEB ExW. *Sittings* Free 25 Other 80. *On 30 March* Afternoon GC 10. *Average* Morning GC 20. *Signed* William Mainprize, Deacon. [522/54]

541 (Wesleyan) Chapel, Brandesburton. *Erected* 1809. SEB ExW. *Sittings* Free 80 Other 122. *On 30 March* Afternoon GC 170 Evening GC 130. *Signed* Joseph Cheesewright, Wesleyan Minister, Hornsea. [522/55].

DRIFFIELD DISTRICT (HO 129/523)

Foston Subdistrict[1]

BEEFORD (Township (P), Population 808)

542 St Leonard, Beeford. Ancient Parish Church. *Consecrated* Before 1800. *Endowment* The Living is endowed with Lands & Tithes, the present Net value of which is about £500, with every probability of diminution. *Sittings* If by Free Sittings are meant those for which no rent is paid, all are Free: Total 360. *On 30 March* Morning GC 180 SS 105 Evening GC 90 SS 30. *Average* Morning GC 200 SS 100 Evening GC 100 SS 50. *Remarks* No regard having been paid to the Ecclesiastical boundaries of the Parish, the parish of Beeford is situated in three different Unions, a fruitful source of confusion and trouble. *Signed* Stephen Creyke, Rector, Beeford, nr Driffield. [523/2]

543 Primitive Methodists, Beeford. SEB ExW. *Sittings* Free 30 Other 60. *On 30 March* SS None Morning GC 41 Evening GC 41. *Average during 12 months* SS None Morning GC 35. *Signed* Thomas Huggard, Steward, Beeford, Driffield. [523/3]

544 Ebenezer Chapel (Independent), Beeford. *Erected* 1810. Entire ExW. *Sittings* Free 40 Other 60 Free Space 30. *On 30 March* Afternoon GC 34. *Average during 10 months* Morning GC 50. *Remarks* This Chapel is connected with that at Frodingham & is supplied by the same Minister in the afternoon of the Lords day. *Signed* David Richardson, Minister, North Frodingham, nr Driffield. [523/4]

545 Wesleyan Methodist Chapel, Beeford. *Erected* Before 1800. SEB ExW. *Sittings* Free 60 Other 104. *On 30 March* Afternoon GC 106 Evening GC 67. *Signed* William Barugh, Society Steward, Beeford Grange, Driffield. [523/5]

NORTH FRODINGHAM (Parish, Population 846)

546 St Elgin, North Frodingham. An ancient Parish Church. *Consecrated* before 1800. *Endowment* Land £39 Glebe £108 OPE £10 Fees £5 Other Categories £0. *Sittings* Free 230 Other 0. *On 30 March* Morning GC 60 Afternoon GC 40. *Signed* Francis Keeling, Minister, North Frodingham, Driffield. [523/6]

547 Bethesda Chapel (Independent), Frodingham. *Erected* 1821. Entire ExW. *Sittings* Free 50 Other 80 Free Space 40. *On 30 March* Morning GC 40 SS 60 Evening GC 75. *Average during 10 months* Morning GC 50 SS 60 Evening GC 80. *Remarks* In connection with this place is Beeford where I preach on the Sunday afternoon a Return for which I have filled up. In the parishes of Foston & Brandesburton there are also chapels at which I minister occasionally to congregations on the week nights, that at Foston averging 30 persons, that at Brandesburton 16 persons. *Signed* David Richardson, Minister, North Frodingham, nr Driffield. [523/7]

---

[1]   No return for the extra-parochial area of Little Kelk (population 63).

548   Primitive Methodist Chapel, North Frodingham. *Erected* 1842. Entire ExW. *Sittings* Free 60 Other 230 Free Space None but Isles. *On 30 March* Morning X Afternoon X Evening 135. *Average during 12 months* Afternoon GC 80 Evening GC 190. *Remarks* Preaching only once a fortnight in the afternoon, on 30 of March a Local Preacher, the congregation is much better when we have an Itenerant Minister. *Signed* Robert Huntsman, Chapel Steward, North Frodingham, nr Driffield. [523/8]

549   Wesleyan Chapel, North Frodingham. *Erected* Before 1800. SEB ExW. *Sittings* Free 77 Other 76 Free Space None But Iles. *On 30 March* Morning 86 Afternoon 88 Evening GC 23. *Average during 12 months* Morning GC 80 Afternoon GC 100 Evening GC 30. *Remarks* There is only preaching twice on a Sunday. The other is a Prayer meeting. *Signed* William Pallister, Steward, Nth Frodingham, Driffield. [523/9]

FOSTON ON THE WOLDS (Township (P), Population 340)

550   Foston Parish Church [All Saints]. *Consecrated* Before 1800. *Endowment* Pew Rents, Fees, Dues, Easter Offerings & Other Sources £89. *Sittings* Free 30 Other 220. *On 30 March* Morning GC 52 Afternoon GC 30 Evening GC X. *Average* Morning GC 57 Afternoon GC 40. *Remarks* Nearly three fourths of the Population are from two to three miles distant from the Church. *Signed* Alfred L. Gibson, [...], Foston, Driffield. [523/10]

551   Bethel Chapel (Independent), Foston. *Erected* 1814. Entire ExW. *Sittings* All Free 150. *On 30 March* Morning GC X Afternoon GC X Evening GC X. *Average during 12 months* Morning GC X Afternoon GC X Evening GC 35. A week evening Service fortnightly. The average attendance is between thirty & forty. *Remarks* There is no Divine Service here on Sundays. It is connected with the Independents Chapel at Frodingham. I did not receive this return till this day April 15th. *Signed* 15 April. *Signed* David Richardson, Minister, North Frodingham, nr Driffield. [523/11]

552   Wesleyan Chapel, Foston. *Erected* 1802. Separate ExW. *Sittings* Free 50 Other 70 Free Space 20. *On 30 March* Evening GC 103. *Average* [sic]Morning GC 120. *Remarks* General congregation about 120. *Signed* Richard Mook & Benjm. Watson, Trustees. [523/12]

BRIGHAM (Township (Foston on the Wolds), Population 139)

553   Wesleyan Chapel, Brigham. *Erected* 1819. SEB ExW. *Sittings* Free 32 Other 48. *On 30 March* Evening GC 45. *Average during 12 months* Evening GC 40. *Dated* 29 March. *Signed* Saml. Robson, Steward, Brigham, nr Driffield. [523/13]

GEMBLING (Township (Foston on the Wolds), Population 110)

554   Primitive Methodist Chapel, Gembling. *Erected* 1845. SEB ExW. *Sittings* Free 6 Other 56. *On 30 March* Morning GC X Afternoon GC 17 SS 16 Evening GC 21. *Signed* George Dobson, Steward. [523/14]

GREAT KELK (Township (Foston on the Wolds), Population 197)

555 Wesleyan Chapel, Kelk. *Erected* 1814. Separate ExW. *Sittings* Free 80 Other 40. *Average during 12 months* Morning GC 24 SS 20. *Signed* Thomas J. Knapton, Wesleyan Chapel, Kelk, nr Driffield. [523/15]

HARPHAM (Parish, Population 266)

556 A Chapelry commonly called Harpham Church [St John of Beverley]. Not known to whom dedicated . *Consecrated* before 1800. *Sittings* Free 70 Other 90 appropriated. *On 30 March* Afternoon GC 80 SS 34. *Signed* Henry Stobart, Asst. Curate, Burton Agnes, Bridlington. [523/16]

557 Methodist, Harpham. *Erected* before 1800. *Sittings* Free all Other none. *On 30 March* Morning GC 35 Evening GC 52. *Signed* John Lovel, Chapel Steward, Harpham. [523/17]

LOWTHORPE (Parish, Population 139)

558 St Martin, commonly called "Lowthorpe Church". It is an ancient Parish Church. *Consecrated* Before 1800. *On 30 March* Morning GC 8. *Average during 12 months* Afternoon GC from 25 to 30. *Remarks* The Services three Sundays in the month are performed in the afternoon and the number of attendants is in general much greater than when the service is in the morning, and the congregations in the Summer months frequently doubles those of the winter months. There is only one House near the Church and in bad weather the congregations are small in consequence of the distance many of the parishioners have to travel. *Signed* Thomas Ibbotson, Perpetual Curate of Lowthorpe, resident at Nafferton Hall, nr Great Driffield. [523/18]

WANSFORD (Township (Nafferton), Population 257)

559 Wesleyan Methodist Chapel, Wansford. *Erected* About 1809. SEB ExW. *Sittings* Free 45 Other 130 Free Space None. *On 30 March* Afternoon GC 60. *Signed* R. Watson, Steward, Wansford, nr Driffield. [523/19]

ROTSEA (Township (Hutton Cranswick), Population 35)

560 Wesleyan Chapel, Rotsea. *Erected* 1847. Separate ExW. *Sittings* Free All. *On 30 March* Morning 35. *Average during 12 months* Morning 36. *Remarks* Private Property. *Signed* Thos. Holtby, Proprietor, Rotsea, Driffield. [523/20]

Driffield Subdistrict[2]

HUTTON CRANSWICK (Township (P), Population 1189)

561 Hutton Parish Church [St Peter], a Vicarage. *Consecrated* In Norman Times.

---

2   No return for the township of Sunderlandwick (population 52) in the parish of Hutton Cranswick.

Sittings Free 300 Other None. *On 30 March* Morning No Service then; Afternoon GC 100 SS 117 Evening GC None. *Average during 12 months* Morning GC 44 SS 100 Afternoon GC 55 SS 100. *Signed* Josh. Rigby, Vicar, Vicarage, Hutton, nr Driffield. [523/22]

562 Partickler Baptist Chaple, Cranswick. *Erected* 1841. SEB ExW. *Sittings* Free 10 Other 80. *On 30 March* Morning GC X Afternoon GC 20 Total 35 [?] Evening GC X. *Signed* John Hodgson, Steward, Cranswick, Driffield. [523/23]

563 Primitive Methodist Preaching Room, Hutton Cranswick. *Erected* cannot say. SEB ExW. *Sittings* Other 60 Free Space 20. *On 30 March* Afternoon GC 45 Evening GC 50. *Average during 12 months* Afternoon GC 50 Evening GC 60. *Signed* David Leaf, Steward; Rev John Hopkinson, Minister, Great Driffield, York. [523/24]

564 Wesleyan Methodist Chapel, Hutton Cranswick. *Erected* about 1800. SEB ExW. *Sittings* Free 40 Other 88. *On 30 March* Afternoon GC 50. *Average during 12 months* Afternoon GC 100 SS 30. *Signed* Rev Samuel Wilde, Wesleyan Minister, Driffield. [523/25]

565 Primitive Methodist Chapel, Hutton Cranswick. *Erected* 1836. SEB ExW. *Sittings* Free 80 Other 160 Free Space 130. *On 30 March* Morning GC 94 Evening GC 220. *Average during 12 months* Morning GC 100 Evening GC 250. *Signed* James Jordan, Steward; Rev John Hopkinson, Minister, Great Driffield. [523/26]

GREAT DRIFFIELD (Township (Driffield), Population 3963)

566 Great Driffield Church, dedicated to All Saints, is an ancient Parish Church consolidated with Little Driffield. *Consecrated* before 1800. *Endowment* [including Little Driffield **571**] Land £85 Tithe Rent Charge (net) £110 Fees £20 Other Sources £0.17.4. *Sittings* Free 195 Other 410. *On 30 March* Morning GC 310 SS 120 Evening GC 152. *Signed* Geo. Allen, Incumbent, Great Driffield. [523/27]

567 (Particular) Baptist Chapel, Chapel Lane, Driffield. *Erected* 1790. SEB ExW. *Sittings* Free 50 Other 170 Free Space 30. *On 30 March* Morning GC 72 SS 36 Afternoon SS 36 Evening GC 120. *Average during 12 months* Morning GC 130 Evening GC 130. *Signed* Thos. E. Wycherley, Minister, Exchange Street, Driffield. [523/28]

568 Providence Chapel (Congregationalists or Independents), Great Driffield. *Erected* 1802. SEB ExW. *Sittings* Free 50 Other 300. *On 30 March* Morning GC 160 SS 59 Evening GC 230. *Dated* 8 April. *Signed* Henry Birch, Minister, Driffield. [523/29]

569 Wesleyan Methodist Chapel, Driffield. *Erected* 1828. SEB ExW. *Sittings* Free 214 Other 406. *On 30 March* Morning GC 180 SS 86 Afternoon GC 130 Evening GC 360. *Average during 12 months* Morning GC 180 SS 86 Afternoon GC 130 Evening GC 400. *Signed* Rev Samuel Wilde, Wesleyan Minister, Driffield. [523/30]

570 Primitive Methodist Chapel, Mill Street, Great Driffield. *Erected* 1821. SEB ExW. *Sittings* Free 110 Other 340 Free Space about 130. *On 30 March* Morning GC 30 Afternoon GC 280 SS 40 Evening GC 330. *Average during 12 months* Morning GC 30 Afternoon GC 270 SS 40 Evening GC 320. *Remarks* We have not a Sermon in the Chapel on Sabbath day morning. Only Some of the Sabbath day Schollars attend alternately the preaching service in the Chapel. *Signed* Thomas Ward, Steward; Rev Thomas Ratcliffe, Great Driffield. [523/31]

LITTLE DRIFFIELD (Township (Driffield), Population 186)

571 Little Driffield Church, dedicated to Saint Peter, is an ancient Church consolidated with Great Driffield. *Consecrated* before 1800. *Endowment* N.B. See Great Driffield [566]. *Sittings* Free 40 Other 57. *On 30 March* Afternoon GC 35 SS 16. *Signed* Geo. Allen, Incumbent, Great Driffield. [523/32]

572 Primitive Methodist Preaching House, Little Driffield. Dwelling House. *Sittings* Free 30 Free Space 20. *Average during 12 months* Evening GC 30. *Signed* Richard Pickering, Steward; Rev John Hopkinson, Minister, Great Driffield. [523/34]

EMSWELL WITH KELLEYTHORPE (Township (Driffield), Population 110)

573 Primitive Methodist Preaching House, Emswell. Part of a Dwelling House. *Sittings* Free 40 Free Space 20. *On 30 March* Evening GC 30. *Average during 12 months* Evening GC 30. *Remarks* We only conduct preaching Services every other Sunday in the Evening it being a thinly populated neighbourhood about 2 miles from Driffield. *Signed* Francis Leppington, Steward; Rev John Hopkinson, Minister, Great Driffield. [523/33]

RUSTON PARVA (Parish, Population 185)

574 Ruston Parva Church [St Nicholas], an ancient Parish Church. *Consecrated* Before 1800. *On 30 March* Afternoon GC 25 SS 20. *Average during 12 months* Afternoon GC 35 SS 20. *Remarks* The Services are generally in the afternoon and in Summer greatly exceed in number of attendants those of the winter term. *Signed* Thomas Ibbotson, Curate of Ruston Parva, Nafferton Hall, nr Great Driffield. [523/35]

575 Wesleyan Methodist Chapel, Ruston Parva. *Erected* 1816. Betwixt two dwellings ExW. *Sittings* Free 12 Other 50. *On 30 March* Morning GC X SS 30 Afternoon GC X Evening GC 40. *Average* SS 30 Evening GC 45. *Signed* John Atkinson, Chapel Steward, Farmer, Ruston Parva, Driffield. [523/36]

576 Wesleyan Methodists, Ruston Parva. *Erected* 1810. Separate Building ExW. *Sittings* Free 20 Other 60 Free Space 20. *On 30 March* Morning GC 80 SS 50 Evening GC 86. *Average* Morning GC 40 SS 40 Evening GC 45. *Signed* Thomas Eastwood, Superintendent, Prospect Row, Bridlington Quay. [524/32]

NAFFERTON (Township (P), Population 1260)

577 <u>All Saints, Nafferton</u>. Ancient Parish Church. *Consecrated* before 1800. *Endowment* Tithe Rent charge from the lay Improprietor £13.6.8 Glebe £104.12.6 OPE (Queen Anne's Bounty) £3.0.4 Fees £11. *Sittings* Free 125 Other 125 An open space for school <u>children</u> 40 Total 290. *On 30 March* Morning GC 60 SS 54 Afternoon GC 100 SS 77 Evening GC X. *Average* Morning GC 70 Afternoon GC 100 Evening GC X. *Remarks* There is a population of about 300 in the township of Wansford, two miles from this Parish Church. The school room there licensed for divine worship, and I gave them a third service there last year in the Summer months. The Sunday school children there only come once a day to church. *Signed* F. O. Morris, Vicar, Nafferton, nr Driffield. [523/37]

578 <u>Wesleyan Chapel, Middle Street, Nafferton</u>. *Erected* 1839 In lieu of one in 1785. SEB ExW. *Sittings* Free 160 Other 310 Free Space None. *On 30 March* Morning GC 140 SS 70 Evening GC 250. *Average during 12 months* Morning GC 150 SS 68 Evening GC 320. *Signed* Jacob Laybourn, Steward, Garden Cottage, Nafferton. [523/38]

579 <u>Primitive Methodist Chapel, Nafferton</u>. *Erected* 1824. SEB ExW. *Sittings* Free 34 Other 106. *On 30 March* Afternoon GC 60 SS 37 Evening GC 90 SS 25. *Signed* Newsome Barker, Steward, Nafferton. [523/39]

SKERNE (Parish, Population 194)

580 <u>Skerne Church [St Leonard]</u>, an ancient Parish Church. Name at Time of Consecration not known. *Consecrated* Before 1800. *On 30 March* Afternoon GC 30. *Average* Morning GC 40 Afternoon GC 60. *Remarks* There would doubtless have been a larger congregation had not a heavy fall of Sleet & Rain come on immediately Before the Service. In Summer the congregations are larger than in Winter to a considerable extent. *Signed* Thomas Ibbotson, Perpetual Curate of Skerne, nr Great Driffield. [523/40]

581 <u>Wesleyan Methodists, Skerne</u>. Schoolroom. *Erected* about 1839. Seperate ExW. *Sittings* Free 55 Other none. *On 30 March* Morning X Afternoon X Evening 43. *Average during 12 months* Morning [sic] GC 50. *Signed* Abraham Robinson, Leader, Skerne. [523/41]

Bainton Subdistrict[3]

WATTON (Parish, Population 315)

582 <u>Watton Church [St Mary]</u>. *Erected* very ancient. *Sittings* Free 310 Total 310.

---

[3] No returns for the township of Bracken (population 32) in the parish of Kilnwick, for the townships of Neswick (population 65) in the parish of Bainton, or for the hamlet of Battleburn (population 26) and the township of Eastburn (population 15) in the parish of Kirkburn.

Usual Number of Attendants Morning GC 30 Afternoon GC 45. *Signed* C. W. Hillaby, Registrar of Births and Deaths, Garton, Driffield. [523/43 Simplified]

[523/44 Mis-filed return relating to Walton, near Wetherby: see West Riding (South) 2667]

583 Primitive Methodist, Watton. Dwelling House occupied by a family. *Sittings* Free 30. *On 30 March* Morning 11 Evening 27. *Average during 12 months* Morning GC 15 Evening GC 35. *Signed* Robert Butler Kirby, Society Steward, Watton, nr Driffield. [523/45]

584 Wesleyan Methodist, Watton. *Erected* not known. Part of a Dwelling House. *Sittings* Free 80 Free Space None. *On 30 March* No Service. *Average during 12 months* Morning GC 20. *Signed* Rev Samuel Wilde, Wesleyan Minister, Driffield. [523/46]

MIDDLETON-ON-THE-WOLDS (Parish, Population 649)

585 [Anglican], Middleton. *Sittings* Free 290 Total 290. *Usual Number of Attendants* Morning GC 50 Afternoon GC 75. *Signed* C. W. Hillaby, Registrar of Births & Deaths, Garton, Driffield. [523/47 Simplified]

586 Wesleyan Methodist Chapel, Middleton. *Erected* About 1809. SEB ExW. *Sittings* Free 50 Other 96. *On 30 March* Morning Total X Afternoon Total X Evening GC 40. *Average during 12 months* Evening GC 50. *Signed* Samuel Dooks, Steward, Middleton, Beverley. [523/48]

587 Wesleyan Methodist Chapel, Middleton Wold. *Erected* 1847. SEB ExW. *Sittings* Free 20 Other 40 Free Space 20. *On 30 March* Afternoon GC 45. *Signed* John Hornby, Chapel Steward, Middleton Wold, Beverley. [523/49]

588 Primitive Methodists, Middleton on the Wolds. *Erected* 1821. Separate ExW. *Sittings* Free 40 Other 100 Free Space 20. *On 30 March* Morning GC X SS 40 Afternoon 64. *Average* Afternoon GC 50 SS 40 Evening GC 60. *Signed* Rev James Phillips, Minister, Westgate, Gt. Driffield. [523/50]

BAINTON (Township (P), Population 404)

589 Parish Church of Bainton [St Andrew]. *Endowment* The Church has no Endowment. Glebe (602 Acres) £800. *Sittings* Ample accommodation for the Parishioners. *Average* SS none, distinct from the Weekly Schools; Morning GC 75 Afternoon GC 75 Evening GC X. *Remarks* The Church is a very old one. The Rectory derives its income from 602 acres of Land, allotted at the Enclosure in 1745, in lieu of all tithes etc. The surplice fees are small. The Church has space enough to seat between 600 & 700 persons. *Dated* 27 March. *Signed* George Thomas Clare, Rector, Driffield. [523/51]

590 Wesleyan (Methodist) Chapel, Bainton. *Erected* 1838. Separate ExW. *Sittings* Free 40 Other 70 Free Space 40. *On 30 March* Morning GC X Afternoon GC X Evening 80. *Average during 12 months* Afternoon GC 40 Evening GC 60. *Signed* John Wallis, Steward, Bainton, Gt. Driffield. [523/52]

591   Primitive Methodist Chapel, Bainton. *Erected* 1837. Separate ExW. *Sittings* Free 40 Other 60 Free Space 40. *On 30 March* Morning GC X Afternoon GC X Evening GC 60. *Average* Morning GC X Afternoon GC 40 Evening GC 60. *Signed* Rev James Phillips, Minister, Westgate, Gt. Driffield. [523/53]

NORTH DALTON (Parish, Population 499)

592   All Saints, North Dalton. Nave, chancel, Norman Tower and Porch. *Erected* unknown as very old. *Endowment* Land £80 Fees £1.10.0. *Sittings* Free 120 Other 60. *On 30 March* Morning X Afternoon GC 75 SS 26. *Average* Morning X Afternoon GC 80 SS 26 Evening X. *Remarks* The average of 106 is far below the number that attend church, as many husbands and wives attend alternately. *Signed* Thomas Rankin, Curate, N. Dalton, Beverley. [523/54]   ·

593   Primitive Methodist, North Dalton. *Erected* 1836. SEB ExW. *Sittings* Free 40 Other 60 Free Space 20. *On 30 March* Morning 60 Afternoon No Service; Evening 40. *Average during 12 months* Morning GC 60 Evening GC 100. *Signed* Rev James Phillips, Minister, Westgate, Gt. Driffield. [523/55]

594   Centenary Chapel (Wesleyan Methodist), North Dalton. *Erected* 1839. SEB ExW. *Sittings* Free 78 Other 96 Free Space 26. *On 30 March* Morning GC 40 SS 40 Afternoon GC X Evening GC 75. *Signed* John Boast, Steward, North Dalton, nr Beverley. [523/56]

SOUTHBURN (Township (Kirkburn), Population 98)

595   Wesleyan Methodist Chapel, Southburn. *Erected* 1848. SEB ExW. *Sittings* Free 24 Other 48. *On 30 March* Morning GC X Afternoon 32 Evening GC X. *Signed* John Simpson, Steward, Southburn, nr Driffield. [523/58]

KIRKBURN (Township (P), Population 140)

596   Kirkburn Church, dedicated to St Mary, is an ancient Parish Church. *Consecrated* before 1800. *Endowment* Land £43 Tithe Rent Charge (net) £73 Fees £2 Other Sources £1.8.0. *Sittings* Free 84 Other 82. *On 30 March* Morning GC 50 SS 34 Afternoon no service. *Average during 12 months* Morning GC 45 SS 40 Afternoon GC 70 SS 40. *Signed* George Allen, Vicar, Kirkburn, nr Driffield. [523/57]

597   (Primitive Methodist) Chapel, Kirkburn. *Erected* 1839. Separate Building ExW. *Sittings* Free 20 Other 68 Free Space 12. *On 30 March* Morning GC 40 SS 40 Evening GC 30. *Average during 12 months* Evening GC 40. *Signed* William Barmby, Steward, Kirkburn, nr Driffield. [523/59]

TIBTHORPE (Township (Kirkburn), Population 271)

598   Wesleyan Methodist Chapel, Tibthorpe. *Erected* 1823 Rebuilt 1850. SEB ExW. *Sittings* Free 30 Other 94 Free Space none. *On 30 March* Morning GC 60 SS 23 Afternoon GC X Evening GC 80. *Average during 12 months* Morning GC 70 SS 23. *Signed* Abram Staveley, Steward, Tibthorpe, Driffield. [523/60]

WETWANG (Township (P), Population 571)

599 St Michael, Wetwang. An Ancient Parish Church. *Consecrated* before 1800. *Endowment* With Land. *Sittings* Free 122 Other 131. *On 30 March* Morning GC Between 50 and 60 SS 59.[4] *Average during 12 months* Morning GC 150. *Signed* J. Matthews, Vicar, Wetwang, Gt. Driffield. [523/61]

600 (Wesleyan Methodist) Chapel, Wetwang. *Erected* 1812. SEB ExW. *Sittings* Free 30 Other 108. *On 30 March* Afternoon GC 102 Evening GC 62. *Average during 12 months* Morning GC 90. *Remarks* On Account of Service in the Established Church in the Forenoon of March 30th we have no Public Service in the Chapel in the Forenoon. When Service in the Established Church is in the Afternoon (which it is every other Sunday) we have no Service in the Chapel in the Afternoon, but in the Forenoon & Evening. *Signed* John Robson, Steward, Wetwang. [523/62]

601 (Primitive Methodist) Chapel, Wetwang. *Erected* 1824. SEB ExW. *Sittings* Free 44 Other 103. *On 30 March* Evening GC 150. *Signed* Michael Sadler, Steward, Wetwang, nr Driffield. [523/63]

FIMBER (Township (Wetwang), Population 179)

602 Chapel of Ease to Wetwang, Fimber. *Consecrated* Before 1800. *Endowment* With Land. *Sittings* Free 70 Other 30. *On 30 March* Upwards of 30. *Signed* J. Matthews, Vicar of Wetwang, Gt. Driffield. [523/64]

603 (Primitive Methodist) Chapel, Fimber. *Erected* 1839. SEB ExW. *Sittings* Free 20 Other 35. *On 30 March* Evening 49. *Remarks* 1 Public Service every Sunday on March 30th it was in the Evening. *Signed* Thomas Horsley, Steward, Farmer, Fimber, Driffield. [523/65]

604 (Wesleyan Methodist) Chapel, Fimber. SEB ExW. *Sittings* Free 20 Other 23. *On 30 March* Evening GC 19. *Remarks* Only one Publick Meeting held in this Chapel, viz in the Evening of March 30th 1851. *Signed* Marmaduke D. Vickerman, Leader, Tailor, Wetwang, Driffield. [523/66]

GARTON-ON-THE-WOLDS (Parish, Population 531)

605 St Michael, commonly called Garton Church, an ancient Parish Church. *Consecrated* Before 1800. *Sittings* Free 154 Other 10. *On 30 March* Afternoon GC 52 SS 46. *Average during 12 months* Morning GC 30 SS 40 Afternoon GC 56 SS 48. *Remarks* The Services are performed here only once each Sunday, Morning & afternoon alternately. The number of Attendants is almost invariably much larger at the afternoon Service than at that of the Morning Service. Indeed this is generally the case in all country Villages. *Signed* Thomas Ibbotson, Vicar of Garton-on-the-Wolds, resident at Nafferton Hall, nr Great Driffield. [523/67]

---

[4]   The form is hard to interpret, but in the light of the remarks on the Wesleyan Methodist Chapel [600] this appears the most plausible reading.

606 <u>Wesleyan Methodist, Garton</u>. *Erected* 1786 and rebuilt 1809. SEB ExW. *Sittings* Free 50 Other 114. *Average during 12 months* Morning GC 30 Afternoon GC 120 Evening GC 100. *Signed* George C[...], Steward, Garton, Driffield. [523/68]

607 <u>Primitive Methodist, Garton-on-the-Wolds</u>. *Erected* 1824. SEB ExW. *Sittings* Free 30 Other 70. *On 30 March* Morning GC 15 Afternoon GC 10 Evening GC 60. *Signed* John Pickering, Steward, Garton, Driffield. [523/69]

Langtoft Subdistrict

TOWTHORPE (Township (Wharram Percy), Population 61)

608 <u>Wharram Percy Church [St Michael]</u>[5], a very antient Building. *Consecrated* Before 1800. *Sittings* Free 48 Other 40. *On 30 March* Afternoon GC 30 SS 32 Total 64 [sic]. *Remarks* The Church at Wharram Percy being three Miles from the Village the congregation entirely depends upon the weather. *Signed* Edmund Day, Curate of Wharram Percy, Norton, Malton. [523/71]

SLEDMERE WITH CROOM (Parish, Population 437)

609 <u>Saint Mary, Sledmere</u>. *Sittings* Total 250. *Usual Number of Attendants* 140 Morning SS 50. *Signed* Jno. Atkinson. [523/72 Simplified]

COWLAM (Parish, Population 35)

610 <u>[St Andrew], Cowlam</u>. *Sittings* Total 80. *Usual Number of Attendants* 10. *Signed* Jno. Atkinson. [523/73 Simplified]

HELPERTHORPE (Parish, Population 140)

611 <u>[St Peter], Helperthorpe</u>. An ancient Parish Church. *Consecrated* Before 1800. *Endowment* Land £130 OPE £20 Easter Offerings £1. *Sittings* Free 50 Other 30. *On 30 March* Morning GC 1. *Average during 3 months* Morning/Afternoon GC 3 Evening GC X. *Remarks* The Church might be pulled down and the Parish united to Weaverthorpe it being close and between the Mother & Daughter Church. *Signed* S. Henry Duntze, Vicar of Helperthorpe, Weaverthorpe, nr Malton. [523/74]

WEAVERTHORPE (Township (P), Population 640)

612 <u>[St Nicholas], Weaverthorpe</u>, an ancient Parish Church. *Consecrated* Before 1800. *Endowment* Land £120 OPE £30 Easter Offerings £1.10.0 Other Sources £5. *Sittings* Free 250 Other 60. *On 30 March* Morning GC X Afternoon GC 100 [or 200?] SS 56 Evening GC X. *Remarks* The Church out of repair. *Signed* S. Henry Duntze, Vicar, Weaverthorpe, nr Malton. [523/75]

613 <u>(Wesleyan) Chapel, Weaverthorpe</u>. *Erected* Before 1800. SEB ExW. *Sittings* Free 100 Other 150. *Average* Morning/Afternoon GC 80. *Signed* Matthew Oliver, Steward, Weaverthorpe, Malton. [523/76]

---

5   For a duplicate return by the church-warden, see Malton District in Vol. 4, North Riding.

614 Primitive Methodist Chapel, Weaverthorpe. *Erected* 1841. SEB ExW. *Sittings* Free 70 Other 80 Free Space 30. *On 30 March* Afternoon GC 40. *Average during 12 months* Afternoon GC 35 Evening GC 90. *Dated* 7 April. *Signed* Rev James Phillips, Minister, Gt. Driffield. [523/77]

EAST AND WEST LUTTON (Township (Weaverthorpe), Population 426)

615 [St Mary], Luttons Ambo. The Church of an antient Chapelry. *Consecrated* before 1800. *Endowment* Easter Offerings £1. *Sittings* Free 60 Other 80. *On 30 March* Morning X Afternoon X Evening X. *Average during 12 months* Morning/Afternoon GC 40 SS 25 Evening GC X. *Remarks* The service at the Chapel only every other Sunday, not on March 30. [undated] *Signed* S. Henry Duntze, Minister, Weaverthorpe, nr Malton. [523/78]

616 (Wesleyan Methodist) Chapel, West Lutton. *Erected* About 1817. SEB ExW. *Sittings* Free 120 Other 120. *On 30 March* Afternoon GC 180 SS 55 Evening GC 70 SS 15. *Average* Afternoon GC 150 SS 50 Evening GC 55 SS 15. *Signed* George Wray, Chapel and Society Steward, West Lutton, Duggleby, Malton. [523/79]

617 (Primitive Methodist) Chapel, West Lutton. *Erected* 1848. SEB ExW. *Sittings* Free 50 Other 50. *On 30 March* Afternoon GC 60 Evening GC 60. *Signed* Robert Bett [?], Society Steward, West Lutton, Duggleby, Malton. [523/80]

BUTTERWICK (Township (Foxholes), Population 109

618 [St Nicholas], Butterwick. *Sittings* Total 100. *Usual Number of Attendants* 12. *Signed* Jno. Atkinson. [523/81 Simplified]

FOXHOLES WITH BOYTHORPE (Township (P), Population 297

619 [St Mary], Foxholes. Name not known. An Ancient Parish Church of a distinct & separate parish. *Consecrated* before 1800. *Endowment* Land £300 Tithe £400. *Sittings* Free 30 There are 7 pews besides the free sittings. *On 30 March* Morning GC 33 SS 22 Afternoon GC 23 SS 21. *Average during 6 months* Morning GC about 31 or 2 SS 35 Afternoon GC about 22 SS 35. *Signed* Richard H. Foord, Rector, Foxholes, Weaverthorpe, Malton. [523/82]

620 Wesleyan Chaple, Foxholes. *Erected* 1820. SEB ExW. *Sittings* Free 60 Other 51. *On 30 March* Afternoon GC 42 SS 28 Evening 70. *Average* Morning GC 7 Afternoon GC 45 SS 25 Evening GC 70. *Signed* John Cook, Class Leader, Foxholes, Malton. [523/83]

LANGTOFT (Township (P), Population 681)

621 St Peter, Langtoft, an ancient Church. *Consecrated* before 1800. *Endowment* Land £310. *Sittings* Free Capable of holding 120 persons; Other [?] Sittings in the Chancel. *On 30 March* Morning 77 [or X?] Afternoon GC 60 SS 30 Evening X. *Dated* 3 April. *Signed* Richard Baldock, Curate, Langtoft, Malton. [523/84]

622   Wesleyan (Methodist), Langtoft.[6] *Erected* About 1810. SEB ExW. *Sittings* Free 35 Other 140 Free Space None. *On 30 March* Morning 105 Afternoon X Evening GC 90. *Remarks* In consequence of the absence of the Minister on the evening of March 30th a prayer meeting was held & a small congregation. The Average number attending divine service in this chapel as far as can be ascertained is not less than 120 at each service. *Signed* Philip Wilson, Steward, Langtoft, Malton. [523/85]

623   Primitive Methodist Chapel, Cotham Road, Langtoft. *Erected* 1839. SEB ExW. *Sittings* Free 32 Other 104 Free Space 20. *On 30 March* Evening 92. *Remarks* Service in the morning once a fortnight. The Evening Congregation smaler than usal as the average from 120 to 140. The cause I believe was a heavy shower of hail and rain near time for divine service. *Signed* Henry Wilson, Society Steward, Farmer, Langtoft, Malton. [523/86]

COTTAM (Township (Langtoft), Population 58)

624   Cottam Chapel [Anglican]. A perpetual Curacy. *Consecrated* [Before?] 1800. *Endowment* Land £130. *Sittings* Free capable of holding 30 persons. *On 30 March* Morning 20. *Dated* 3 April. *Signed* Richard Baldock, Curate, Cottam, Driffield. [523/ 87 Form torn]

KILHAM (Parish, Population 1247)

625   All Saints, Kilham. An ancient parish Church. *Consecrated* Before 1800. *Endowment* Tithe £21 Glebe £209 Fees £10. *Sittings* Free 144 Other 304. *On 30 March* Morning GC 42 SS 14 Afternoon X Evening GC 70. *Average during 12 months* Morning GC 60 SS 15 Afternoon GC X Evening GC 90. *Remarks* The Chancel is nearly as large as the Nave and if seated would contain 200 persons. Forms are now placed there for the school children. *Signed* E. F. B. B. Fellowes, Minister, Kilham, nr Driffield. [523/88]

626   Baptist Chapel, Kilham. *Erected* 1819. Entire with a Vestry adjoining ExW. *Sittings* Free 60 Other 240. *On 30 March* Morning GC 30 SS 21 Afternoon GC X SS 21 Evening GC 30 SS X. *Average during 12 months* Morning GC 50 SS 21. *Remarks* Observe there are but few sittings let, the remainder may therefore be considered as free, the cause of so few sittings being let is we have not had any settled Minister amongst us for several years. Two or three familys from home March 30th. *Signed* John Hithersay, Occasional Minister, Kilham, nr Driffield. [523/89]

627   Wesleyan Methodist Chapel, Kilham. *Erected* 1815. SEB ExW. *Sittings* Free 168 Other 212 Free Space none. *On 30 March* Morning GC X SS X Afternoon GC 150 SS 120 Evening GC 140 SS X. *Signed* Richard Knaggs, Chapel Steward, Kilham Field, nr Driffield. [523/90]

628   Primitive Methodist, Kilham. *Erected* 1824. SEB Both [Place of Worship and Sunday School?]. *Sittings* Free 48 Other 82 Free Space 20. *On 30 March* Morning GC None Afternoon GC 100 Evening GC 120. *Signed* X [mark?] George Hardy, Steward, Kilham, nr Driffield. [523/91]

---

6   For a duplicate return by the minister, filed under the Bridlington district, see **657**.

Skipsea Subdistrict[1]

BURTON AGNES (Township (P), Population 345)

629 St Martin's, Burton Agnes. Ancient Parish Church. *Consecrated* Before 1800. *Endowment* Land nearly 200 acres Tithe above £730 Fees about £7. *Sittings* Free 166 Other 174. *On 30 March* Morning GC 55 SS 50 Afternoon GC 160 SS 50 Evening GC X. *Average during 12 months* Morning GC 55 SS 50 Afternoon GC 170 SS 50 Evening X. *Signed* Wm. Nawton, Churchwarden, Burton Agnes, nr Bridlington. [524/2]

630 Wesleyan Chapel, Burton Agnes. *Erected* 1837. Separate Building ExW. *Sittings* Free 55 Other 136 Free Space all occupied by free Seats. *On 30 March* Evening GC 100. *Signed* John Hutty, Steward, Burton Agnes, Bridlington. [524/3]

HAISTHORPE (Township (Burton Agnes), Population 122)

631 Wesleyan Meeting House, Haisthorpe. Dwelling House. *Sittings* Free 50. *On 30 March* Afternoon 25. *Signed* John Purey, Householder or Tenant, Haisthorpe, Bridlington. [524/4]

632 Ranters, Haisthorpe. A dwelling House. *Sittings* Free 35 Free Space 35. *On 30 March* Evening 25. *Signed* Jabez Walker, Tenant of the House, Haisthorpe, Bridlington. [524/5]

THORNHOLME (Township (Burton Agnes), Population 100)

633 Ranters, Thornholme. Dwelling House. *Sittings* Free 50 Free Space 50. *On 30 March* Morning GC 35 Afternoon GC X Evening GC 35. *Signed* Mark Nonnundale, Occupier & Leader, Thornholme, Bridlington. [524/6]

634 Wesleyan Meeting House, Thornholme. A Dwelling House. *Sittings* Free 30. *On 30 March* Morning GC 25. *Signed* Robert Boynton, Tenant & Leader, Thornholme, Bridlington. [524/7]

GRANSMOOR (Township (Burton Agnes), Population 83)

635 Gransmoor Chapel [St Mary]. A licensed building. *Consecrated* 1839 No Church here before. It is more than 2 miles from Burton Agnes Parish Church. *Erected* W. Duesbury Esqre. *Endowment* There is no endowment. *Sittings* Free 20 Other 70. *On 30 March* Morning GC 16 SS 0 Afternoon GC X SS 0 Evening GC X SS 0. *Average during 12 months* Morning GC 30 SS 0 Afternoon GC 30 SS 0 Evening GC 30 SS 0. *Remarks* There is only one Service here each Sunday. During the winter

---

1   No return for the township of Dringhoe, Upton and Brough (population 163) in the parish of Skipsea.

it is alternately morning and afternoon, during the summer it is in the evening. *Signed* John Medforth, Chapel Warden, Gransmoore, Bridlington. [524/8]

636 Wesleyan Meeting House, Gransmoor. Part of a Dwelling House. *On 30 March* Afternoon 25. *Signed* John Medforth, Overlooker, Gransmoore, Bridlington. [524/9]

LISSETT (Township (Beeford), Population 123)

637 Chapel of St James', Lissett. *Consecrated* before 1800. *Endowment* Land/ Tithe/Glebe/OPE included in the Rectory of Beeford Fees 5s or 6s Other Categories None. *Sittings* Free 75 Other 5. *On 30 March* Morning X Afternoon GC 26 SS 4 Evening X. *Average during 12 months* Morning GC 30 SS 15 Afternoon GC 40 SS 20 Evening X. *Remarks* The services are alternate morning and afternoon. On this afternoon there were only 4 schoolchildren at church owing a very prevalent sore throat which kept them & grown up at home. *Signed* Thos. Fred Simmons, Curate, Beeford, Driffield. [524/10]

638 Wesleyan Methodist, Lissett. Part of a Dwelling House. A private dwelling occupied as a Farm House. *Sittings* will contain 50 persons. *On 30 March* Morning GC X Afternoon GC X Evening GC 25. *Signed* Jarvis Cheesman, Minister, Bridlington Quay. [524/11]

ULROME (Township (Skipsea), Population 221)

639 [St Andrew], Ulrome. A small church, built part with stone & part with Brick & tiled, situated in the North East End of Ulrome. *Consecrated* Built three or four hundred years ago. *Endowment* Tithe payment £15 Glebe £35 OPE £7 Easter Offerings £3. *Sittings* Free 2 Other 17. *On 30 March* Morning GC 17 SS 11. *Average* Morning GC 20 to 30 SS 11 or 12. *Remarks* The Service at the church is alternate, morning & afternoon, 1/2 past 10 & 3 o'clock. *Signed* Charles Cory, Perp. Curate, Ulrome, nr Driffield. [524/12]

640 Wesleyan, Ulrome. *Erected* March 1848. SEB ExW. *Sittings* Free 46 Other 45 Free Space 20. *On 30 March* Afternoon 72 Evening 44. *Signed* John Day, Steward, Tailor, Ulrome, Driffield. [524/13]

SKIPSEA (Township (P), Population 435)

641 Independent, Skipsea. *Erected* About 1801. SEB ExW. *Sittings* Free 50 Other 110. *On 30 March* Morning GC X Afternoon GC 80 SS 14 Evening GC 26. *Signed* Thomas Poole, Minister, Hornsea. [524/14]

642 Primitive Methodist Chapel, Skipsea. *Erected* 1844. SEB ExW. *Sittings* Free 18 Other 58 Free Space None. *On 30 March* Evening GC 24. *Average during 12 months* SS X Evening GC 24 SS X. *Signed* Robert Langham, Minister, Hornsea. [524/15]

643 [Skipsea] Church dedicated to St Nicholas. about 5 or 6 hundred years ago. *Endowment* Land £42.10.0 Tithe Payment £15 OPE (Queen Anne's Bounty

Money) £33.19.2 Fees £3 or £4 Other [except Glebe] Categories £0. *Sittings* Free 50 Other 31 pews holding 210 persons. *On 30 March* Afternoon GC 85 SS 51. *Average Morning* GC from 80 to 90 SS 50. *Remarks* In No. 5 – The Glebe is included in the Lands purchased with Queen Anne's Bounty money. The Service at the Church is alternate, morning & Afternoon 1/4 past 10 & 1/2 past 2 o'clock. *Signed* Charles Cory, Vicar, Skipsea, nr Driffield. [524/16]

644   Wesleyan, Skipsea. *Erected* About 1800. SEB ExW. *Sittings* Free 80 Other 114. *On 30 March* Morning GC 45 SS 20 Afternoon GC X Evening GC 140. *Signed* John Brounbridge [?], Trustee & Local Minister, Skipsea, Driffield. [524/17]

BARMSTON (Parish, Population 249)

645   All Saints Church, Barmston. Ancient Parish Church. *Consecrated* before 1800. *Endowment* Tithe £654 Glebe 111 acres; Easter Offerings £19.0.9. *On 30 March* Morning GC 49 SS 12 Afternoon GC 22 SS 10. *Average during 12 months* Morning GC 110 SS 12 Afternoon GC 22 SS 10. *Remarks* The Glebe land is put down in acres which is worth about 26s per acre. *Signed* John William Bower, Rector, Barmston Rectory, Driffield. [524/18]

646   Wesleyan Methodists, Barmston. *Erected* 1839. Separate Building ExW. *Sittings* Free 40 Other 60 Free Space 40 persons. *On 30 March* Evening GC 80. *Average during 3 months* Evening GC 60. *Dated* March 1851. *Signed* Thomas Eastwood, Superintendent, Prospect Row, Bridlington Quay. [524/19]

FRAISTHORPE (Township (P), Population 83)

647   [St Edmund], Fraisthorpe. Chapel united with Carnaby Vicarage. *Endowment* Fees £30. *Sittings* Free 40 Other 30. *On 30 March* Morning GC 25. [undated] *Signed* Francis Rounding, Church Warden, Kingsfield, Bridlington. [524/20]

Bridlington Subdistrict[2]

BESSINGBY (Parish, Population 92)

648   St Magnus, Bessingby. I think a church of an ancient Chapelry belonging to Bridlington but now a separate parish. *Endowment* Land £30.14.6 OPE £20 Fees £0.5.0 Other Categories £0. *Sittings* Free 0 Other 135. *On 30 March* Morning X Afternoon 22 Evening X. *Average during 12 months* Morning X Afternoon 35 Evening X. *Remarks* I dont know the income of the benefice but believe it to be about £51 and derived from land and interest of money in Queen Anne's Bounty the fees do not amount to 5s per annum. *Signed* James Thompson, Curate of Bessingby, Parsonage, Bridlington Quay. [524/21]

---

2   No returns for the township of Auburn (population 21) in the parish of Fraisthorpe, or for the hamlet of Easton (population 19) and the townships of Holderthorpe with Wilsthorpe (population 147) and Buckton (population 182) in the parish of Bridlington.

CARNABY (Parish, Population 161)

649 St John, Carnaby. *Sittings* Free 30 Appropriated 60. *Usual Number of Attendants* Morning GC 50 SS 25 alternately [with] Afternoon GC 50 SS 25. *Signed* Thomas Major. [524/22 Simplified]

650 Wesleyan Methodists, Carnaby. Robinson's Cottage. *Erected* Before 1800. It is an inhabited Cottage. *Sittings* Free Space 30. *On 30 March* Morning Total X Afternoon Total X Evening GC 25. *Average during 4 months* Evening GC 23. *Signed* John Mainprize, Steward, Carnaby, nr Bridlington. [524/23]

BOYNTON (Parish, Population 113)

651 Saint Andrew, Boynton. *Sittings* Free 20 Appropriated 40. *Usual Number of Attendants* Morning GC 30 SS 6 alternately [with] Afternoon GC 30 SS 6. *Signed* Thomas Bell. [524/24]

BRIDLINGTON AND QUAY (Township (P), Population 5839)

652 St Mary's or The Priory Church, Bridlington. An Ancient Parish Church. *Consecrated* Ages before the Reformation. *Endowment* Land £69 OPE £60 Fees £40. *Sittings* Free 250 Other 1000. *On 30 March* Morning GC 300 SS 148 Afternoon GC 193 SS 149 Evening GC 195. *Average during 3 months* Morning GC 500 SS 206 Afternoon GC 600 SS 206 Evening GC 300. *Remarks* As Bridlington Quay is a Watering place in the Summer, the number of attendants at the Parish Church varies very much. *Signed* Henry Frederick Barnes, Perpetual Curate, Bridlington Quay. [524/25]

653 Christ Church, Bridlington. A District Chapelry. *Consecrated* Sept. 1841. As a chapel of Ease to St Mary's Bridlington but since created an Incumbency by Queen Annes Bounty and District annexed by Church Commissioners. *Erected* By Parishioners, the money being raised by voluntary contribution Church Commissioners £200 Church Building Soc. £100 Private Subscription £2000. *Cost* Total £2300. *Endowment* Land £18 OPE £40 Pew Rents £90 Fees £5. *Sittings* Free 320 Other 291. *Average during 12 months* Morning GC 350 SS 60 Afternoon GC X Evening GC 500 SS 20. *Remarks* The Church has been closed during the last four months. *Signed* James Thompson, Perpetual Curate of Christ Church, Parsonage, Bridlington Quay. [524/26]

654 Wesleyan Chapel, St John's Street, Bridlington. *Erected* Before 1800. SEB ExW. *Sittings* Free 250 Other 420. *On 30 March* Morning GC 207 SS 70 Afternoon GC X SS X Evening GC 426 SS X. *Signed* Edward Stokes, Minister, St Johns Street, Bridlington. [524/27]

655 Primitive Methodist Chapel, St John's Street, Bridlington. *Erected* Built 1834 and Re-built 1849. SEB ExW. *Sittings* Free 40 Other 171. *On 30 March* Morning GC X Afternoon GC 97 Evening GC 169. *Signed* Charles Kendall, Minister, No 4 Church Green, Bridlington. [524/28]

656   Primitive Methodist Chapel, Esplanade, Bridlington Quay. *Erected* 1833. SEB ExW. *Sittings* Free 40 Other 160 Free Space 60. *On 30 March* Morning X Afternoon GC 55 Evening GC 167. *Signed* Jonathan Wardill, Chapel Steward, King Street, Bridlington Quay. [524/29]

657   Wesleyan Methodists, Langtoft.[3] *Erected* 1809. SEB ExW. *Sittings* Free 36 Other 134 Free Space 40. *On 30 March* Morning GC 110 SS 36 Afternoon none Evening GC 140. *Average* Morning GC 100 SS 28 Afternoon None Evening GC 120. *Signed* Thomas Eastwood, Minister, Superintendent, Prospect Row, Bridlington Quay. [524/30]

658   Wesleyan Chapel, Dock Street, Bridlington Quay. *Erected* Before 1800. SEB ExW. *Sittings* Free 200 Other 500 Free Space about 60. *On 30 March* Morning GC 230 SS 100 Afternoon GC 90 Evening GC 500. *Average during 4 months* Morning GC 180 SS 94 Afternoon GC 80 Evening GC 420. *Signed* Thomas Eastwood, Minister, Superintendent, Prospect Row, Bridlington Quay. [524/31]

[524/32: Misfiled return relating to Ruston Parva: see **576** above.]

659   Zion Chapel (Congregational or Independent), Saint John's Street, Bridlington. *Erected* Before 1800. SEB ExW. *Sittings* Free 64 Other 386 Free Space None except the Ailes. *On 30 March* Morning GC 200 SS 40 Evening GC 290. *Remarks* Bridlington Quay, being a Town to wh. great numbers resort, in summer time for the purpose of sea-bathing, the Sabbath Congregations are much larger, from June to October, than they are during the winter months. I have, however, taken the average number of our Congregation, not from the Summer increase, but from that of Residents who regularly attend the Services of Religion in Zion Chapel. *Signed* George Frederick Ryan DD, Minister, Bishop's Terrace, Quay Road, Bridlington Quay. [524/33]

660   (Particular) Baptist Chapel, Bridlington. *Erected* 1699. SEB ExW. *Sittings* Free 50 Other 150 Free Space Abt. 50. *Average during 1 month* Afternoon GC 70 SS 30. *Remarks* Why not have ascertained the income of each Minister and the extent of endowment connected with each religious cause? *Signed* George Herbert Orchard, Baptist Minister, Quay Road, Bridlington. [524/34]

SEWERBY WITH MARTON (Township (Bridlington), Population 356)

661   St John the Evangelist, Sewerby-cum-Marton. Ecclesiastical District within the Parish of Bridlington. The church built under the provisions of 1 & 2 Willm. IV. *Consecrated* April 27 1848 as an additional Church situated one mile & an half from the Parish Church. *Erected* by & at the sole cost of Yarburgh Greame Esq. of Sewerby House, in the District aforesaid. *Cost* Private Benefaction, Total within a little of £6000. *Endowment* OPE £109.10.0 per annum in the funds. The Clergyman has £100 Clerk £5 Church Cleaner £3 Churchwardens (for expenses, besides the legal provision for repairs & some pew rents) £1.10.0. Sittings Free 108 Other 104.

---

3   For a duplicate return by the steward, filed under the Driffield district, see **622**.

On *30 March* Morning GC 85 SS given in educational return; Evening GC X. *Average* Morning GC 80 Afternoon GC winter 100 summer 220 Evening GC X. *Remarks* The Sunday School opened only on the 14th July 1850, in connexion with a day school opened on the 8th of the same month. The school & school House erected by the same individual who built the church. The School not endowed, but all the expenses borne by the same Gentleman. The attendance both at Church & School is most satisfactory. *Signed* Frederick Osborne Smith, Minister, Incumbent of Sewerby with Marton, Bridlington Quay. [524/35]

662   Wesleyan Methodist, Sewerby. *Erected* 1825. SEB ExW. *Sittings* Free 20 Other 72. On *30 March* Morning X Afternoon X Evening 76. *Average* Morning [sic] GC 70 SS None. *Signed* Jarvis Cheesman, Minister, Prospect Row, Bridlington Quay. [524/36]

FLAMBOROUGH (Parish, Population 1297)

663   The Parish Church of Flamborough [St Oswald]. *Consecrated* Before 1800. *Endowment* Land £61 OPE £16 Fees £3. On *30 March* Morning GC 150 SS 100 Afternoon GC 70 SS 50. *Remarks* The congregation is estimated from an inaccurate report of the numbers actually present on March 30th 1851, is somewhat less than the average attendance owing to weather. *Signed* John Furniss Ogle, Perpetual Curate, Flamborough, nr Bridlington. [524/37]

664   Wesleyan Methodists, Flambro. *Erected* 1799. SEB ExW. *Sittings* Free 70 Other 199 Free Space 60 persons. On *30 March* Afternoon GC 260 SS 104 Evening GC 250. *Average* Afternoon GC 240 SS 86 Evening GC 250. *Signed* Thomas Eastwood, Superintendent, Prospect Row, Bridlington Quay. [524/38]

665   Primitive Methodist Chapel, Flambro. *Erected* 1821. SEB ExW. *Sittings* Free 100 Other 202. On *30 March* Morning X Afternoon 50 Evening 130. *Average during 12 months* Morning SS X Afternoon 60 Evening 200. *Signed* Anthony Hall, Local Preacher & Steward, Flambro. [524/39]

BEMPTON (Parish, Population 342)

666   St Michael, Bempton, a donative the parish church of Bempton. In an ancient document styled "Conventio inter Robertum Prioreim de Bridlinton et inhabitatores & c "A. D. 1441. 19 Hen. VI" it is called an ancient chapel within the parish of Bridlington. Now a donative. *Consecrated* before 1800. *Endowment* OPE £51 & augmented with £800 Q. A. B. *Sittings* Free 80 Other 170. On *30 March* Morning GC 44 SS No School Afternoon GC X Evening GC X. *Average during 1 month* Average number of attendants is 53. *Remarks* Having been resident for a few weeks only, as officiating Minister I cannot give any more information respecting the endowment. The return is taken from the History of the East Riding; but should this be not sufficient, no doubt the incumbent Rev: J. Banks, Horndon on the Hill; Romford, will give any information required. *Signed* John Duffin, Curate (pro tem:), Bempton, nr Bridlington. [524/40]

667 Bempton Primitive Methodist Chapel. *Erected* 1843. SEB ExW. *Sittings* Free 40 Other 60 Free Space none. *On 30 March* Morning GC 27. *Average during 12 months* Morning GC 30. *Signed* John Woohouse, Chapel Trustee, Bempton. [524/41]

668 Wesleyan Methodists, Bempton. *Erected* 1825. Separate Building ExW. *Sittings* Free 30 Other 130 Free Space 50 persons. *On 30 March* Morning GC 120 SS 70 Afternoon GC 150 SS 70 Evening GC 150. *Average during 3 months* Morning GC 100 SS 50 Afternoon GC 130 SS 70 Evening GC 140. *Signed* Thomas Eastwood, Minister, Superintendent, Prospect Row, Bridlington Quay. [524/42]

Hunmanby Subdistrict[4]

SPEETON (Township (Bridlington), Population 150)

669 Speeton Chapel [St Leonard], a perpetual Curacy in the Parish of Bridlington. *Licensed* before 1800. *Endowment* OPE £50. *Sittings* Free 34 Other 38. *On 30 March* Morning GC X Afternoon GC 28 SS 13 Evening GC X. *Average during 1 month* Average attendants about 50. *Remarks* Having only been officiating Minister of this place for a few weeks I cannot give any more information respecting it. shd. more be required I refer you to the incumbent Rev: J. Banks, Howdon on the Hill: Romford, Essex. The return respecting the endowment is from the Eccles: Gazette. *Signed* John Duffin, Curate (pro tem:) of Speeton, Bempton, nr Bridlington. [524/44]

670 (Wesleyan) Chapel, Speeton. *Erected* 1847. SEB ExW. *Sittings* Free 50 Other 30. *On 30 March* Morning GC 33 Afternoon GC X Evening GC X. *Average during 12 months* Morning GC 50. *Signed* John Seller, Chapel Steward, Speeton, nr Bridlington. [524/45]

GRINDALE (Township (Bridlington), Population 153)

671 [St Nicholas], Grindall. Ancient Chapelry in the Parish of Bridlington. *Consecrated* before 1800. *Erected* The present Fabric erected, upon the foundations of the old Building, by the late Patron John Greame, Esq. of Sewerby House, Bridlington in 1830. *Endowment* Land £37 OPE £44 Fees £0.2.6 Total £81.2.6. *Sittings* Free 8 Other 52. *On 30 March* Afternoon GC 27 SS 14 Evening X. *Average* Morning GC 20 SS 15 Afternoon GC 30 SS 15 Evening GC X. *Signed* Frederick Osborne Smith, Minister, Incumbent, Bridlington Quay. [524/46]

672 Wesleyan Methodist Chapel, Grindale. *Erected* 1826. SEB ExW. *Sittings* Free 28 Other 32. *On 30 March* Evening GC 30. *Signed* John Smith, Trustee. [524/47]

673 Primitive Methodist, Grindale. *Erected* 6 year. *Average during 12 months* Morning GC 18. [undated] *Signed* George Walkington, Class Leader, Carrier, Grindall. [524/48]

---

4   No return for the parish of Argam (population 40).

RUDSTON (Parish, Population 599)

674   All Saints, Rudston, an Ancient Parish Church. *Endowment* Land 253 Acres; Fees £2.10.0 Dues £40. *Sittings* Free 200 Other 100. *On 30 March* Morning GC 41 SS 50 Afternoon GC 67 SS 50. *Average during 12 months* Morning GC 50 SS 50 Afternoon GC 90 SS 50. *Remarks* I am not aware at what rent the Glebe land is let. *Signed* P. G. Bartlett, Curate, Rudston, nr Bridlington. [524/49]

675   Primitive Methodist Chapel, Rudston. *Erected* 1830. SEB ExW. *Sittings* Free 30 Other 60. *On 30 March* Morning GC 17 Afternoon GC X Evening GC 60. *Signed* Charles Kendall, Minister, No. 4 Church Green, Bridlington. [524/50]

676   Wesleyan Methodist, Rudston. *Erected* 1811. SEB ExW. *Sittings* Free 40 Other 125 Free Space None. *On 30 March* Morning X Afternoon X Evening 130. *Average* Morning [sic] GC 130. *Signed* Jarvis Cheesman, Minister, Bridlington Quay. [524/51]

THWING (Parish, Population 444)

677   [All Saints], Thwing. *Sittings* Free 12 Other 150. *On 30 March* Morning GC 40 SS 12 Afternoon GC 70 SS 13 Evening GC X. *Average during 3 months* Morning GC 40 to 60 SS 12 Afternoon GC 60 to 80 SS 12 Evening GC X. *Remarks* Having but recently entered on the Curacy part of this Paper is left unfilled. *Signed* H. N. Bousfield, Licensed Curate, Thwing, nr Bridlington. [524/52]

678   Wesleyan Methodist Chapel, Thwing. *Erected* about 1810 Rebuilt & enlarged in 1839. SEB ExW. *Sittings* Free 65 Other 126. *On 30 March* Morning GC 70 SS 60 Evening GC 113. *Average during 12 months* Morning GC 70 SS 60 Evening GC 160. *Remarks* The morning Congregation near an average. On account of a Special Service held in a Neighbouring village the Evening Congregation was below an average. *Signed* Edward Braithwaite, Society Steward, Thwing, nr Bridlington. [524/53]

679 [duplicate] Centenary Chapel (Wesleyan Methodists) Thwing. *Erected* 1839. SEB ExW. *Sittings* Free 60 Other 125 Free Space 50. *On 30 March* Morning GC 100 SS 50 Afternoon None Evening GC 180 SS none. *Average during 6 months* Morning GC 160 SS 50 Afternoon None Evening GC 170 SS none. *Remarks* The congregations differ in attendance between Summer and Winter. [undated] *Signed* Thomas Eastwood, Minister, Superintendent, Bridlington Quay. [524/54]

680   Primitive Methodist Chapel, Thwing. *Erected* 1840. SEB ExW. *Sittings* Free 36 Other 64. *On 30 March* Morning GC X Afternoon GC 5 Evening GC 19. *Signed* Charles Kendall, Minister, Church Green, Bridlington. [524/55]

WOLD NEWTON (Parish, Population 276)

681   [All Saints], Wold Newton. Ancient parish church. *Consecrated* before 1800. *Sittings* Free 126 Other 14 Total 140 exclusive of the accommodation for children. *On 30 March* Morning GC 65 SS 38 Afternoon X Evening X. *Average during 12 months* Morning X Afternoon GC 120 SS 45 Evening X. *Remarks* The Services are alternately in the Morning and Evening of Sunday. The afternoon congregation generally fills the Church. *Signed* J. Skelton, Vicar, Wold Newton, Bridlington. [524/56]

682 (Weleyan) Methodist Chapell, Wold Newton. *Erected* 1839. SEB ExW. *Sittings* Free 60 Other 104. *On 30 March* Morning GC 50 Afternoon GC X SS X Evening GC 100 SS X. *Remarks* The Sunday Scholars atend the Church in the afternoon and likewise maney of the Pipel as we no preaching when the servis is in the Church. *Signed* George Knaggs, Trustee For the Chappill, Wold Newton, nr Bridlington. [524/57]

683 Primitive Methodist, Wold Newton. *Erected* Since 1841. *Sittings* Free 40 Other none. *On 30 March* Morning none Afternoon GC 10 Evening none. *Average during 12 months* Morning GC 10 SS none. *Signed* Michael Gibson, Minister, Kilham, nr Driffield. [524/58]

BURTON FLEMING (Parish, Population 574)

684 Parish Church of North Burton otherwise Burton Fleming [St Cuthbert]. Ancient Parish Church. Distinct & Separate Parish. *Consecrated* 1828 [?]. *Erected* Before 1800. *Endowment* Land £62 Tithe (monies payment in lieu of the Inclosure) £15 OPE £15.14.9 Fees £2 Easter Offerings £0.10.0 [Total] £95.4.9. *Sittings* Free 40 Other 110 Appropriated by Custom to Houses. *Average* Morning GC about 50 SS for 12 Months last past 30 Afternoon GC about 30. *Remarks* Only one Service on the Sunday morning and afternoon alternately. *Signed* Richard Duggleby, Churchwarden, North Burton Grange, Bridlington. [524/59]

685 Wesleyan Methodist, Burton Fleming. *Erected* 1800. SEB ExW. *Sittings* Free 20 Other 150 Free Space None. *On 30 March* Morning GC 100 SS 40 Afternoon X Evening GC 160. *Average during 3 months* Morning GC 120 SS 38 Evening GC 140. *Signed* Jarvis Cheesman, Minister, Bridlington Quay. [524/61]

686 [duplicate] Wesleyan Chapel, Burton Fleming. *Erected* About 1803. SEB ExW. *Sittings* Free 30 Other 120 Free Space None. *On 30 March* Morning X Afternoon X Evening 36. *Average during 6 months* Morning GC 90 SS 55. *Signed* Richard Gray, Steward, Burton Fleming, nr Bridlington. [524/63]

687 Primitive Methodist Chapel, Burton Fleming. *Erected* 1838. SEB ExW. *Sittings* Free 22 Other 100 Free Space none. *On 30 March* Morning GC 49 Afternoon GC X Evening GC 70. *Signed* Jonathan Guforth, Steward, North Burton [Burton Fleming], Bridlington. [524/62]

REIGHTON (Parish, Population 247)

688 Reighton Parish Church [St Peter]. *Consecrated* Before 1800. *Endowment* Land £120 OPE £65 Fees £1 Easter Offerings £5. *Sittings* Free 20 Other 84. *On 30 March* Afternoon 20. *Remarks* The 31st of March was here very Stormy, the morning average may be 30, the afternoon 50, but no account has been kept (nothing but a dame School). *Signed* John Wilkinson [?], Curate, nr Bridlington. [524/64]

689   Wesleyan Methodist Chapel, Reighton. *Erected* 1818. SEB ExW. *Sittings* Free 28 Other 52 Free Space 20. *On 30 March* Morning GC 34 SS 17. *Average* Morning GC 35 SS 25 Afternoon GC 55 SS 25 Evening GC 30. *Remarks* Divine Service in this Chapel is conducted in the Morning on one Sabbath and in the Afternoon on the Alternate Sabbath. Consequently the avarage congregation will be 45 and 25 Sabbath School Children. In the evening a prayer meeting is conducted average attendance 30. *Signed* Joseph Holtby, Chapel Steward, Reighton, Bridlington. [524/65]

690   Primitive Methodist, Reighton. *Sittings* Free 40 Free Space 30. *On 30 March* Evening GC 30. *Average* Evening GC 30. *Remarks* Divine service is conducted in this place in the afternoon on one sabbath and the afternoon and evening on the alternate sabbath. The average number at the prayer meetings 20. *Signed* Robert Holmes, Class Leader, Reighton, nr Bridlington. [524/67]

HUNMANBY (Township (P), Population 1291)

691   All Saints, Hunmanby. Ancient Parish Church. *Consecrated* Before 1800. *Endowment* Glebe £350. *Sittings* Total 300 None appropriated. *On 30 March* Morning GC 130 SS 40 Afternoon GC 80 SS 40. *Average during 12 months* Morning GC 180 SS 50 Afternoon GC 150 SS 50. *Signed* Robert Milford Taylor, Vicar, Hunmanby. [524/68]

692   Particular Baptists, Hunmanby. *Erected* 1816. SEB ExW. *Sittings* Free 40 Other 120 Free Space 20. *On 30 March* Morning GC X Afternoon GC 60 SS 20 Evening GC 70 [also figures of Afternoon 70 and Evening 80]. *Average during 3 months* Morning GC X Afternoon GC 60 SS 22 Evening GC 70. *Signed* John Frankish, Deacon, Builder, Hunmanby. [524/69]

693   Wesleyan Chapel, Hunmanby. *Erected* Before 1800. SEB ExW. *Sittings* Free 120 Other 260 Free Space 50. *On 30 March* Morning GC X SS X Afternoon GC 250 SS 76 Evening GC 200 SS X. *Average during 3 months* Afternoon GC 240 SS 70 Evening GC 180. *Signed* William Reynolds, Superintendent of Sunday School, Draper, Hunmanby. [524/70]

694   Primitive Methodist Chapel, Hunmanby. SEB ExW. *Sittings* Free 84 Other 50 Free Space 40. *On 30 March* Morning GC 70 Afternoon GC X Evening GC 110. *Average* Morning GC 90 Afternoon GC X Evening GC 120. *Remarks* We have no Sabbath School. *Signed* Charles Parker, One of the Ministers, 9 St Mary Street, Scarbro'. [524/71]

FORDON (Chapelry (Hunmanby), Population 55)

695   Ancient Chapelry of Fordon. *Consecrated* Before 1800. *Endowment* Land £52. *Sittings* Free 35. *Remarks* Service once a Month & on certain Holy days. Average attendance 28. *Dated* 24 March. *Signed* Robert Mitford Taylor, Curate, Hunmanby. [524/72]

INDEX OF DENOMINATIONS

Anglican

Acaster Malbis, 61
Acomb, 76
Aike, 338
Aldbrough, 514
Allerthorpe, 168
Askham Bryan, 65
Askham Richard, 67
Atwick, 529-30
Aughton, 232
Bainton, 589
Barmby on the Marsh, 246
Barmby Moor, 170
Barmston, 645
Beeford, 542
Bempton, 666
Bessingby, 648
Beswick, 333
Beverley, 306, 311-12
Bielby, 200
Bilton, 495
Bishop Burton, 317
Bishop Wilton, 135
Bishopthorpe, 63
Blacktoft, 268
Bossall, 122
Boynton, 651
Brandesburton, 539
Brantingham, 288
Bridlington, 652-3
Bubwith, 235
Bugthorpe, 139
Burnby, 196
Burton Agnes, 629
Burton Fleming, 684
Burton Pidsea, 482
Buttercrambe, 126
Butterwick, 618
Carnaby, 649
Catwick, 536
Cheapside, 270
Cherry Burton, 320
Clifton, 52
Copmanthorpe, 57
Cottam, 624
Cottingham, 358
Cowlam, 610
Dringhouses, 59
Drypool, 392
Dunnington, 102
East Cottingwith, 160
Eastrington, 260
Ellerker, 287
Ellerton, 229
Elloughton, 289

Elstronwick, 489
Elvington, 99
Escrick, 94
Etton, 323
Everingham, 202
Fangfoss, 151
Fimber, 602
Flamborough, 663
Flaxton, 118
Fordon, 695
Foston on the Wolds, 550
Foxholes, 619
Fraisthorpe, 647
Fridaythorpe, 132
Fulford (Gate Fulford), 87
Full Sutton, 144
Garton, 487
Garton-on-the-Wolds, 605
Gate Helmsley, 112
Goodmanham, 209
Goxhill, 524
Gransmoor, 635
Great Driffield, 566
Great Givendale, 183
Grindale, 671
Halsham, 478
Harpham, 556
Harswell, 207
Haxby, 47
Hayton, 197
Hedon, 382
Helperthorpe, 611
Hemingbrough, 243
Heslington, 83
Hessle, 378
Hilston, 486
Holgate, 54
Hollym, 472
Holme on the Wolds, 327
Holme-on-Spalding-Moor, 224
Holmpton, 469
Holtby, 106
Hornsea, 525
Hotham, 267
Howden, 251
Huggate, 187
Hull, 393, 411-13, 417, 422-5
Humbleton, 490
Hunmanby, 691
Huntington, 50
Hutton Cranswick, 561
Keyingham, 450
Kilham, 625
Kilnsea, 466

Baptist (see also Particular Baptist, Scottish Baptist)

Beswick, 334
Bishop Burton, 319
Hull, 403, 408-9, 421
Kilham, 626
Skidby, 297

Brethren

York, 10

Catholic: see Roman Catholic

Church of England: see Anglican

Congregationalists: see Independents

English Presbyterian (Unitarian)

York, 31

Independents

Beeford, 544
Beverley, 313
Brandesburton, 540
Bridlington, 659
Cottingham, 363
Elloughton, 291
Foston on the Wolds, 551
Great Driffield, 568
Heslington, 86
Hornsea, 526
Howden, 252
Hull, 404-5, 426, 431-2, 436
Long Riston, 507
Mappleton, 519
Market Weighton, 214
Meaux, 348
North Frodingham, 547
North Newbald, 281
Pocklington, 174
Sancton, 222
Skipsea, 641
South Cave, 286
Swanland, 372
Thorngumbald, 442

Welton, 366
Witham, 352
York, 8, 32

Independent Methodist

Hull, 435

Jews

Hull, 415

Latter Day Saints (Mormons)

Ellerton, 231
Hull, 427
Preston, 389

Methodist (see also Independent Methodist, Methodist New Connexion, Primitive Methodist, Wesleyan Methodist, Wesleyan Methodist Association, Wesleyan Methodist Reformers)

Harpham, 557
Seaton Ross, 205

Methodist New Connexion

Dunswell, 359
Sculcoates, 395, 402

Mormons: see Latter Day Saints

New Church: see Swedenborgian

Nondenominational

Hull, 410, 429, 434

Particular Baptist

Beverley, 315
Bridlington, 660
Great Driffield, 567
Hunmanby, 692
Hutton Cranswick, 562

Presbyterian: see English Presbyterian, United Presbyterian

Primitive Methodist

Acomb, 78
Aike, 339
Aldbrough, 515
Asselby, 250
Atwick, 532
Bainton, 591
Barmby Moor, 172
Barmby on the Marsh, 248
Beeford, 543
Bempton, 667
Beverley, 314
Bewholme, 535
Bilton, 496
Bishop Wilton, 137
Bridlington, 655-6
Brough, 292
Bugthorpe, 141
Burstwick, 446
Burton Fleming, 687
Burton Pidsea, 484
Catwick, 538
Cherry Burton, 322
Claxton, 123
Cottingham, 362
Dunnington, 104
Easington, 467
Eastrington, 262
Emswell, 573
Etton, 324
Fangfoss, 153
Faxfleet, 272
Ferriby, 371
Fimber, 603
Flamborough, 665
Flaxton, 119
Fridaythorpe, 134
Garton-on-the-Wolds, 607
Gembling, 554
Gilberdyke, 265
Goodmanham, 211
Great Driffield, 570
Grindale, 673
Haisthorpe, 632
Harton, 121
Haxby, 49
Hayton, 198
Hedon, 384
Hemingbrough, 245
Hessle, 381
High Catton, 148
Holme-on-Spalding-Moor, 228

Hornsea, 528
Howden, 253
Huggate, 189
Hull, 396, 399, 430, 433, 437
Hunmanby, 694
Hutton Cranswick, 563, 565
Kexby, 101
Keyingham, 451
Kilham, 628
Kirkburn, 597
Langtoft, 623
Leven, 346
Lillings Ambo, 117
Little Driffield, 572
Lockington, 336
Long Riston, 506
Lund, 331
Market Weighton, 213
Melbourne, 167
Meltonby, 181
Middleton-on-the-Wolds, 588
Millington, 186
Nafferton, 579
New Village, 274
North Cave, 277
North Dalton, 593
North Frodingham, 548
North Newbald, 282
Patrington, 459
Paull, 441
Pocklington, 176
Preston, 387
Reighton, 690
Rimswell, 477
Roos, 480
Rudston, 675
Ryhill, 448
Seaton Ross, 206
Seaton, 522
Shiptonthorpe, 218
Skipsea, 642
Skirlaugh, 503
South Cave, 285
Stamford Bridge, 150
Strensall, 116
Sutton, 355
Swanland, 374
Swine, 499
Thornholme, 633
Thwing, 680
Tunstall, 484
Walkington, 300
Warter, 192
Watton, 583
Weaverthorpe, 614
Welton, 367
Welwick, 462
West Lilling, 117

West Lutton, 617
Wetwang, 601
Wilberfoss, 156
Willerby, 364
Withernsea, 471
Withernwick, 510-1
Wold Newton, 683
Wressle, 241
Yapham, 180
York, 5

Quakers: see Society of Friends

Roman Catholic

Beverley, 307
Everingham, 203
Hedon, 383
Holme-on-Spalding-Moor, 226
Houghton, 221
Howden, 254
Hull, 406
Marton, 501
Pocklington, 177
Sancton, 221
York, 3, 36

Scottish Baptist

Beverley, 310

Society of Friends (Quaker)

East Cottingwith, 162
Hull, 418
North Cave, 278
York, 19

Swedenborgians (New Church)

York, 13

Unitarian

Hull, 420
Welton, 368
York, 31

United Presbyterian

Hull, 416

Wesleyan Methodist

Acaster Malbis, 62
Acomb, 77
Aldbrough, 516
Allerthorpe, 169
Anlaby, 377
Arram, 343
Askham Bryan, 66
Askham Richard, 68
Asselby, 249
Atwick, 531
Aughton, 233
Bainton, 590
Barmby Moor, 171
Barmby on the Marsh, 247
Barmston, 646
Beeford, 545
Bempton, 668
Beverley, 308-9, 316
Bewholme, 534
Bielby, 201
Bishop Burton, 318
Bishop Wilton, 136
Bishopthorpe, 64
Blacktoft, 269
Bolton, 182
Brandesburton, 541
Breighton, 238
Bridlington, 654, 658
Brigham, 553
Broomfleet, 273
Bubwith, 236
Bugthorpe, 140
Bursea, 225
Burstwick, 447
Burton Agnes, 630
Burton Fleming, 685-6
Burton Pidsea, 483
Carnaby, 650
Catwick, 537
Cherry Burton, 321
Claxton, 124
Copmanthorpe, 58
Cottingham, 361
Dringhouses, 60
Dunnington, 103
Easington, 468
East Cottingwith, 161
Eastrington, 261
Ellerby, 500
Ellerton, 230
Elloughton, 290
Elvington, 100
Fangfoss, 152
Faxfleet, 271
Fimber, 604
Flamborough, 664

Swine, 498
Thixendale, 131
Thorganby, 96
Thorngumbald, 443
Thornholme, 634
Thornton, 164
Thwing, 678-9
Tibthorpe, 598
Tickton, 305
Ulrome, 640
Upper Poppleton, 56
Walkington, 301
Wansford, 559
Warter, 191
Warthill, 110
Watton, 584
Weaverthorpe, 613
Welton, 369
Welwick, 463
West Ella, 376
West Lilling, 117
West Lutton, 616
Wetwang, 600
Wheldrake, 98
Wilberfoss, 155
Witham, 353
Withernwick, 512-3

Wold Newton, 682
Wressle, 242
Wyton, 494
Yapham, 179
York, 7, 26, 30, 39
Yorkfleet, 257
Youlthorpe, 138

Wesleyan Methodist Association

Heslington, 84
Hull, 397
York, 34

Wesleyan Methodist Reformers

Acomb, 78
Hull, 407
Knapton, 79
Nether Poppleton, 75
York, 2, 38